SPENSER

and

BIBLICAL

POETICS

SPENSER

and

BIBLICAL POETICS

CAROL V. KASKE

CORNELL UNIVERSITY PRESS

ITHACA AND LONDON

THIS BOOK HAS BEEN PUBLISHED WITH THE AID OF A GRANT FROM THE
HULL MEMORIAL PUBLICATION FUND OF CORNELL UNIVERSITY

First published 1999 by Cornell University Press

Printed in the United States of America

Library of Congress Cataloging-in-Publication Data
Kaske, Carol V. 1933–
    Spenser and Biblical poetics / Carol V. Kaske.
      p.   cm.
    Includes bibliographical references and indexes.
    ISBN 0-8014-3679-6 (cloth)
    1. Spenser, Edmund, 1552?–1599—Religion.   2. Christianity and literature—
England—History—16th century.   3. Christian poetry, English—History and
criticism.   4. Bible—In literature.   5. Poetics.   I. Title.
    PR2367.R4K37   1999
    821'.3—dc21   99-41666

Cornell University Press strives to use environmentally responsible
suppliers and materials to the fullest extent possible in the publishing
of its books. Such materials include vegetable-based, low-VOC inks
and acid-free papers that are recycled, totally chlorine-free, or partly
composed of nonwood fibers. Books that bear the logo of the FSC
(Forest Stewardship Council) use paper taken from forests that have
been inspected and certified as meeting the highest standards for
environmental and social responsibility. For further information, visit
our website at www.cornellpress.cornell.edu.

Cloth printing   10 9 8 7 6 5 4 3 2 1

In Memoriam
Robert E. Kaske
1921–1989

But when thou famous victorie hast wonne,
And high emongst all knights hast hong thy shield,
Thenceforth the suit of earthly conquest shonne,
And wash thy hands from guilt of bloudy field:
For bloud can nought but sin, and wars but sorrowes yield.

(I.x.60)

Bloud is no blemish; for it is no blame
To punish those, that doe deserve the same.

(VI.i.26)

CONTENTS

ACKNOWLEDGMENTS

Since I have been working on versions of this project off and on for some thirty years, individual debts are difficult to acknowledge, and many mentors and helpers are now beyond reach of this message. Chief among those who have critiqued chapters in recent years are Joseph Dallett, Michael Twomey, Thomas D. Hill, Barry Adams, Mark Hazard, Stephen Barney, Thomas P. Roche, Nicole Clifton, Richard Peterson, William J. Kennedy, and Debora Shuger. Special thanks are due to my two readers for Cornell University Press, William Oram and Anne Lake Prescott. The American Philosophical Society partially funded a research trip to Cambridge. I wish to thank the libraries and librarians of Cambridge University, of Pembroke College, Cambridge, and of the Center for Renaissance and Reformation Studies at the University of Toronto for their hospitality; the Folger Library and the Library of Congress for microfilms and photostats; and the University of Toronto Press for permission to quote and paraphrase parts of my articles "Bible" and "Amavia, Mortdant, Ruddymane" from the *Spenser Encyclopedia,* and Yale University Press for permission to quote from *Yale . . . Shorter Poems.* Scholars whom I have not been able to cite but who have nevertheless influenced my thinking on images and contradictions are Robert Heilman and Donald Stauffer on Shakespeare and A. S. P. Woodhouse, Robert Hoopes, Paul Alpers, Maurice Evans, Haruhiko Fujii, and Alan Sinfield on Spenser. I am grateful to my parents for introducing me to the Bible at an early age. My deepest debt is acknowledged in the dedication.

C. V. K.

NOTE ON TEXTS AND TRANSLITERATION

I have used the following texts of Spenser:

J. C. Smith, ed., *The Faerie Queene.* Oxford English Texts. Oxford, 1909.

With the kind permission of Yale University Press, William Oram, Einar Bjorvand, Ronald Bond, Thomas H. Cain, Alexander Dunlop, and Richard Schell, eds., *The Yale Edition of the Shorter Poems of Edmund Spenser.* New Haven, 1989.

Rudolph Gottfried, ed., *Prose Works.* Baltimore, 1949. Unnumbered vol. in *Works . . . A Variorum Edition.* Baltimore, 1932–57.

I have normalized *u-v-w* and *i-j-y.*

ABBREVIATIONS

Am.	*Amoretti*
Arg.	the arguments or epigraphs to cantos
BCI	Elizabeth Leedham-Green, *Books in Cambridge Inventories*
BCP	Book of Common Prayer
CCCHA	*Colin Clouts Come Home Againe*
CP	Peter Martyr Vermigli, *Common Places,* followed by book, part, page, and column
CR	Corpus Reformatorum, the series in which Melanchthon's Latin *Opera* appears
DNB	*Dictionary of National Biography*
FQ	*Faerie Queene*
Glossa	*Glossa Ordinaria,* by chapter and gloss-letter or lemma
HL, HB, HHL, HHB	*Fowre Hymnes: of Love, Beautie, Heavenlie Love, Heavenlie Beautie*
King, SPRT	John N. King, *Spenser's Poetry and Reformation Tradition*
King, TRI	his *Tudor Royal Iconography*
LB	Erasmus, *Opera omnia*
MCLI	R. E. Kaske, *Medieval Christian Literary Imagery*
MHT	*Mother Hubberd's Tale*
Nicolas	Nicolas of Lyra as printed with Glossa, by chapter and lemma

NT	New Testament
OED	*Oxford English Dictionary*
OT	Old Testament
PL	Migne, *Patrologia Latina,* followed by volume in Arabic numerals and column, or *Paradise Lost,* followed by book in Roman numerals and line
SC	*Shepheardes Calender*
SE	*Spenser Encyclopedia,* by author and entry
SPRT, see King	
ST	*Summa Theologiae,* by part, article, quaestio, etc.
STC	A. W. Pollard and G. R. Redgrave et al., *A Short-Title Catalogue of Books Printed in England, Scotland, and Ireland, and of English Books Printed Abroad, 1475–1640*
TJ	Tremellius-Junius Latin Old Testament and/or Apocrypha, by chapter and verse, and gloss number or letter
TRI, see King	
Var.	*Works of Edmund Spenser: A Variorum Edition,* ed. Edwin Greenlaw et al.
YSP	*Edmund Spenser, Shorter Poems*
*	See "Appendix 1. Statistics" for exemplars available to Spenser and his immediate audience at Cambridge University.

Biblical poetics comprises, first, in its most central meaning, the poetic practice of the biblical authors, especially the prophets and psalmists; then, what biblical commentators and Judaeo-Christian literary critics have perceived that poetics to be—a branch of hermeneutics; and finally, in the remoter sense in which we use it in literary criticism, that poetics which a poet might have derived from these two sources.[1] Biblical poetics in the third sense would involve certain rhetorical devices and methods of presentation which are either peculiar to Scripture (such as negative poetics for portraying the deity) or prevalent in expressing certain of its favorite topics (such as paradoxes on the topic of law). I concentrate on aspects of such poetics—chiefly, various kinds of oppositions—which are both interrelated and underplayed or overlooked. I hope to illuminate these by reference to certain medieval and sixteenth-century exegetes also seldom considered in such a context. Comparative illustrations of applied biblical poetics to be cited occasionally include the *Divine Comedy, Piers Plowman,* and the works of George Herbert and of John Milton; these place Spenser in a long tradition of religious poetry.

Barbara Lewalski pioneered the explicit study of biblical poetics, properly so called, with her *Protestant Poetics and the Seventeenth-Century Lyric,* bringing a wealth of polyglot religious sources into the scholarly conversation. Although many Spenserian scholars have pursued typology, biblical genres, and the prophetic mode with enduring results, no one to my

1. The term "biblical poetics" was used by Curtius, as Lewalski explains, in a rather different sense, that of divinely inspired poetry, in which sense Nohrnberg applies it to Spenser. Lewalski, *Protestant Poetics,* 7; Nohrnberg, *Analogy,* 676–77. I will devote a separate study to Spenser and the Psalms.

knowledge has ever explicitly applied the general term "biblical poetics" to Spenser.[2] Yet the attempt is worth making, because even though Spenser's style is often ornate and seldom plain, as conventional wisdom considers that of the Bible to be, if one lays the Bible beside Spenser's work as a whole, many similarities emerge.

In recent years three quite different books have been devoted to the general topic of Spenser and religion: John N. King's *Spenser's Poetry and the Reformation Tradition,* Harold Weatherby's *Mirrors of Celestial Grace,* and Darryl Gless's *Interpretation and Theology in Spenser.* (The books on this general topic by Richard Mallette and Linda Gregerson appeared too late to be included here.) I share some methods and presuppositions with each of these three scholars. At the same time, some of my differences from them indicate why my book is needed. Naturally, I pay the most attention to form. Each of us employs a body of source materials that is different from and complementary to that of the others—and happily so, since no one can cover all of the relevant religious discourse. Only King and I consider any Spenseriana outside of *The Faerie Queene.* King examines English and popular late-medieval and sixteenth-century iconographic topoi, techniques, and conventions; he finds that they support a consistently—or at least fairly consistently—Protestant theology. Weatherby brings to bear principally on FQ I, II, and VII the Greek Fathers, widely read in Spenser's day. Weatherby argues that Greek orthodoxy contributed something to Spenser's immanentist theology and ascetic ethics. Gless brings to bear, principally on FQ I, English theologians of Spenser's time and slightly after it, along with the popular and already translated Calvin, thus achieving a "Reformed" but also a pluralistic interpretation. In this group Weatherby alone considers continental texts in Latin, as I do, and he concentrates on the Greek Fathers. This information gap represents one reason why a thorough survey of Spenser's Latin sources would be valuable, a project to which this study makes a small contribution. (Unless otherwise noted, translations from these texts are my own.)

Although all four of us invoke medieval texts to varying degrees, I invoke them the most. King and Weatherby, while acknowledging Spenser's theological multivocality (King endorses my concept of *correctio* and

---

2. John N. King comes closest to doing so in SPRT: he explores Spenser's adoption of biblical genres; he devotes discussions to Spenser's debt to Revelation (70–75) and to Despair's Satanic misuse of Scripture (213–216); he explores Spenser's performance of biblical genres; but he subsumes these under the in some ways more capacious, in other ways more limited rubric of "Reformation poetics." Cullen's chapter "Guyon *Microchristus*" in *Infernal Triad* explores typology in FQ II. Both Wittreich in *Visionary Poetics* and Fletcher in *Prophetic Moment* explore Spenser's prophetic mode.

Weatherby acknowledges Spenser's contradictions), give the least attention to it, Gless and I the most. But Gless locates the heterogeneity in the
minds of differently conditioned audiences of a single given passage, I in
a single ideal reader of successive passages. King and Weatherby speak less
about the reader's line-by-line perception; they tend to look at the text and
the views expressed therein as static, perhaps because they understand-
ably feel that the static reading is the only reading one can talk about.

 This book is a partial and tentative essay on a few aspects of Spenser's
biblical poetics, not a comprehensive survey of it (for an abbreviated survey, see my entry "Bible" in SE). Its germ was the now well-known relationship, discovered by C. S. Lewis, between the Garden of Adonis and
the Bower of Bliss. What has not previously been realized is that Spenser
performs this sort of tergiversation again and again. In Chapter 1, "Spenser's Bible," I give, for once, a comprehensive survey of my announced
topic on a factual and elementary level, emphasizing those strategies
which this book presupposes. Throughout the book, I alternate between
the approach of the intentionalist and that of the reader-response critic;
that is, I consider both the Bible's stylistic features and Elizabethan ways
of reading it; I consider Spenser's methods derived therefrom as sometimes conveying meaning, sometimes constructing it with the help of the
individual reader.

 I next address three principal aesthetic problems. In Chapter 2 I begin
with a formal concern, Spenser's image-patterns. They unify most of
Spenser's poems, especially the FQ and the *Amoretti,* where they sometimes become a theme in their own right. The problem is, he repeats images first in an honorific sense, then in a disparaging one, or vice versa (at
least twenty-six of them, by my count; see Appendix 2). In so doing, I
propose, Spenser imitates the variation of repeated imagery revealed in
the Bible by that medieval method of tracing a repeated image known as
"distinguishing" *in bono et in malo,* in a good sense and a bad (Chapters 2
and 3).

 In Chapters 3 and 4, "Images That Correct Their Predecessors" and
"Propositional Contradictions and Their Resolutions," I observe that
Spenser presented certain themes, too, in a contradictory way—sometimes irreconcilably so, sometimes in ways that are resolvable. In so doing, he imitates the contradictions—sometimes on these very topics—
that certain exegetes of the Middle Ages and the Renaissance saw in the
Bible. My discussion proceeds from unifying strategies to those that are
agonistic and thus hermeneutically unsettling. Most of it is organized
around one or another practice of biblical exegesis and brings Spenser's
text in piecemeal, albeit in either large or related pieces.

To obviate the distortion that quoting out of context may entail, in my fifth and final chapter I focus on one episode, that of the Nymph's Well, resuming previous strategies and revealing a new one as prompted by the text. This new strategy represents an opposition between image and meaning and constitutes the third aesthetic problem: that is, in three places in *The Faerie Queene*, Spenser symbolizes Christ by or compares him to something repulsive. This breach of decorum follows the model of the Hebrew Scriptures as they were then read by Christian exegesis. Each of Spenser's three aesthetic problems can be found in the Bible as viewed by one or another group of exegetes, who then give at least a rationale if not a resolution.

My basic approach is text-centered. My focus is on intertextuality in the sense of literary imitation. Given the nature of the subtext, this imitation is fairly reverential (God is a father whom few would attempt to slay); but it is not rigidly so, in that the ways of appropriating the Bible are numberless and God's word can even be pitted against itself. I did not preselect these approaches and critical role models; when text-centered intertextuality could not solve a problem, I chose whatever approach the text seemed to invite.

In Chapters 3 and 4, I employ a type of reader-response criticism and affective stylistics. When I say "the reader," I mean the individual perceiving psyche as implied in the text at hand, whom I gender as feminine because she might well be; when I say "the audience," I mean the historically conditioned immediate reading public, chiefly the court and Cambridge, a culture that is empirically deducible from other texts, an external indicator of what H. R. Jauss calls "the horizon of expectation" for a poet's sources and doctrines. Cambridge represents the widest of Spenser's intellectual communities and the only one for which we have comprehensive statistics.

Ecclesiastical politics comes up frequently throughout. (Secular politics will be considered apropos of the image of shields.) Instead of the anachronistic terms "Puritan," "Catholic," and "Anglican," I employ as their closest approximation the labels that would have been understood at the time: "precisian," "popish" or "Romanist," and "Establishment" or "Church of England" (as exemplified in the Thirty-nine Articles and the Book of Common Prayer). The precisian, the Establishment, and the Romanist overtones of an image or provenance of a doctrine or practice will always be distinguished. "Protestant" embraces both precisian and Establishment. I do not prejudge the case by calling Spenser's poetics "Protestant"; Spenser's precise doctrinal allegiance, whether "Anglican" (whatever that means in the sixteenth century), Reformed, or patristic, is still being debated and may be eclectic, depending on the passage or the issue. Nor do I rule out any source on the grounds that it "must have been" unpalatable to Spenser; I do so only if the work (e.g., that of Hans Denck) is not attested at Cambridge.

For my source materials, I have mapped out two vaguely defined and somewhat overlapping groups of exegetes, one for images and another for contradictions. My exegetes who focused on imagery, referred to predominantly in Chapter 2, consist of a few patristic exegetes, some late medievals, and some sixteenth-century Romanists. Those exegetes, theologians, or pastors who recognized contradictions, predominant in Chapter 4, include mostly Bible-centered Protestants, since they were the keenest to solve the problem. Chapter 5 uses a combination of the two. All these exegetes would disagree with one another about theology; but theology can be separated from poetics; and each had something to say about one of the three aesthetic problems Spenser poses. Both cadres are in one way or another linked to Spenser's specific place and time. This satisfies current concerns for cultural specificity, both spatial and temporal, especially as to the material production of texts and their reception; it also seems to me valuable as a check on the critic's imagination.

To indicate a source's popularity and physical availability at Cambridge, I have consistently referred to three reference works. The first tool is H. M. Adams's *Catalogue of Books Printed on the Continent of Europe, 1501–1600, in Cambridge Libraries.*[3] Adams specifies the college that owns each one (as of 1967), and that presumably owned it in Spenser's time. Admittedly, Adams can furnish only an approximate index of popularity: since he gives no acquisition dates, donors, or owners, we cannot be sure that a given book was there for Spenser or his immediate audience. Adams leaves out the following: MSS and incunabula, which are covered for Pembroke by my third tool; and books in English, on which I am not concentrating because they are less numerous and scholarly, and because Gless, King, and Anthea Hume have already covered them.[4]

My second tool is Elizabeth Leedham-Green's invaluable *Books in Cambridge Inventories.*[5] BCI prints the usually dated probate inventories of books that were in the possession of individuals somehow related to Cam-

---

3. Hereafter cited parenthetically as Adams or simply by *, which means, "See holdings listed in Appendix 1."

4. See Leedham-Green, BCI I:xviii: "Few scholarly texts were published in Great Britain." While informative, Hume (*Edmund Spenser*) is too reductive to be part of my conversation: she reduces Spenser to "Immerito" and any poet to his historical background, yet for this she relies heavily on Perkins, on whom see historicist strictures below.

5. Hereafter cited as BCI or simply by * (see note 3). References are to Volume 2.

bridge (both small and great, including a few booksellers, but mostly fellows, the rank held by Spenser's friend Gabriel Harvey) who died in harness; thus it conveys a representative sample of the books privately owned there with chronological precision.

My third tool, M. R. James's *Descriptive Catalogue* of the library of Pembroke College, Cambridge, establishes what books were most immediately available to Spenser, his tutors, his friends, and his chapel preachers, though it tells us less about the tastes of Spenser's cohort than about those of Pembroke's previous generations. James lists its printed books to 1500 and all its MSS, with some donors and acquisition dates.[6] As for books published from 1500 to 1599, Adams specifies those which are at Pembroke. Thus he and James together supply a conspectus (incomplete only because of the scarcity of acquisition dates) of the imprints held by Pembroke.[7] My Bibliographical Appendix summarizes the numbers of copies listed in Adams (noting those at Pembroke), BCI, and James of the sources I cite. I assemble the picture projected by these three indicators because it is informative and as yet unattempted; but I by no means reject, and sometimes appeal to, such tried-and-true indicators of readership as publication history, indicators that in some cases project an admittedly different picture.

My scholarly scruples and liberties include the following.

1. The liturgy and the Book of Homilies will be scanted "as an independent context" because, as Lewalski says of her similar avoidance, "it is often not possible or profitable to distinguish between general

6. M. R. James, *Descriptive Catalogue of MSS in the Library of Pembroke College, Cambridge,* hereafter cited as James or simply by *, as above. James also notes any book listed as seen by Bale, whose *Scriptorum Illustrium Maioris Brytanniae Catalogus* received its first complete edition in London in 1559.

7. Of course, we can never determine from external evidence alone what anyone actually read. In his undergraduate years, Elizabeth Leedham-Green has kindly informed me, Spenser could not browse freely like an American undergraduate of today. To the books in his own college (James), Spenser would have had access only after earning his B.A. in 1573, for only readers of this rank and above were normally admitted there. Before his B.A., his friend Gabriel Harvey, who was elected Fellow of Pembroke in November 1570, could have escorted him in or obtained these books for him. Leedham-Green claims that to the reading of undergraduates, BCI, even though it records books in private hands and only those of some commercial value, is a better index than are the library catalogues because "the University and College libraries do not seem to have undertaken to supply the standard texts required by junior, as opposed to senior members, and the responsibility for providing them was shouldered by many tutors" (xx). Again, with regard to the MSS, although Spenser certainly possessed the competence to read them—full of ligatures though they are—she informs me that MSS were beginning to be more the object of antiquarian reverence than of reading.

biblical influences conveyed through private reading, study, sermons, and the like, and biblical influence conveyed through the liturgy" (11).

2. Except as a contrast, Calvin will receive little attention. His doctrine dominated the Elizabethan religious scene.[8] Calvinism is represented in the glosses to the Protestant Bibles, which will receive considerable attention. On doctrine, Calvin and Spenser resemble each other chiefly in their untypical statements and parenthetical qualifications, whereas straightforward parallels to Spenser lie ready to hand in other theologians such as Melanchthon. Calvin seldom comments on style or acknowledges hermeneutic difficulties such as contradictions.

3. A focus on Spenser's ideal reader and his courtly and Cambridge audiences, not just on sources, allows the critic to cite works that were not demonstrably known to Spenser but only to one of his audiences (e.g., Ochino's *Labyrinthi,* demonstrably known to Queen Elizabeth and her bishops); these can indicate to us what Spenser surmised—whether by reading them or by word of mouth or some other kind of osmosis—his audience's readerly tastes to be. I do not confine Spenser's Cambridge audience to those who were there at the same time he was, 1569–76; I have not limited myself to books published before 1576, just to books published before 1590.

4. My *terminus ad quem* is 1589, or, in one or two cases, 1590, early 1590 being the date when the first instalment of the FQ was published—an instalment including Books I and II, where the major theological statements of the FQ appear. True, the *Fowre Hymnes* were not published until 1596, and the last two of them also deliver major theological statements; they will be both treated in themselves and cited as evidence, but they neither merit nor require so much contextualization as does the FQ. As to their value as evidence, the conscientious historicist will not privilege them as the final revelation of "Spenser's thought," if such a monolith ever existed, and read them back into the first instalment, because they may reflect only what Spenser believed in 1596, not what he believed in 1590. To cite sources published after 1590 for the theology of the FQ is to court anachronism. On the one hand, post-1590 sources can be useful as capturing in writing opinions that before 1590 existed only in the air. On the other hand, people after 1590

8. See, for example, Wallace, *Puritans,* 27–28.

argued about and even reversed themselves on doctrines of free will, predestination, and the perseverance of the elect, so that for all we know, such sources can mark a change in Spenser's milieu and thus mislead us. For example, in the course of the 1590s, William Perkins's opinions changed; this is why, unlike some of my predecessors, I eschew the works of Perkins, all published in 1590 or after.[9] I make exceptions for Spenser's friend Sir Walter Raleigh, for my poetic analogues Herbert and Milton, and for Streat's hermeneutics, because Streat spells out precisely the stages of reading a contradictory text. In the chronologically precise BCI, I have limited my survey to owners who died before 1590, thus ruling out, as one cannot do with the books in Adams and in much of James, any works that were acquired after 1590. This scruple about dates will reveal a more innovative Spenser than is pictured by Hume and Gless.

5. Licenses. Although my *terminus ad quem* is strict, my *terminus a quo* is not; as I have indicated, I consider medieval sources, provided the work in question was available to Spenser or to one of his immediate audiences. Where fundamental Reformed doctrine is not an issue (as it is not in the *distinctiones*), and sometimes even when it is (as in the Seven Corporal Works of Mercy), if the stylistic similarities are compelling and unequaled in any Protestant source of the time, I even use Romanist sources—not as a clue to Spenser's personal denominational allegiance, which has not so far been ascertained and perhaps never will be, but as representing one of the several competing discourses that are inscribed, as we are now coming to realize, in the FQ.

9. On the disputes in general, see Tyacke, *Anti-Calvinists;* on Perkins's changes of opinion, see, for example, Schuldiner, *Gifts and Works,* 37, n. 3

SPENSER'S BIBLE

The discussion in this chapter lays a foundation not only for ensuing chapters but for further explorations of Spenser's biblical poetics on my part and that of others as well. In the sixteenth century, the Bible represented a major source of legitimacy and cultural capital. In Elizabethan culture—more than ever before, though less than under the Commonwealth or in New England—the Bible and its associated discourses bulked at least as large as did the combined works of classical antiquity and its associated discourses; for women and the poor, it constituted almost the whole of literary culture. Women had access to it because households rich enough to afford books would normally have owned a Geneva Bible and used it daily for private and family devotions. The literate poor could find a Great or a Bishops' Bible displayed for their use, chained to a desk for safekeeping, in every parish church. Elizabethans also had the Bible read to them with documentable frequency. Besides family devotions, everyone was expected to attend church on Sunday; in addition, the universities compelled daily attendance at their own chapels. In the BCP, the services of Morning and Evening Prayer required the recitation of the whole Psalter each month, the Old Testament once a year, and the New Testament thrice. The service of Holy Communion always involved public reading of the Lesson (usually a passage from an Epistle) and—if it was a Sunday or a feast day—of the Gospel prescribed.

Spenser uses the Bible more than does Shakespeare because he is a learned and a thematic poet, but less than Milton because he shifts more often into a secular mood and retains more of the Romanist heritage. Many of Spenser's translations are biblical: four of the sonnets he apparently translated in *Theatre* versify subjects taken from Revelation; and among his lost works are translations of *The Seven Psalms,* Ecclesiastes, and *Canticum canticorum* (Song of Solomon). Spenser often mentions the Bible explicitly. In the Letter to Ralegh, he cites Ephesians to explain the symbolism of Red Cross's armor as "the armour of a Christian man." In FQ I, Red Cross gives Arthur as a parting gift "his Saveours testament" (I.ix.19). In the House of Holiness, Fidelia holds a book "signd and seald with blood," out of which she teaches "Of God, of grace, of justice, of free will" (I.x.13; 19). Since for Spenser the Old Testament too is written with blood (I.x.53.7), and since Fidelia's syllabus is comprehensive, her book seems to be the entire Bible. These references do not, however, mean that Spenser thought the Bible held direct answers to all of life's problems.

More so than either Shakespeare or Milton, Spenser wavers between biblicism, syncretism, and secularism in different works or sections of the same work. The presence of the Bible is insistent, for example, in FQ I and the *Hymne of Heavenly Love.* No biblical references, and scant traces of biblical poetics (an occasional rhetorical figure or archetypal resemblance), appear in secular poems such as *Prothalamion* and *Muiopotmos* (note their absence from Landrum's tabulation, 538–44).[1] This localization of references has the effect of foregrounding or thematizing its use and non-use; where use is frequent, it is not just a reflection of the general culture but a conscious choice. In certain passages this sharp distinction between biblical and secular content is admittedly blurred by syncretism, exemplified in FQ II and HHB, especially by Spenser's insertion of "those *Idees* . . . which *Plato* so admired" into the biblical heaven of blessed souls (82–83).

Versions

The history of sixteenth-century versions of the Bible is too complicated for a literary critic to take into account at every turn, but it can be mastered with respect to the phrasing of a few important verses. Spenser exhibits some familiarity with Hebrew in that he puns on *Sabbaoth* and *Sabaoth* in FQ VIII.viii.2.[2] Since the Greek and Hebrew originals were

1. Landrum, "Spenser's Use," 517–44, hereafter cited parenthetically in text. This source contains faulty reasoning and data (on which see Shaheen, *Biblical References*) but provides our only statistics on the shorter poems and the prose. Much of the material in this chapter (along with other information on the subject) was first published in my entry "Bible" in the *Spenser Encyclopedia.*

2. Allen, "On the Closing Lines," 93–94; Shaheen, *Biblical References,* 171–72, hereafter cited in the text.

part of the curriculum at Merchant Taylors' School, and since BCI lists twenty-one Greek and thirty-seven Hebrew Bibles or testaments at Cambridge before 1590, Spenser may have read it in these languages.

But Latin Bibles outweigh all others by far. Including Bibles currently in a fragmentary state, and of course the five polyglots, in the years from 1535 (the first Latin copy in BCI) or 1538 (first English copy) through my *terminus ad quem* of 1589, Cambridge scholars owned approximately 187 whole Bibles in Latin and only 37 whole Bibles in English. By odds of about five to one, then, Cambridge scholars preferred Latin Bibles to English. This supports Sears Jayne's generalization: "In general, Elizabethans who could read at all could read Latin and expected to have to read in Latin anything really worth reading. The tendency of modern scholars to believe that they can understand Elizabethan England adequately in terms of its English works alone is one reason why so much remains to be learned about that period."[3]

They had a wide choice of Latin versions: the Vulgate; Erasmus' translation of the New Testament (he included his Greek text and, in some editions, annotations); the Old Testaments of Münster, of Pagninus, and of Leo Jud; Calvin's translation incorporated in his commentaries on most of the Bible; the classicizing translation of Sebastian Castellio; and, finally, the Junius-Tremellius-Beza Bible. BCI and Adams testify that all these were available at Cambridge, but a single study cannot do justice to all of them. I have always checked the Vulgate, sometimes used by Spenser, according to Naseeb Shaheen (34–35, 186).[4] I emphasize the aforementioned composite, which has been dubbed "the Protestant Vulgate": it consisted of the Tremellius-Junius OT, the Junius Apocrypha (which two parts I will hereafter abbreviate TJ), and the Beza NT. The parts were usually published separately. This composite deserves more attention than it has received from critics because it has glosses that are at once philological, sensitive to rhetoric and dialectic, relatively heavy for a Protestant Bible, and influential (especially Beza's NT) on the Geneva glosses. It was well attested at Cambridge before 1590*. Moreover, Junius' and Tremellius' commentary was known to Spenser's dedicatee, patron, friend (in some sense), and fellow poet, Sir Philip Sidney.[5]

In English, Spenser could have known the Great Bible (1539, revised 1540), the Bishops' Bible (1568, revised 1569 and 1572), the Rheims New

---

3. Jayne, *Library Catalogues,* 53.

4. Shaheen is the principal statistical work on our subject in the FQ; he occasionally misses an allusion, but he is cautious, distinguishing remoter ones with a "cf." He and Landrum cover only English versions, though Shaheen occasionally mentions the Vulgate as well. In an area so blurry as allusion, statistics can at best be only approximate.

5. Van Dorsten, "Sidney," 1–13; C. Kaske, "Another Echo," 83–86.

Testament (1582), and the unauthorized but popular Geneva (1560, revised 1576). In BCI, on the few occasions when the version of an English
Bible is specified, it is the Bishops' and the Geneva. The rare copies of
the pioneering English translations by Tyndale, Coverdale, "Matthew,"
and Taverner probably did not influence Spenser directly (Shaheen, 13–
14). Apart from the many instances when assignment is impossible, Shaheen distinguishes Spenser's use of the Great and its predecessors, the
Bishops', and the Geneva (34–35). The Geneva was the most popular
version by the last quarter of the sixteenth century, and it is the one most
often cited by Spenser critics. Spenser thus lived in a translational inter-
regnum when no single Latin or English version enjoyed such overriding
verbal authority as Jerome's Vulgate held for Romanists and the King
James version (1611) for later centuries of English-speaking readers.

Any study of biblical influence is further complicated by the status
of the Bible as a heard or spoken text. A liturgical reading of the Bible is
incantatory and would therefore tend to affect poetics and reader response in subliminal ways; in the customary post-mortem discussions
on any sermon, however, lections would be analyzed thematically and
contentiously.

The Book of Psalms

That Spenser was devoted to the Bible as a poetic model and not just as
a repository of doctrine is indicated by his love of the Psalms. True, his
culture impelled him thereto, for the Book of Psalms was arguably the
best-known book of the Bible. They were drummed into everyone's con-
sciousness in almost every church service. The Book of Psalms dramatizes the possibility of a biblical poetics. Sidney says in effect that the
Psalms are a divine model both inspiring and authorizing the poet, especially the religious poet. So are the Song of Songs, Ecclesiastes, Proverbs,
Job, and the hymns sung by Moses and by Deborah.[6] The Psalms were
also translated into meter in whole or in part by many important poets:
Wyatt, Surrey, Gascoigne, Sidney (in collaboration with his sister Mary),
Campion, Bacon, Crashaw, Carew, and Milton.

In this period the Psalms existed in other versions besides those listed
above. Beza did a Latin version which was popular at Cambridge. Three
English versions were authorized for use in churches: the Bishops', the
Sternhold and Hopkins metrical version, and Coverdale's, incorporated
(with a few changes) first into the Great Bible and then into the BCP.

6. Sidney, *Miscellaneous Prose*, 80.3–11.

In addition to his own translation of the seven Penitential Psalms (6, 32, 38, 51, 102, 130, and 143, among his lost works), Spenser borrows from Psalms more than from any book other than Revelation.[7] Moreover, his use of Psalms is pervasive, whereas his use of Revelation is localized. Some borrowings and allusions are straightforward: for instance, "And eke with fatnesse swollen were his eyne" (FQ I.iv.21) from "Their eyes swell for fatnesse" (Psalter of BCP, Ps. 73:7). Others are purely stylistic imitations, such as that sentential syntactic and semantic parallelism which is characteristic of the FQ and elegantly exemplified in Una's lament (I.vii.22–25). The frequency as well as the range of Spenser's use of the Psalms reflects the status of the Psalms in the period, which in turn exemplifies in the extreme both the omnipresence and the verbal confusion of the Bible as a whole.

Even when Spenser is at his most biblical, he is no Bunyan; his Bible is still encrusted with patristic and medieval traditions derived from the Apocrypha and pseudepigrapha and from commentaries, devotions, homilies, idealistic literature, the liturgy, and religious art. Spenser's most biblical piece is HHL: its tone is one of psalmic earnestness; Christ's life is recounted twice, chiefly from the Gospels (133–68; 234–45). Yet even these biographies are organized around Bonaventuran meditational "compositions of place"; they recount events of which the Bible contains only hints: the preincarnate generation of the Son (22–42; cf. John 1:1–18) and the Fall of the Angels (78–105; cf. Isa. 14:12–15). Tradition colors Spenser's portrayal even of Christ.

Apocrypha

The Apocrypha would be considered a full-fledged part of the Bible by Romanists but an encrustation by precisians. It held a fascination for Spenser which seems unusual in view of its subsequent eclipse. In his time this fascination was not quite so remarkable in that all Bibles contained these books; English Protestant Bibles inserted them en masse between the Old Testament and the New (except the "Prayer of Manasseh," inserted between 2 Chronicles and Ezra). Although the Geneva Bible cautions that originally these books were "not received by a commune consent to be red and expounded publikely in the Church" ("The Argument" to the Apocrypha), Article Six accepted them, and the Book of Common Prayer—anti-Calvinist on this issue—ordered most of them to be read in church. Judith, Tobit, Wisdom of Solomon, Ecclesiasticus

---

7. Landrum, *Spenser's Use*, 517; Shaheen, *Biblical References*, 181.

(or the Wisdom of Jesus Son of Sirach), and Baruch formed most of the Old Testament lessons for Morning and Evening Prayer in October and November of the liturgical year. Grace Warren Landrum finds thirty-three uses of the Apocrypha in all of Spenser's works. A long-recognized, striking, and pervasive use of the Apocrypha is the portrayal of Sapience in *An Hymne of Heavenly Beautie* (183–288).

Commentaries

We can infer that Spenser knew and used biblical commentaries both from their prevalence in Cambridge at large (Adams and BCI) and within this in the library of his own college, Pembroke (James), and from his professional association with the commentary on Revelation in Van der Noot's *Theatre.* The first thing one learns about Spenser's Duessa—that her biblical model, the Whore of Babylon, represents the Roman Church—is the product of exegesis. In this dependence Spenser was not alone. One T. Grashop, in his hermeneutical preface, "Howe to take profite in reading of the holy Scriptures," prefixed to some editions of the Geneva Bible (e.g., London: Barker, 1594), counsels the reader to "reade interpreters, if he be able"—so long, of course, as they do not contradict the Creed and Ten Commandments. Although one watchword of the Reformation was *sola Scriptura* (Scripture alone), this could be taken not radically, to mean that the Bible alone is its own interpreter to the eye of faith, but conservatively, to mean that no doctrine or practice may stand unless based on Scripture. Even the Geneva Bible (on most issues more Protestant than the Church of England) contains glosses, which doubled in number in the Tomson revision of 1576.

Besides the Latin Fathers, especially Augustine, English Protestants such as Cranmer and Andrewes used an astonishing number and variety of Greek Fathers, presumably "to go behind" medieval and Romanist formulations "to the meaning of 'original' Christian texts."[8] To judge by the availability of such sources at Cambridge*, English Protestants did not eschew even Romanist commentaries; they frequently consulted not only the Reformers but also Erasmus, the *Glossa ordinaria,* Nicolas of Lyra, and Hugh of St. Cher. Commentaries are the principal source for biblical poetics; they also help us to read the Bible in the light of older meanings, to unearth religious commonplaces available to Spenser in forms now lost to us, and to document the possibility that a given idea

---

8. Weatherby, *Mirrors,* 162.

or poetic strategy could have occurred to a writer of his place and time—
a possibility that has been questioned, sometimes justifiably so, by scholarly Spenserians.

The Four Allegorical Senses

One poetic strategy that a poet would derive from commentaries, particularly those on the OT, was allegory. The symbolic modes are most con-
veniently organized under the four exegetical senses. They are defined in
the mnemonic jingle "Littera gesta docet, quid credas allegoria, / Moralis
quid agas, quo tendas anagogia" (The *letter* teaches the events, the *allegory* [*figura*, or typology] what you should believe, the *moral* [sense,
or tropology] what you should do, the *anagogy* where you should be
headed).[9] The four senses are useful chiefly as pigeonholes for the different kinds of subject matter, the different semantic fields, that an allegorical image or story can simultaneously contain, though all four of them are
seldom found simultaneously in any single passage either in the Bible
or in secular literature. Although some exegetes denied the possibility,
the four senses were affirmed in secular literature by Dante or whoever
wrote the *Epistle to Can Grande,* by Boccaccio (*De genealogia deorum*), and
vaguely by Spenser's contemporary and admirer and Queen Elizabeth's
godson Sir John Harington in both his preface and his notes to his translation of the *Orlando furioso* (1591).

In Spenser as elsewhere, the anagogical sense is rare; in the FQ, only
the last two stanzas of the *Mutabilitie Cantos* and the "New Jerusalem"
which Red Cross glimpses from the Mount of Contemplation are pure
anagogy, "where you should be headed" (FQ I.x.55–57; VII.viii.1–2). Tro-
pology, however, is or was thought to be practically ubiquitous in both
sacred and secular texts; Spenser's character Despair (I.ix) is pure tropol-
ogy, "what you should—or should not—do," especially since he functions as Red Cross's inner voice. This moral sense was usually conveyed
in one of two modes: either in concrete examples, scarcely distinguishable
from the literal, which Protestants generally preferred to see in the Bible,
or in personifications such as Sapience or Wisdom which are alien to the
strictly canonical Scriptures (except for Proverbs 9 and brief tropes else-

---

9. See *Glossa ordinaria,* Nicolas de Lyra's opening "Prologus" and "Additiones" thereto
by Paul of Burgos, PL 113:28c and 33c; see Henri de Lubac, *Exégèse médiévale* 1:23. Since page
or signature numbers are often missing and in any case vary with the edition, I will cite the
Glossa and the frequently appended Nicolas by chapter and verse number only, or in this case
by section.

where) but frequently imposed upon them by medieval and Romanist exegetes. Spenser abounds in personifications, even in his most religious moments. In view of the foregoing, he would seem to have considered them biblical because he still read the Bible through the spectacles of medieval and Romanist exegesis.

Typology

Among the four senses of the term, "allegory" in its limited sense of "what you should believe" is better known by the medieval term *figura* or the modern typology. Surprisingly but fortunately for poets, *quid credas* means not abstract doctrine but narratives of salvation history—Creation, Fall, vicissitudes of Israel, Redemption, Second Coming, and Last Things. Strictly defined, it is the analogy between two events in salvation history. This narrative focus betrays its origin in the Christian project to appropriate the Hebrew Bible. Since Paul himself had employed typological exegesis in order to read prophecies of Christ into seemingly irrelevant Old Testament history, typology was recognized in the Bible even by the usually literalistic Reformers. The FQ contains four clear and widely recognized Christ figures: Arthur's rescue of Red Cross from Orgoglio's dungeon (I.viii) reenacts the credal Harrowing of Hell (with suggestions from 2 Thess. 2:8 and Rev. 12, 17, and 19); Red Cross's rescue of the King and Queen of Eden from their prison by killing the Dragon in three days (I.xi) recalls Christ's death, Harrowing of Hell, and Resurrection; his betrothal to Una (I.xii.37–40) prefigures the Marriage of the Lamb to the New Jerusalem (cf. Rev. 21:2); and Guyon's undergoing a three-day temptation and then lying apparently dead at the mouth of a cave guarded by an angel recapitulates a moment both in Christ's temptation in the wilderness and in the Resurrection (II.vii. 65–viii. 9; cf. Matt. 4:11; 28:1–8). Two striking reenactments of the Fall are the initial exile of Adam and his Queen from Eden (Letter to Ralegh and in I.vii.44, II.i.5) and Mordant's drinking Acrasia's wine in a garden and magically bequeathing it to his infant son Ruddymane as a bloodstain symbolizing original sin (II.i.35–ii.11).

Typology exfoliates into two borderline cases. Sometimes typology straddles the boundary with the moral sense, as in the imperative to imitate Christ (e.g., FQ I.x.40). This "applied typology" recapitulates an event in salvation history on the smaller stage of a private life.[10] Insofar

10. Charity, *Events*, 160–61; Lewalski, *Protestant Poetics*, 13.

as Red Cross's figuration of Christ is imitable, it exemplifies applied typology. Prophetic typology, by contrast, merges with apocalypticism—
"what you should believe" will happen at the end of the world. Apocalypticism thus straddles the line between time and eternity, typology and anagogy. It is exemplified in the binding of Archimago and his predicted escape (I.xii.35–36; see Rev. 20:1–3) right before the marriage/betrothal of Red Cross as the Lamb to Una as the New Jerusalem (Rev. 21). Thus, Book I embraces on its intermittent typological level all of salvation history from Genesis to Revelation. In his uses of Revelation, Spenser sometimes (e.g., V Proem) seems to be writing about the Last Days; sometimes he seems to be merely exploiting the apocalyptic mood and its imagery; and sometimes, as in Duessa's escape or in the betrothal, merely availing himself of John's anticipatory apocalypticism: "Antichrist shal come, even nowe are there many Antichrists" (1 John 2:18).[11]

Literary uses of typology are less precisely definable, because there the literal level is usually fictional (see Eric Auerbach's essay "Figura"), as it is in Spenser.[12] But the very presence of some typology in his poem undergirds his minutely topical political allegories (such as Sir Burbon abandoning his shield, V.xi.46, 52–57) with at least the appearance of a philosophy of world history. In the many places such as this where Spenser tells both a moral and a political story simultaneously, the political level takes the place of the medieval allegorical or typological level; Elizabethans would call this substitution a legitimate variation on typology, since all worldly politics, in a providentialist view of history, is a part of salvation history. (Without providence, typology looks like history repeating itself cyclically and for no apparent reason, except possibly the fulfillment of an archetype.) By allusions to the Bible, by imitations of its structure, style, and method of presentation, by calling on prevalent habits of Biblical reading and listening, Spenser shapes his poem so as to make his audience read, mark, and inwardly digest it as if it were the Bible.

11. Apocalypticism in the FQ has been explored by Sandler, "Elizabethan Apocalypse," and King both in SPRT, 70–75, and in *English Reformation Literature*, 446–49.
12. Auerbach, *Scenes*, 11–76.

STRUCTURE, MEANING, AND

IMAGES REPEATED *in bono et in malo*

Throughout the FQ, Spenser repeats with greater or lesser variation countless images—such as ladies, altars, cups, wells, gardens, boats, and armor. He also repeats what one might broadly call "motifs"—themes, characters, and actions, such as pride, fasting, magic, glory-praise-honor, and abandoning one's shield. Those pairs and chains which vary significantly and which therefore will serve as the database for this chapter and the next are listed in Appendix 2. This list shows not only numbers but also distribution, not only how plentiful such repetitions are but also how pervasively, mostly radiating from Book I, they stitch together all the books of the FQ, particularly I, II, V, and VI. Book I in particular, as has sometimes been remarked, seems to have two of everything. Indeed, this network constitutes one of the poem's few unifying devices. Such a network—altars, pride, a laurel leaf—also helps to unify the *Amoretti and Epithalamion* (1595). Critics have noticed local instances in passing.

In the heyday of New Criticism (except for Lewis's insight in 1936 about the Garden of Adonis and the Bower of Bliss), imagistic structure was studied only in shorter works of English literature, where there is no question of the audience's ability to keep it in mind. Yet Joyce, Yeats, Eliot, Woolf, Robert Penn Warren, and others of those modernist writers who shaped the taste of the New Critics were often practicing a leitmotivic method of presentation in longer works; Thomas Mann enunciated it as a program.[1] In the 1940s and 1950s, Shakespeare's plays were revealed to be stitched together by images or even structured around them. In the 1960s, Northrop Frye and A. C. Hamilton established that repeated im-

---

1. See Mann's essay "Leitmotiv," 571.

ages constitute one important structure in the FQ, and that their intra-
textual relations must be considered before allegoresis is attempted or allusions traced; the structure thus revealed is often not "organic" like that
sought by the New Critics but schematic and/or allusive. In the 1970s,
James Nohrnberg and Stephen Barney also emphasized repeated images,
mingling them, however, with larger repetends and with external allusions of all kinds. In this chapter and the next, I am carrying on this tradition but at once narrowing, complicating, and historicizing it.[2] More
recently still, in the 1980s, on the smaller scale of word and phrase, John
Hollander describes the "self-echo" in *Paradise Lost,* "the poem's memory
of itself," "the almost leitmotivic reappearance of phrases and cadences . . .
to which sophisticated critical attention of the past few decades has been
so attentive" and conjectures in a note that it "probably derives from *The
Faerie Queene.*" He concludes the note with a challenge: "Spenserian
echoing is a most complex matter. Where, and why, this sort of thing
happens in Spenser is worth studying."[3] Although Hollander's "echoes"
are not always coextensive with my images and motifs, he is calling for
the sort of "concordantial" reading that I will be doing in this chapter
and the next.

In a literary work, almost anything can be repeated significantly, thus
earning the status of a motif; motif hunting is a fruitful critical method.
Milton repeats, first, rhetorical devices, "phrases and cadences," then sit-
uations and kinetic images such as single combats, temptations, descents
and ascents, councils, and lone defiers thereof.[4] Again, in chivalric romance, virtuous ladies and evil sorceresses, jousts, disguises, visits to
castles, interludes of rest beneath trees, comparisons of fighters to wild
beasts, and miscellaneous accoutrements of knighthood are repeated;
such "romance doubling" may involve entire plots. Sometimes these motifs are even biblical, such as those of fall and redemption. I also concede
that the Bible shares a vocabulary of motifs—call it the racial uncon-
scious or what you will—with other works of comparable size and cultural significance. Thus it would be pointless to trace to the Bible a motif so vague and general as descent into oneself or proof of knighthood
because of its archetypal nature and the danger that the similarity may lie
in the way the critic has labeled it. But I hope to show that Spenser repeats concrete, sharply outlined motifs in a distinct pattern that is more

2. Frye, "Structure of Imagery," in Hamilton, *Essential Articles,* 155–56. Hamilton, *Structure of Allegory,* 12, 43, 82–83 et passim; Nohrnberg, *Analogy,* 595–98 et passim; Gilman, *Iconoclasm,* 62; and Barney, *Allegories of History,* 114–125, esp. 124–25 et passim.

3. Hollander, *Figure of Echo,* 51.

4. See also Oram, "Invocation," 121–39, esp. 124.

biblical than that followed by all but a few authors before him, but one that Herbert and Milton may well have copied.

Length raises doubts based on readerly perception. Some of those repetitions that Hollander and I celebrate are widely spaced, seemingly too far-flung to have registered on readers without concordances. I answer that, as was once argued by defenders of image-patterns in Shakespeare, Spenser's audiences had memories that were more capacious than ours because more exercised. Besides, with a written text, one can supplement memory by going back and rereading.

One can read the Bible, too, looking before and after with some common thread in mind—including images, words, and phrases.[5] Jean Leclercq postulates such a process of reading Scripture when he speaks of "hook-words" in the compositions of monks, whose scriptural meditations have made them living concordances:

> Verbal echoes so excite the memory that a mere allusion will spontaneously evoke whole quotations and, in turn, a scriptural phrase will suggest quite naturally allusions elsewhere in the sacred books. Each word is like a hook, so to speak; it catches hold of one or several others which become linked together and make up the fabric. . . . [Q]uotations by means of the "hook-words," group themselves together in their minds and under their pen, like variations on the same theme.[6]

Such "rumination" was made easier, first, by marginal cross-references, available in most Bibles then as now.[7] In the Renaissance, in all confessions, and in Protestantism even among the laity, one did not have to devote one's entire life to Scripture like a monk to be able to meditate and compose like this; printed concordances were widely available at Cambridge in Spenser's day.[8] BCI lists an overwhelming fifty decedents before

5. In modern biblical criticism, *Leitwörter* and "keywords" are traced in individual Psalms and other biblical poems by Alter, *Biblical Poetry,* 32, 60–61, 83, 119, 135, 144; for widely spaced situational parallels, see Nohrnberg, *Like unto Moses,* 269–307.

6. Leclercq, *Love,* 91. Since Spenser was not a monk, I use *distinctiones* to prove he read in this way. Leclercq mentions the *distinctiones* as being an artifical, academic, and scholastic outgrowth of this habit of reading (see 95–96, 98, and 366–67, n. 15); this schematism makes *distinctiones* less relevant for monks but more akin to Spenser. Leclercq concedes about his authors a criticism I will rebut about Spenser: the monastic repeater is "not . . . necessarily referring to what he has already said" (91). Leclercq does not mention varying images *in bono et in malo.*

7. They were supplied, for example, in all editions of the Geneva Bible and all of the some half-dozen editions I have seen of the "Protestant Vulgate."

8. To Spenser's Vulgate (before the Clementine Revisions, 1590), there were many printed concordances in the sixteenth century; see MCLI, 5, 8. Herrey's *Twoo* [sic] *Concordances* to the Geneva Bible were printed sometimes with it, sometimes separately.

1590 who owned them*. And these concordances and cross-references, along with the distinctions discussed later in this chapter, were more than a convenience: they constituted a statement about the common threads with which God had stitched his book together and about the proper way to read it—a hermeneutics and thus a biblical poetics in the second sense sketched in my introduction.

Renaissance exegetes urged readers to follow up internal cross-references. Grashop urges them to "consider the . . . agreement that one place . . . hath with another, whereby that which seemeth darke in one is made easie in another." About forty years later, George Herbert exemplifies this way of reading when he exclaims in "The H. Scriptures, II": "This verse marks that, and both do make a motion, / Unto a third that ten leaves off doth lie." Similarly, in Herbert's "A Priest to the Temple, or, The Country Parson," the third means to understand Scripture is "a diligent collation of Scripture with Scripture. For all Truth being consonant to it self, and all being penn'd by one and the self-same Spirit, it cannot be, but that an industrious, and judicious comparing of place with place must be a singular help for the right understanding of the Scriptures."[9] Luther affirms this same principle:

> Such is the way of the whole of Scripture: it wants to be interpreted by a comparison of passages from everywhere and understood under its own direction. The safest of all methods for discerning the meaning of Scripture is to work for it by drawing together and scrutinizing passages.[10]

This image-hopping shows that the Bible was regarded as one book, not many; if so, it could provide a poet with a divinely sanctioned model for his global structures. I propose that Spenser—who, like all good Protestants, must have spent considerable time in meditating on the Scriptures—developed themes in pieces scattered throughout a work and related them with hook-words.

Consequently, in reading the FQ, and also *Amoretti and Epithalamion*, I submit that we should pay attention to the signifiers, collate those passages that contain the same hook-word, and compile a mental concordance. Because the Bible was perceived as requiring this kind of reading, and because every Protestant was required to read the Bible, Spenser could count on readers to read his work in the same way, provided he dropped enough hints.

Now, medieval and Renaissance Bible reading (e.g., Herbert's herme-

---

9. Herbert, "The Parsons Knowledg [*sic*]," chap. 4, in *Works*, 229.
10. *Word and Sacrament 3* (vol. 37 of *Works*), 21.

neutics) often sought to derive a consistent unitary meaning from such repetitions, and this can often be done with repetitions in the FQ as well. Medieval or Renaissance, topical or imagistic, concordantial exegetes also sometimes noted their diversity. For example, in the quotation above, the application of concordantial reading has just led Luther to discover a narrative inconsistency, so that his manifesto acknowledges that such collation could kindle friction as well as light. John of Chalons recommends "distinguishing" as the basis for constructing a sermon:

> The preacher should . . . note the *dictio* on the basis of which the division is to be made; he should at once look up that principal *dictio* in the Concordance, and, according to the diversity of authorities written therein, he should note in how many different ways this *dictio* is treated.[11]

Evidence abounds—both external and internal—as to the biblical origin of Spenser's repeated images; but since he could also have devised this strategy independently, or learned it from several previous writers, it is not uniquely biblical.

Let us look for a distinctive biblical trademark. As one pursues a given image concordantially through the FQ, one usually, though not always, finds it occurring here in a good sense, there in a bad, here in an honorific sense, there in a derogatory one. The need to distinguish such shifts was something of which many "New" as well as archetypal critics, for all their concordantial reading, were unaware. As A. C. Spearing says, rebuking the pre–New Critical D. W. Robertson, Jr., and Bernard Huppé, "they would arbitrarily make the 'higher' meaning of images totally present at any point" instead of looking for "development."[12]

Nowadays we read with an eye for internal differences. Spenserians should do so because in at least four places in the FQ a reversal of value is explicitly remarked upon. In the Dragon-Fight, when Red Cross's armor is heated by the spark and sears his body, the poet-speaker comments on the paradox: "That erst him goodly armed, now most of all him harm'd" (I.xi.27). When Paridell and Hellenore send love messages by means of a cup of wine, the poet-speaker calls it "A Sacrament prophane in mystery of wine" (III.ix.30–31), recalling the truly mysterious sacrament, the Eucharist, which has been represented straightforwardly in Fidelia's cup (I.x.13). Guyon's discovery that the pure well will not wash

---

11. In his unpublished "Art of Making Sermons . . . ," summarized from two MSS in the Bibliothèque Nationale in Rouse and Rouse, *Preachers,* 192–93.

12. Spearing, "Development," 252.

blood from Ruddymane's hands drives him "into great amaz'ment" and cleaves "into diverse doubt his wavering wonder" (II.ii.3). Besides upsetting Guyon's normal expectations for blood and water, this upsets the reader's as well; she recalls five cantos earlier the Hermit's command to Red Cross to "wash [his] hands from guilt of bloudy field" (I.x.60) and just four cantos earlier the Well of Life that could "guilt of sinfull crimes cleane wash away." When introducing the bad Genius of illusion in the Bower of Bliss, the poet-speaker admonishes us that he is "Not that celestiall powre, to whom the care / Of life, and generation of all / That lives, pertaines in charge particulare" (II.xii.47); this good Genius or something like him is duly introduced in a parallel garden in the next book (III.vi.31–33). These examples lay bare many aspects of Spenser's way with images. They make clear that the reader cannot always assign the same meaning to every occurrence of an image. When the alteration occurs in adjacent sentences (Guyon's three conjectures about the blood, the poet's classification of Genii), it can often be labeled antithesis, or definition of a thing by its contrary; it is common to all discourse. But when widely separated, I will argue, it is distinctively biblical; it has no counterpart, for example, in Renaissance rhetorical manuals and occurs with much less frequency elsewhere.

The Practice of "Distinguishing" Repeated Images in the Bible

The Bible, too, repeats a given image in an honorific and a derogatory sense: in Matthew 13:33 (see also Luke 13:21) Christ says, "The kingdome of heaven is like unto leaven," but in 16:6 (see also Mark 8:15, Luke 12:1) he warns: "Take heede and beware of the leaven of the Pharises and Sadduces." This bipolarity—manifested also in good and bad cups, gardens, altars, trees, mountains, cities, holy men, warriors, and women—had been noticed there by patristic, medieval, and Counter-Reformation exegetes. (I merely note the last three images in passing, pervasive though they are in the FQ, because, besides possibly deriving from romance, they fall into the category of foil characters, discoverable in almost any fiction.) When a word was repeated in such a bipolar way, exegetes said that it was to be understood *in bono [sensu] et in malo* or *in meliorem et peiorem partem*. Nicolas de Byard, for example, distinguishes leaven, "Fermentum," *in bono et in malo*. Some exegetes mention this polarization regularly; some silently exhibit it by the arrangement in which they "distinguish," as R. H. Rouse and M. A. Rouse put it, "multiple spiritual meanings for terms in the text." [13] The habit of "distinguishing" an image gives rise to a list of meanings called a *distinctio* (plural, *distinctiones*), which purports to exhaust all the meanings of a given word, object, or concept in Scripture. It gives scriptural references and sometimes also quotations for each meaning, wherein it resembles a concordance entry.

On the exegetical page, the presence of a *distinctio* is often typographically highlighted. Sometimes it begins with paragraph signs or rubrication. Often the various meanings are stacked in columnar form, sometimes connected by branching lines (in MSS) or a bracket (in print) to the word; [14] thus they capture the eye, the memory, and the imagination. Though still called *distinctiones,* this hermeneutical practice sometimes distinguishes "in fact only one symbolic meaning for the scriptural term, followed by a sequence of several justifications or explanations of the symbolism" (Rouse and Rouse, "Biblical *Distinctiones,*" 35) with scriptural verses for each; it does so when the Bible does not vary the image but repeats it in approximately the same sense. Some motifs in the FQ do not vary, for example, "giant" (always *in malo*) or the phrase noted by Hollander, "x who knows not x," which always signals authorial self-reference.

Scholars and critics of *distinctiones* tend to privilege one or another aspect of them. Judson Allen and Maren-Sophie Røstvig (discussed below) tend to privilege concepts over images; I find concepts too vague to base an argument on. Focusing properly on images, J. W. Blench and the Rouses privilege minute analyses of objects from nature such as birds, a focus I find too narrow for accuracy. Other ways of distinguishing that are both exegetical and useful for Spenser include good-better-best, bad-worse-worst, earthly and temporal versus celestial and eternal (e.g., Spenser's kinds of glory), general versus special, [15] inner versus outer, and moral versus mystical. Spenser distinguishes images more frequently *in bono et in malo* than in other ways. A *distinctio* serves for the poet as a bag of tricks, a list of ways in which he can deepen a given image and vary its repetitions; it serves the reader as a checklist of hermeneutical possibilities.

While *distinctiones* do not include exhaustive theoretical treatments of allegory, one of their ways of "distinguishing" is in terms of the famous

13. Rouse and Rouse, "Biblical *Distinctiones,*" 35.

14. For a rough idea of how they looked, see Gellrich, *Idea,* 72, transcribing "cathedra," "chair," from Bersuire's *Repertorium,* or, for a less visual impression, my quotations of "gloria" from Alexander Carpentarius and of "calix" and "vinum" from Hugh of St. Cher later in this chapter.

15. See Barney, *Allegories,* 98; this resembles Queen Elizabeth's "two persons," monarch and lady, in the Letter to Ralegh.

four senses. The classic example both of a biblical distinction and of the four senses is the four senses of "city" or "Jerusalem." Spenser reflects them in his variations on the image of the city. His heavenly Jerusalem corresponds perfectly to its biblical counterpart on the anagogical level, and it has certain moral implications, too, as we shall see. Spenser celebrates also Lincoln (III.ix.51), Troynovant (II.46; III.ix.45), and Cleopolis (I.x.58–59; II.x.72; III.ix.51). Lincoln and Troynovant—geographic, historical, and political cities devoid of moral coloring—exemplify the literal level corresponding to the earthly Jerusalem. Troynovant represents the historical London with an onomastic twist to stress its role in the Tudors' foundation myth. Moreover, Spenser's several significant uses of typology in or near these passages (see Introduction) and the Christian element in the Briton Monuments (II.x.5–68) imply a providential view of history which ties all history into salvation history, the political into the figural. Cleopolis and its history (II.x.70–76), being Fairy and thus secular, can be figural only in a weak sense; Cleopolis is moral, representing, as we shall see in the next chapter, a worldly, competitive lifestyle. As a contrast to these, the biblical city *in malo*, Babylon, is alluded to in connection with Lucifera's dungeon (I.v.47).

Though not always straightforwardly biblical in content, then, Spenser's image-chain of cities varies according to two biblical patterns; it is biblical not in a slavish but in a sophisticated way. Distinguishing figural-versus-moral combined with general-versus-special explains how Una can represent one thing to Sansloy and the Satyrs, namely, revelation and the True Church (figural), and not only this but also another thing to her knight—his indwelling Christ or Holy Spirit (moral). General-versus-special, outer-versus-inner, and figural-versus-moral together make up an equivalent to the important distinction public-versus-private in the Letter to Ralegh.

As late as the seventeenth century, preachers distinguished images according to the four-level scheme. Lancelot Andrewes and Donne (in his sermons on Psalms and Ezekiel) employ it with the same modifications—the omission of anagogy and the politicization of typology to refer to the sovereign—as does Spenser.[16]

Nevertheless, Spenser uses the four-level scheme either strikingly but

16. For Donne, see Lewalski, *Protestant Poetics*, 136–39; for Andrewes, see Blench, *Preaching*, 67 and notes. According to his usual practice, Andrewes derives his meanings here from some of his (and Spenser's) favorite sources: the *Glossa ordinaria*, Nicolas of Lyra, and Hugh of St. Cher, a copy of which last he owned and willed to Pembroke College (see Hugo of Vienna in James's *Descriptive Catalogue*).

very locally, for cities, or else pervasively but vaguely, that is, where he politicizes typology. The scheme is thus attenuated in his later, secular books and in the secular poems because they too, like the Elfin Chronicles, do not invoke those religious doctrines of the afterlife and of salvation history which it presupposes. As we can see from this example, the four senses are quite different from repeating images *in bono et in malo:* although the two principles of distinction may happen to coincide (e.g., glory on the anagogical level is good, while on the tropological it may be bad, as in I.iv.9), nevertheless the good and the bad can both coexist on the same level, usually the tropological (e.g., good and bad fasting) so that they constitute an entirely different classification. Spenser's practice of repeating images *in bono et in malo* is as recognizably biblical as that of repeating them on the four levels; moreover, it is pervasive in the FQ. Whether far-fetched or plausible, biblical or secular, a *distinctio* suggests a structure that a poet can build in order to deepen and vary an image and that a reader can use as a checklist of its hermeneutical possibilities.

In Book VI, Spenser repeats the word "grace" and the motif of a vision on a mountain from Book I. In the Bible, too, images often recur a long time after their first appearance. We can be the more confident that Spenser and his audience learned about such recurrences from the Bible in that the standard how-to for poets, the rhetorical manual, fails to mention any repetitions that are so far-flung, any echoes of word or phrase that are so long-range. In fact, according to Richard A. Lanham, "The term 'imagery' as it is used today in literary criticism was not part of the traditional rhetorical nomenclature."[17] Terms such as "imago," "similitudo" (at least as a figure of style), "translatio" (metaphor), and "permutatio" (allegory) receive small elaboration there. The implication is that when a given image is repeated, it will retain the evaluation with which it first appeared; however preoccupied the manuals are with praise and blame, they do not mention repeating images *in bono et in malo.*

The shock or alienation effect of the reversal is akin to ambivalence and irony, whether verbal, dramatic, or cosmic, but it is not the same. In verbal irony and ambivalence, a single occurrence can be read either honorifically or disparagingly, depending on one's point of view; repeating an image *in bono et in malo* is reversing the value in a different passage. It is a strategy that is applicable to secular works because it does not require allegory or any religious dogma beyond the categories of good and evil.

---

17. Lanham, *Handlist of Rhetorical Terms,* s.v. "Image."

Distinctions *in bono et in malo* in the Bible,
in the *Distinctiones,* and in Spenser:
Fasting, Birds, Altars, and Glory

An individual *distinctio* can often be found embedded in almost any kind of biblical or religious study aid, even encyclopedias, and especially in the more expansive commentaries such as Hugh of St. Cher (Hugo of Vienna in Pembroke College's copy) on the whole Bible. They first appear in the Fathers. The much-discussed locus classicus for images repeated *in bono et in malo* is Augustine in *De doctrina Christiana* (III.xxv.35–36), adducing among others the images of leaven, serpents, and lions. Augustine presents these diversities not as a poetic strategy but as a pitfall for the interpreter of Scripture. They occur in Gregory's *Moralia in Job,* of which Pembroke owned at least one copy in Spenser's time, and in Cassiodorus' *Expositio Psalmorum*.[18] Such Latin Fathers were still revered in the Church of England—a reverence voiced, for example, in Jewel's Apology and the Thirty-nine Articles.

In the Middle Ages and the Renaissance, these distinctions were sometimes culled and collected in their own freestanding book, properly called a *distinctiones* (hereafter, this plural noun when it governs singular verbs and articles will denote such a work). The *distinctiones* is an alphabetical dictionary of symbols, a selective concordance with quoted contexts and comments.[19] Spenser composed concordantially, by which I mean that he imitated the Bible as portrayed by the *distinctiones,* in that he wrote with a concordance of his own poem in mind and expected readers to compile one too. What my Appendix of Images does for the FQ, a *distinctiones* does for the Bible. Devoting an entire work to a hermeneutical strategy calls attention to it. The *distinctiones* I discuss in what follows are related in one way or another to Spenser.

18. I have adapted my survey from Rouse and Rouse, "Biblical *Distinctiones,*" esp. 28–29. For Pembroke's copies of Gregory's *Moralia in Job,* see James's *Catalogue,* MSS 13–15, 178–79; hereafter cited as James with MS or book number. Pembroke also owned a *Tabula* to it (no. 242) and several compilations derived from it. In the various *distinctiones* they survey, the Rouses mention distinctions *in bono* and *in malo* on 29 and 35 and a similar feature in the marginal cross-references, "contrasting material . . . distinguished by a 'contra,'" on 33.

19. On *distinctiones,* see Wilmart, "Répertoire," 335–46; Smalley, *Study of the Bible,* 246–49; Rouse and Rouse, "Biblical *Distinctiones,*" 27–37; Barney, "Visible Allegory," 87–107; MCLI, 32–40. For applications to literature, see Robertson and Huppé, *Piers Plowman,* 5–6, though they use them primarily for their content, not as stylistic models; Spearing, "Development," 252; Mann, "Eating and Drinking," 37; Allen, *Ethical Poetic,* 73, 117–28; and idem, "Malory's Diptych," 237–55.

In several of these freestanding *distinctiones, in bono et in malo* is the preferred way of distinguishing images. It is the most frequent distinction drawn by perhaps the very first exemplar of the genre, the *Distinctiones Abel* of Peter the Chanter (d. 1197 or 1198), according to Stephen Barney.[20] Pierre Bersuire's *distinctiones,* called the *Repertorium* or *Dictionarium,* fairly well represented in Cambridge at large*, explicitly distinguishes every image in this way, just as Spenser explicitly distinguishes the good from the bad Genius.[21]

Hieronymus Lauretus, in the Preface to his *Sylva Allegoriarum* (sixteenth century), makes a similar distinction:

> This [principle] only we have observed, not, however, invariably, that what is interpreted as being about God should have first place, then about angels, good people, and virtues: lastly about demons, heretics, evil people, and vices.

The sixteenth-century date of this work (as well as of two other less popular *distinctiones*) and its availability at Cambridge* prove that neither the genre nor its clientele died out; in the world at large, Lauretus went through twelve editions.[22] Bersuire even carried this exegetical pattern over into his mythography, which was separately printed as *Metamorphosis Ovidiana Moraliter . . . Explanata* (sometimes wrongly attributed to Thomas Waleys). In his introductory survey (chapter 1), Bersuire offers for most of its seventeen pagan gods meanings *in bono et in malo.*[23] Although Venus is not one of those so distinguished, being condemned throughout, this exegetical pattern could have inspired Spenser's shifting

20. Barney, "Visible Allegory," 97.

21. Bersuire (Petrus Berchorius; fourteenth century, a friend of Petrarch's; wrongly called Berthorius or Bercarius), *Dictionarium vulgo Repertorium morale,* hereafter cited as *Repertorium* by entry. Even a neutral word like *neque* is assigned meanings *in bono et in malo,* though of course disparaging words like *nequitia* cannot have a meaning *in bono.* The meanings I cite from the convenient *Repertorium* Spenser may have derived from Bersuire's cumbersome study aid, the *Reductorium morale super totam bibliam;* this work is a running commentary on "omnes figurae bibliae," "the images in the whole Bible," book by book—a work whose huge *tabula* at the end makes it usable as a *distinctiones;* see MCLI, 23, 38, 46. Of this, Pembroke itself owned in Spenser's time one and probably two copies—a MS (James, no. 197) given by a medieval donor, and Book no. 21 (Cologne, 1477).

22. I refer to the Lyons 1622 edition, cited in text by entry (ed. princ. Barcelona, 1570). See MCLI, 39.

23. Available at Cambridge*. See MCLI, 113. I have employed the transcription of the Paris, 1509 edition, *De formis figurisque deorum* (= a separate printing of *Reductorium morale,* 15.1). Cf. Allen, *Mysteriously Meant,* 171–73.

evaluations of his recurring myth of Venus and Adonis (III.i.34–38 *in malo;* III.vi.45–49 *in bono*).

An author one of whose works is cited by Spenser wrote another of these freestanding *distinctiones*—Alain de Lille (Alanus de Insulis, 1128–1208). While not attested at Cambridge, it was printed in Deventer in 1477, so Spenser could conceivably have known it. Under "calix," Alain distinguishes cups *in bono et in malo* (col. 726) much as does Spenser. Spenser cites Alain's poem *De planctu naturae* (called by Spenser *Plaint of kindes,* FQ VII.vii.9).[24]

While BCI lists no freestanding *distinctiones* in private hands, Pembroke, Spenser's own college, possesses three MSS bearing that title, of which certainly one, and almost certainly all, were there in Spenser's time. One of them—that of Nicolas de Byard (James 238.3)—was given by a medieval donor and therefore was certainly there in Spenser's student days. James plausibly conjectures that another of these three, that of Simon de Boraston (or Burneston; James 156), represents an unattributed *distinctiones* given by one John Spenser in 1383–89 (List of Donors, xiv); if so, it was at Pembroke during Spenser's stay there. Moreover, looking at this Renaissance donor list, Spenser may have conjectured the donor to have been a member of his own "house of auncient fame" (*Prothalamion* 131, especially if John was also the name of the social climber's own father), and read his book for that reason. The third work of this title was seen there by John Bale in the course of his bibliographical survey about twenty years before Spenser matriculated, though it has since been lost.[25] In 1599, too late to have influenced Spenser or his immediate audience, Smart gave Pembroke several works titled *distinctiones* (e.g., James 99–101), as part of the treasure trove of medieval books emanating from the dissolved monastery at Bury; this fact may indicate the continued appeal of such books.

24. PL 210, cols. 685–1012. Neither the *De planctu naturae,* cited by Spenser, nor the *Distinctiones* I have cited was owned by Cambridge, by Cambridge decedents, or by Pembroke College Library before 1590. Cambridge University Library owns a copy of another poem by Alain, however, the *Anticlaudianus.* Although some have suspected that when Spenser cites the "*Plaint of kindes,*" he is merely echoing *The Parliament of Foules,* John E. Hankins invokes all three works of Alain—the *Distinctiones* and the two poems—in his *Source and Meaning.* On Spenser's estimate of the *De planctu* and the probability that he knew it in MS, see Quilligan, *Milton's Spenser,* 161–65, esp. 162 and n. 30.

25. We know neither the author nor the title, but its incipit (not found in Stegmüller's, Vatasso's, or Haureau's lists) is "Nunc ad ea que contra naturae cursum edita" (James, *Descriptive Catalogue,* xviii). With regard to the name of Spenser's father, see Judson, *Life,* 8. On Boraston and Byard, see Pfander, "Medieval Friars," 19–29, esp. 23.

Some images repeated with variations in Spenser—fasting, birds, altars, and glory—are also "distinguished" in the Bible by exegesis which Spenser could have known. We first receive the impression in I.iii.14 that fasting is evil because it is performed by the ignorant, ineffectual, unhospitable, and grotesquely Romanist Corceca. Yet the normative Hermit Contemplation also fasts (I.x.48.5–9) and tells Red Cross to do the same (I.x.52).[26] Fasting is portrayed *in bono et in malo* in the Bible; for example, although fasting is often commended, nevertheless Saul's frequent fasts cannot prevent his losing the favor of God, so that they take on a legalistic quality (1 Sam. 14:24–30; see also 28:20; and Jezebel in 1 Kings 21:8–12). Christ himself enunciates a distinction: when the disciples of John suspect him because his disciples do not fast like them, he replies that fasting does not befit his disciples in their present circumstances but will in future circumstances (Matt. 9:14–15). To illustrate a typical *distinctio,* Christina von Nolcken picks the entry on fasting in the *Rosarium theologie,* called, in its longer version, the *Floretum.* Fasting in the Bible is double, fruitful and unfruitful, that is, good and morally vapid, each of which in turn is divided into four sorts. The unfruitful fasting is stigmatized as such by the circumstances, such as "from necessity" and "by hypocrites"—categories that are applicable to the signally unfruitful Corceca.[27] Fasting is treated by Spenser much as it is in the Bible as constructed by this hermeneutical method. From those scholars (Wilmart and Rouse and Rouse) who have read Boraston and Nicholas de Byard, we learn that Boraston, suggestively for Fradubio (I.ii.28–45) and for "*The tree of life,* the crime of our first fathers fall" (I.xi.46), remarks that man is like a tree and distinguishes "Arbor" *in bono et in malo.* Byard (who, though French, worked in England) distinguishes at least two images *in bono et in malo*—"fermentum" ("leaven") and "abscondere" ("concealment")—and he remarks suggestively for the FQ, "civitas triplex est."[28]

26. See Hamilton ed. at I.iii.14. For my interpretation of this shift, see Chapter 3.

27. Von Nolcken, "Some Alphabetical Compendia," 271–88. Of the *Floretum,* Cambridge University owned not only a MS copy of the Latin original but also a MS of a Middle English translation thereof, of which von Nolcken prints the entry "Jejunium," 285. This work exemplifies the genre *distinctiones.* See MCLI, 32, 37–38.

28. Nicholas (de) Byard (Biard, Biart), *Distinctiones* (James, no. 238.3), was donated in the Middle Ages by John de Stratton and seen by Thomas James in his survey of 1600. Different meanings of the same word, e.g., "abscondo," are punctuated by paragraph signs, under which the meanings of a given word are grouped into what Rouse and Rouse call "families" under several chapter headings and are divided, among other ways, according to the principle of *in bono et in malo,* e.g., chap. 3. "Abscondere non debet . . . ," 4, "Abscondendus est . . . ," 5, "Abscondenda non est . . ." (Rouse and Rouse, "Biblical *Distinctiones,*" 34; Wilmart, "Répertoire," 43–44). I have glanced through Pembroke's manuscripts of both Byard

Rouse and Rouse quote or summarize from Byard and two other *distinctiones* the entries on birds ("aves," and "volucres," 28–34). The mounting eagle occurs in these; it stands for Christ and for the just or the contemplative man; Spenser uses the image for Red Cross after his bath in the Well of Life (I.xi.34). Images of avian flight "rich in resonance and significance" pervade the work of Spenser, as Patrick Cheney has shown.[29] Thus Spenser may have derived not just this or that particular bird image but the idea of repeating bird images from the Bible, in part because these were highlighted by the *distinctiones*.

Under the title "Altar," Byard has, according to Wilmart, the following entry:

> Altar means the mind in which good thoughts should be offered to the Lord . . . both because it is hollow and empty through humility, that it may receive the fire, . . . and because it ought always to have this fire: see Lev. 6: "let a fire be always burning on the altar." (Wilmart, 344, n. 5)

This is suggestive for Spenser's erotic altars, perhaps in the FQ (III.xi.47 and IV.x.38) and certainly in *Am.* 22 (YSP):

> There ["within my mind"] I to her as th'author of my blisse,
> will builde an altar to appease her ire:
> and on the same my hart will sacrifise,
> burning in flames of pure and chast desire:
> The which vouchsafe O goddesse to accept.

Here, the humility and the *cogitationes* are offered to the lady instead in syncretic or potentially idolatrous *Frauendienst.* Then in the *Epithalamion* printed with the *Amoretti,* and arguably as a partial generic correction to it, after the lover and lady have transcended the Petrarchan religion of love, a wholly good altar provides the locus of their wedding (215, 223, 230), thus yielding in the little volume a simple pattern of altars *in bono et in malo.* Again, the similarity of pattern is as important as that of meaning. Now, Boraston, like many other authors of *distinctiones,* was English and thus possessed another local appeal for Spenser besides his donor to counter his mustiness. Boraston was seen at Pembroke by Thomas James in 1600. It is tempting to suppose that reading Byard and Boraston as a student provided Spenser with a model of his future poem's

---

and Boraston, verifying Wilmart's transcription of "abscondere," Byard's first entry; for the rest, I rely on the selections transcribed by him and the Rouses.

29. See Cheney, *Spenser's Famous Flight,* 16–17 et passim.

imagistic structure. Such an argument is unnecessary, however, for in arguing the influence not of any one *distinctiones* but of the genre, one can resort to other *distinctiones* then available and now more accessible, or speak merely of kindred methods of presentation.

Among its printed books, Pembroke (and Cambridge at large*) owned several copies of those alphabetical preacher's manuals or moral encyclopedias derived from *distinctiones* and still loosely called by that name. Again, many are by Englishmen; the prestige of such works would have been augmented, not decreased, by their being nevertheless written in Latin and printed on the Continent. These topical *distinctiones* or moral encyclopedias, like the *loci communes* which they resemble, devote more entries to abstractions (such as doctrines or virtues and vices) than to images (such as altars) and motifs (such as fasting); they comprise "not so much . . . scriptural terms in want of definition, as . . . topics in search of scriptural discussion" (Rouse and Rouse, "Biblical *Distinctiones*," 34). Exegesis even on this level of abstraction is still relevant to Spenser as a model of how the Bible develops a theme; from such moral encyclopedias, for example, he could have derived his way of exploring a topic in pieces interspersed with other topics and with "mere" narrative, since that is the way in which moral encyclopedias describe the Bible. (I must admit that their value to my case is ancillary because they sometimes draw extensively on secular learning, for instance in their treatment of true and false friendship, making them less distinctively biblical.)

Among these preacher's manuals at Pembroke is the popular *Destructorium Vitiorum* of Alexander Carpenter/Alexander Anglicus.[30] A "Tabula Alphabetica" in the front gives an entry in the form of a paradigmatic *distinctio* of different kinds of glory in the Bible:

> Gloria aliqua est vera & aliqua vana, et gloria vera dividitur in gloriam veram, veriorem, verissimam. . . . Gloria vana dividitur in gloriam diabolicam, gloriam mundanam, gloriam humanam. . . .
> Gloria vana diabolica septem habet filias. . . .

As this *distinctio* is expounded in the text itself, each species and subspecies merits a chapter, be it large or small, and each chapter has an initial illuminated in red or blue. This treatment of glory exemplifies the

---

30. The Cologne, 1485, edition, given by a medieval donor (= James, Book no. 28); Pembroke also owns an incomplete copy of the Cologne, 1480, edition (Book no. 26); and BCI lists eleven copies owned by Cambridge decedents before 1590. I cite from the Nuremberg, 1496, edition.

medieval penchant for articulating both the topic and the page on which it is written. Furthermore, it shows how the author of a *distinctio* characteristically frames the "branches" or divisions of the word's meaning in alliteration and in homoioptoton or syntactic parallelism. *Distinctiones* project this articulation onto the Bible and the world it purports to describe.[31] *Gloria vana diabolica* and her daughters suggest Lucifera and Philotime. Alexander assures us that the testimony of a good conscience (2 Cor. 1:12) is true glory, albeit the lowest grade thereof; this thought casts a favorable light on Guyon's controversial feeding of himself with "his owne vertues, and praise-worthy deedes" (II.vii.2).

Pembroke also owned the immensely popular *distinctiones* or preacher's encyclopedia the *Summa praedicantium* by John (de) Bromyard, another Englishman, and that of Rainer de Pisis.[32] It could have been this book and/or habituation to this method of Bible reading which led Spenser to split up his treatments of glory among various protagonists and passages of the poem as he did. Either or both experiences could have led Spenser's reader to reassemble them; she would distinguish *in bono* from *in malo,* in this case *vera* from *vana;* she would find an extraordinarily rich pattern of images and characters—the many and various allies, associates, and antitypes of Arthur and Gloriana in the poem.[33]

Finally, not only in the sixteenth century, with Lauretus and others, but in the seventeenth as well, the tradition continued with a local and Protestant vitality: a *distinctiones* grew again out of English soil when Benjamin Keach (1640–1704) (helped, according to some, by Thomas De Laune [d. 1685]), published *Tropologia: A Key to Open Scripture Metaphors.*[34] One part of it catalogues scriptural metaphors, especially those

31. Gellrich, *Idea,* 69, 74 et passim; see also Barney, "Visible Allegory," on "parallelism" (93), and on its refractions from the Bible to exegesis, to sermons and other literature, to literary criticism (102–3).

32. Bromyard's *Summa** (James, Book no. 35); other Cambridge colleges currently own four other sixteenth-century copies of it. It was completed by 1352; see van Nolcken, "Some Alphabetical Compendia," 272–73. Pembroke possessed a printed copy of Rainerius de Pisis' huge *Pantheologia** (James, Book no. 31; from my inspection, now only the first of the two volumes); and other Cambridge colleges currently own nine sixteenth-century copies.

33. See Rathborne, *Meaning,* chap. 1, "The Glory of This World"; McNamee, *Honor,* chap. 8, "Magnanimity in Spenser"; and Nohrnberg, *Analogy,* chap. 1.3, "Arthurian Torso."

34. Published London: J[ohn] R[ichardson] and J[ohn] D[arby] for Enoch Prosser, 1682. A work of almost the same title had been issued by the same publishers in 1681 under the name of Thomas DeLaune; cf. Norton, *History of the Bible,* 246–49, 262, 350. For our purposes the authorship of either work is immaterial. Lewalski discusses *Tropologia* in *Protestant Poetics* and traces it to the material on metaphor in Salomon Glass's comprehensive *Philologia Sacra* (Jena, 1623), 82–83.

standing for God and for Scripture (a scope that precludes imagery *in malo*). The author(s) of *Tropologia* believe(s) that scriptural rhetoric, including images, is divinely inspired, not a mere veil to be stripped from the inspired truth beneath. So Augustine believed: "Not only can nothing seem to me more wise than they are, but also nothing can seem more eloquent. . . . [I]t should not have been said in any other way." According to John Alford, so did all those writers who imitated Scripture, such as Richard Rolle and Langland.[35] This view represents an older and less restrictive competitor to Aquinas' famous theory of allegory cited by Lewalski, and one more encouraging to poets.[36] Lewalski notes in *Tropologia* a typical Protestant trend: it continues to allegorize, but only typologically.

True, Rouse and Rouse assert that the genre was "moribund" by the fourteenth century. Even if they mean that *distinctiones* were copied but not created, this report of the genre's demise is premature and is refuted by the Renaissance *distinctiones* chronicled above. In fact, Dom André Wilmart says their "succès" was "durable, jusqu'au début de l'époque moderne" (345). True, J. W. Blench implies that sermons obviously constructed around the *distinctio* (that is, according to his trademark, around allegorizing the properties of some object in nature) ceased to be composed after the second decade of the sixteenth century.[37] My trademark of repeating images *in bono et in malo* is unmentioned but well exemplified in his quotations (11, 15–16). Although Blench does not realize it, Lancelot Andrewes renewed the enterprise of building sermons around the *distinctio* (in both definitions), just as he did the use of the four levels. In any case, the composition of new imagistic *distinctiones* (e.g., Lauretus), and the reprinting of older ones (e.g., Bersuire, well into the eighteenth century), indicates that they continued to be read by someone— by those few preachers who renewed the enterprise; by any preacher who employed images locally; and by any and all readers of the Bible engaged in illuminating a given image or topic by its recurrences and in appreciating the overall design of Scripture.

This survey has historicized in biblical exegesis of the time, the place, or both not simply concordantial reading of images but reading with the

35. Augustine, *Christian Doctrine*, 123; Alford, "Biblical *Imitatio*," 1–23, esp. 3–5.

36. This older hermeneutics of the Alexandrian and Latin Fathers (especially Paschasius Radbertus), which was adopted by English preachers, "has behind it the theory of 'verbal dictation' by God" and "founds the spiritual sense upon the basis of the verbal expression, even in the case of figurative expression." Blench, *Preaching*, 2, citing Smalley, *Study*, 300.

37. Blench, *Preaching*, 2, 8–9.

expectation that their meanings will vary. Thus, what modern biblical criticism sometimes regards as evidence of multiple authorship, older criticism regarded as a poetic strategy of the one divine author, showing his exemplary many-mindedness.

Modern Critics and Imagistic Variation: Dragons and Serpents, Cities and Mountains

The phrase *in bono et in malo* is mentioned in passing on rare occasions in whole or in part by those medievalists who are preoccupied with medieval hermeneutics, either biblical or mythographic, but no Spenserian devotes attention to this variation. Alastair Fowler has identified a part of the pattern in his own phraseology: "Moral emblems, mythological entities, and symbolic attributes often appear twice over, in true and in false forms . . . pairs of iconographically similar passages in close moral relation, even at a wide spatial remove." [38] He situates this incisive formulation within a Neoplatonic framework: the good instance represents the idea or reality; the bad or limited one, the copy or appearance. This explains some of Spenser's pairs—the true and false Unas, Red Crosses, Geniuses, and Florimells and the scales of Astraea (V.i.11) in relation to those of the Giant (V.ii.30ff.)—but not all, as will emerge in the next chapter.

In 1960, Northrop Frye perceived that in Spenser, "any symbol may be used ambivalently [cf. my distinction above] and may be virtuous or demonic according to its context"; he somewhat reductively called the principle "symbolic parody" and the disparaged images "demonic counterparts." I agree that the true and false Unas, Red Crosses, Geniuses, Florimells, and scales exemplify not only Neoplatonism but Frye's relationship between the images as well—which for brevity we can call "demonic parody." Frye did not, at least in his printed work, explicitly trace demonic parody to the Bible but instead embedded it in his idiosyncratic Blakean version of the four levels of existence, which he wrongly ascribed to the Bible. Patricia Parker comes closer to the mark in tracing it to a

38. See Fowler, "Emblems," 146; "Emanations," 53–82 passim; quotation, 69. Barney says that "the House of Holiness . . . resembles *in bono* the House of Pride" (*Allegories*, 115; see also 122). Preceded by one or two such users of the phrase locally and in passing, I drew attention to the pervasiveness of Spenser's variations *in bono et in malo*, first in a paper at the Modern Language Association in 1980 (whence I am credited with the phrase by King; see SPRT, 68, n. 56), then in 1990 in my article "Bible" in SE.

loosely defined "biblical romance": "A crucial debt of Spenserian [romance] to biblical romance is the conception of evil as a false look-alike of good . . . making the quest of both Redcrosse and the reader an education in distinguishing between parody doubles." [39]

Neither Fowler nor these critics employ *distinctiones* or the term *in bono et in malo;* and their discussions, while often accurate so far as they go, fail to cover the entire field of images *in bono et in malo.* Only a small percentage of the images *in malo* masquerade as good, and only about half of them are explainable as demonic parodies or false material copies. That dragon which Red Cross destroys is not a demonic parody or false copy of the good dragon on Arthur's helmet (FQ I.vii.31); the Satyrs who give Hellenore their characteristic treatment (III.x.36–52) are not a demonic parody or false copy of the Satyrs who rescue and cherish Una (I.vi). *In bono et in malo* is a more capacious term and one that existed in Spenser's day.

The only critic who has explicitly asserted that Spenser frequently repeats images *in bono et in malo* according to a pattern in biblical exegesis is Maren-Sophie Røstvig. In her book *Configurations: A Topomorphical Approach to Renaissance Poetry,* she asserts the repetition of images and loosely defined topoi—sometimes *in bono et in malo*—in Spenser, Tasso, and Milton alike; she traces the procedure ultimately to the Bible by way of the Fathers. I am grateful for Røstvig's independent confirmation of my insight and for her additional sources. She relies principally on discussions in Augustine and Cassiodorus, I on those in *distinctiones* and other late-medieval and Renaissance sources that can be linked to Spenser's precise place and time. In the *Gerusalemme,* she affirms three instances, of which one—rejections of honor—is convincing, of a topos *in bono et in malo;* [40] in Spenser, she discovers one image that does indeed vary in this way, garlands in FQ I (297–98); in Milton, she discovers the topos of harmony *in malo,* the harmony of the devils and their universe of death (475). I will not engage Røstvig's book at every point because my reasoning is incommensurable with hers. She defines her topoi so loosely—such as boldness or descent into the self—that a critic could manipulate them to form almost any pattern.

As to the artistic purpose of the variation, she sees it as harmony: "In

39. Frye, "Structure"; quotation, 158; see also 162–63; for ascription of Blakean four levels of existence to the Bible, 161; Frye exemplified demonic parody in the image of gold. See also Parker, "Romance" in SE.

40. Honor is rejected once admirably (by the shepherds), once sophistically (by Armida), 237.

Renaissance epics one way of establishing linkage between parts is to take the same 'sign' (or topos) in a good and a bad sense, a technique far better than mere repetition." The strategy acquires value, as she rightly says, because it "teaches us to perceive logical discriminations" (143). Cassiodorus says in his *Expositio Psalmorum*, well represented at Cambridge*: "It [the Bible] often uses the one concept in both the bad and the good sense, so that what has a shared name is seen to differ in its qualities."[41] Such Fathers treat this biblical feature only as a hermeneutic obstacle. I see the strategy as generating pluralistic meaning, at least initially.

Some of those sharp-edged Spenserian images repeated *in bono et in malo* are themselves so repeated in the Bible and are therefore derived from it in whole or in part. This fact marks the entire pattern as biblical in provenance and resonance. Although "horror" at reptilians is inevitable, being one of the few truly universal human traits, Spenser went out of his way to include one or more good instances of each species—dragons and serpents—so as to create two biblical moral polarities. Dragons in Spenser, as in the Bible, are of course almost without exception malefic. In the Bible there are two instances of dragons who are at least potentially good: the dragons who are exhorted along with other recalcitrant creatures to praise the Lord (Ps. 148:7 and Isa. 43:20). Spenser's one good dragon is that on Arthur's helmet:

> His haughtie helmet, horrid all with gold,
>   Both glorious brightnesse, and great terrour bred;
>   For all the crest a Dragon did enfold
>   With greedie pawes, and over all did spred
>   His golden wings: his dreadfull hideous hed
>   Close couched on the bever, seem'd to throw
>   From flaming mouth bright sparkles fierie red,
>   That suddeine horror to faint harts did show;
> And scaly taile was stretcht adowne his backe full low.
> (I.vii.31)

The caesura-less alexandrine mimes on the page the trailing length of the tail.

---

41. Cassiodorus, *Expositio,* Preface, xv:20–21, trans. P. G. Walsh, *Explanation.* Røstvig paraphrases Cassiodorus as follows: "The same word or thing may be construed *in bono* or *in malo,* and . . . this teaches us to perceive logical discriminations" (*Configurations,* 143). Besides the evidence of Cassiodorus' popularity given in my Appendix, MSS of this work were owned, according to M. Adraien in his introduction, by Corpus and Trinity. On images *in bono et in malo,* see also Cassiodorus, *Introduction to Divine and Human Readings,* Book I, xv:4.

Taken out of context, this helmet could be that of a villain; but it bears favorable political connotations because it hints at Arthur's lineage and destiny, as yet unknown to him, in that it symbolizes the position he is to inherit, the title of his father, "Pendragon" (alluded to in FQ II.x.68). This title is a symbol of "supreme power" in ancient British or Welsh tradition: it means literally "head dragon-standard," from the fact that ancient British or Welsh battle standards had a dragon on them, and metaphorically "a leader in war" (OED s.v. "Pendragon"). A. C. Hamilton notes in this place that Geoffrey of Monmouth attributes a dragon helmet to Arthur. It is morally exemplary by being at once strange and appropriate, thus manifesting, like the rest of Arthur's elaborately described costume, the ability to spend money well, a part, according to its strict Aristotelian sense, of Arthur's virtue of magnificence. Spenser devotes an entire stanza to this good dragon, partly, I suggest, to provide a counterweight to the reptilian antagonists in Book I and thus to call attention to his own imagistic balancing act. Thus, Spenser's strategy of having a good dragon is biblical even though the source of his good dragon is not.

Spenser's bad reptilians are of course the monster Error (I.i), Duessa's Beast (I.viii.6; 15–17), the Dragon that Red Cross kills (I.xi), the serpent on which Envy chews (I.v.30–32 and V.xii.28–39), and others of less importance. Of Spenser's two good serpents, again, one is not biblical. It is the ouroboros twining about the feet of the statue of Venus in the Temple of Venus, whose tail-eating symbolizes both intercourse and death in a paradoxical creation-in-destruction and whose endless form symbolizes the resulting perpetuity of the cycle of generations. Like Arthur's dragon, it evokes a vague frisson which befits the destructive side of its paradox.

The Bible varies serpents *in bono* also, introducing two good serpents among many bad. One is reproduced in Spenser's other good though bone-chilling serpent—the one in Fidelia's cup. Its principal or only source is now agreed to be the ambivalent brazen serpent which when gazed upon healed the Israelites from the bites of real serpents (Num. 21: 8–9) and which Christ designates as a type of himself (John 3:14). The second good biblical serpent is a figurative one which Spenser does not echo, that in Christ's injunction "be ye therefore wise as serpents, and innocent as doves" (Matt. 10:16).

For his intertwined image-pattern of mountains and cities, Spenser dipped into and modified paired images of mountains and cities *in bono et in malo* in Hebrews 12:18–24. In his epic simile for the Mount of Contemplation, Spenser invokes three mountains—Sinai, Olivet, and Parnassus (I.x.53–54). Ostensibly the purpose of Spenser's simile is celebratory, and the first mountain, Mount Sinai, is as honorific as the others;

but readers cannot fail to notice its grimness as contrasted to the "flowring girlond" on the next mountain, the Mount of Olives, a grimness implying that while all three afford true visions, it is Mount Sinai that conveys the bad news:

> Such one, as that same mighty man of God,
> That bloud-red billowes like a walled front
> On either side disparted with his rod,
> Till that his army dry-foot through them yod,
> Dwelt fortie dayes upon; where writ in stone
> With bloudy letters by the hand of God,
> The bitter doome of death and balefull mone
> He did receive, whiles flashing fire about him shone.
>
> Or like that sacred hill, whose head full hie,
> Adornd with fruitfull Olives all arownd,
> Is, as it were for endlesse memory
> Of that deare Lord, who oft thereon was fownd,
> For ever with a flowring girlond crownd.
> (I.x.53–54)

Spenser's "writ in stone" of course refers to the stone tablets upon which God himself inscribed the law. Once we realize the biblical context, the chilling overtones are intensified from the biblical verb "to stone" (quoted below); stone is set in contrast to the gospel in "ye are . . . the Epistle of Christ . . . written . . . not in tables of stone, but in fleshly tables of the heart" (2 Cor. 3:3). Spenser's idea that the Old Testament was written with blood is not biblical; he must be extending the idea that the Old Covenant was sealed with blood, namely, the blood of animal sacrifices (see, e.g., Exod. 24:6–8; Heb. 10:29). Thus we actually have one mountain *in malo*. Spenser took his one unpleasant mountain most directly from Hebrews 12:

18   For yee are not come unto the mount that might be touched, nor *unto burning fire,* nor to blacknes and darknesse, and tempest,

19   Neither unto the sounde of a trumpet, and the voyce of wordes, which they that heard it, excused themselves, that the word should not be spoken to them any more,

20   (For they were not able to abide that which was commanded, yea, thogh a beast touch the mountain, it shalbe *stoned,* or thrust through with a dart:

21   And so terrible was the sight which appeared, that Moses said, I feare and quake.)

22   But ye are come unto the mount Sion. . . . (emphasis mine)

This Mount Sinai, like Spenser's, clearly symbolizes the Mosaic law given thereon in all the grimness with which Paul surrounds it. This contrast of mountains consists of a series of antitheses contrasting law and gospel like Christ's "Antitheses" in the Sermon on the Mount (Matt. 5:21–48). Spenser's theological reason for this disparagement is not made clear in the immediate context, but it becomes clear in his succeeding portrayals of Mosaic law (I.xi.26–28 and II.i.35–ii.9; see Chapters 4 and 5). For the good biblical mountain, Mount Sion or Zion, Spenser substitutes the less Jewish and more Christian Mount of Olives, seemingly in order that its flowers might contrast more sharply with Sinai's thunderbolts, its pastoral Christ with a lawgiving Moses. Olivet is listed along with Sinai and Sion under "mons" in *distinctiones;* and Dante models his Mount Purgatory on various biblical mountains: Sion, Sinai, Pisgah, and the Mount on which Christ preached his famous sermon in Matthew.[42]

That Spenser did indeed have this biblical passage in mind, so that it rates not simply as a model but as a source and perhaps even a target of allusion, is shown when he shifts to the image of a city, "The new Hierusalem," a few stanzas later (I.x.55–57), especially:

> . . . he might see
> The blessed Angels to and fro descend
> From highest heaven, in gladsome companee,
>
> . . . .
>
> ". . . Hierusalem that is,
> The new *Hierusalem,* that God has built
> For those to dwell in, that are chosen his,
> His chosen people purg'd from sinfull guilt,
> With pretious bloud, which cruelly was spilt
> On cursed tree, of that unspotted lam,
> That for the sinnes of all the world was kilt.

The author of Hebrews shifts from a mountain to a city in this very verse:

> 22   . . . and to the citie of the living God, the celestial Hierusalem, and to the company of innumerable Angels,
> 23   And to the assemblie and congregation of the first borne, which are written in heaven . . .
> 24   . . . and to the blood of sprinkling.[43]

The qualifier "new" glances at an "old" or earthly Jerusalem. Spenser juxtaposes to his Jerusalem an earthly city, Cleopolis (58–59), but not a bib-

---

42. See Kaske, "Mount Sinai"; Demaray, *Invention.*
43. Cf. Frank Kermode on the "New Hierusalem" in his *Selections.*

lical one. This parallels his adding a classical mountain to the two bibli-cal mountains. In the space of seven stanzas (53–59), he thus repeats ad-jacently two pairs of images repeated adjacently in the source—moun-tains and cities—not slavishly but in a biblical pattern. He is following out creatively the biblical principle of repeated and distinguished images: for in the Bible "civitas" though not "mons" is "triplex," as Byard remarks in his *Distinctiones* (Rouse and Rouse, "Biblical *Distinctiones*," 35).

The three mountains respectively metonymize not only three kinds of vision but also *The Three Laws,* as John Bale called them in his interlude of that name (1538), the three covenants of God with man in history, in Spenser's order, that of Mosaic law, that of grace, and that of natural man. These constitute the traditional successive *status* of mankind—in histori-cal order, Nature (in the period "from Adam to Moses," Rom. 5:14), Law, and Grace; they also constitute, according to Stephen Barney ("Vis-ible Allegory," 98), a standard *distinctio:* naturalia/mosaica/evangelica. By putting nature last, Spenser violates evolutionary order, giving the im-pression that the *status* or covenants are all of equal validity—that he is a syncretist.[44]

Spenser includes many more images of mountains to unify the FQ: the Mount of Venus in the Garden of Adonis in III.vi, Mount Acidale in VI.x, and Arlo Hill[45] in VII.vii.3ff.; all his mountains, bad and good, are settings, if not for visions, at least for some sort of encounter with the di-vine. Mount Acidale in VI.x is a displaced Parnassus-Helicon, inhabited by Colin and the Graces instead of their divine exemplars Apollo and the Muses. In the Bible and exegesis, the divine presence constitutes the good aspect of Sinai; this motif Spenser carries to all his mountains.

Distinguishing Eucharistic Cups

In both the Bible and the FQ, the image of a cup refracts a spectrum of meanings so complex and pervasive that it constitutes my strongest evi-dence of indebtedness. As can be seen from the Appendix of Images, Spenser's chain of cups extends all the way through Book V; it consists of nine complex instances, varied *in bono et in malo* and in other ways. Hugh of St. Cher gives at different points various tables or *distinctiones* of biblical cups, drinks, and wines and their respective meanings. One of them not only organizes its "calices" around the four levels but also sub-

---

44. Bale, *Comedy;* on this simile, see Phillips, "Spenser's Syncretistic Religious Imagery."
45. Arlo Hill is really a mountain, as Spenser's contemporaries would have known, and Spenser uses the terms "mountain" and "hill" interchangeably in "July."

divides them *in bono* and *in malo* according to who bears them, what is in them, and so on.[46] As Lauretus notes, the Bible itself specifies cups *in bono et in malo:* "Ye cannot drinke the cup of the Lord, and the cup of the devils" (1 Cor. 10:21 [Vulgate 10:20]).

A brief and obvious example lends weight to subsequent attributions. In FQ V.i.15, when the squire wishes with regard to the decapitated lady "That I mote drinke the cup, whereof she dranke," he echoes Christ's question, "Are ye able to drinke of the cup that I shal drinke of?" (Matt. 20:22). The obvious meaning is given by Hugh in the last-mentioned *distinctio* of cups; he says Christ's cup means "mortis angustiae, Matt. 26d," that is, the anguish of death, citing Christ's use of the metaphor in Matthew 26:39. Even the ultra-Protestant Geneva Bible supplies a little *distinctio in bono et in malo* on Matthew 20:22–23, saying that "the Hebrewes understand by this word Cup, sometimes . . . punishment . . . to sinne, as Psal. 11.6. or the joy that is given to the faithfull, as Psal. 23.5. and sometimes a lot or condition, as Psal. 16.5." "Cup" was and still is a byword for one's lot; and it still bears biblical overtones, as the OED confirms. This echo is not profoundly significant for the poem; but its straightforwardness lends credibility to more oblique and complex echoes. My *distinctio* of Spenser's cups in my Appendix of Images indicates that some of them might be more richly suggestive when considered in a group.

To call Paridell's adulterous scribbles in wine "a sacrament prophane in mystery of wine" (III.ix.30) gives his act biblical and eucharistic overtones and invites us to look for such overtones in other cups, even seemingly secular ones. Obviously biblical is the cup of Duessa when she appears in full regalia as the Whore of Babylon in I.viii.14–15.

The cup of the biblical Whore and of Spenser's Duessa can be shown to be eucharistic. Now, Fidelia's cup is precisely the Eucharist, and it is linked imagistically with Duessa's. Duessa's occurs just two cantos before with no other cups in between. They are obviously employed *in malo et in bono* in a polemical adaptation of the biblical *distinctio*—the cup of the Lord and the cup of devils (1 Cor. 10:21). Duessa's cup must have eucharistic overtones because the pair of biblical cups to which it alludes has them. Just as Duessa embodies the biblical Whore's symbolism (according to Protestant exegesis) of the Roman Church, so Duessa's cup, as D. Douglas Waters has convincingly argued, represents the Romish Mass in general.[47]

---

46. *Opera*, 7, fol. 100.3, on 1 Cor. 10:21.

47. FQ I.viii.14; and stanza 25.1–3 parallels Rev. 14:8 and 17–19:3; see also the female personification of "Babylon" in the prophets. Waters finds some sources and connects them to

What has not been noticed is that this eucharistic symbolism and its biblical background explain what Duessa's cup does to Timias. When Duessa sprinkles its contents over him, it makes him fall down before her, her cup, and her beast:

> Then tooke the angrie witch her golden cup,
>> Which still she bore, replete with magick artes;
>> Death and despeyre did many thereof sup,
>> And secret poyson through their inner parts,
>> Th'eternall bale of heavie wounded harts;
>> Which after charmes and some enchauntments said,
>> She lightly sprinkled on his weaker parts;
>> Therewith his sturdie courage soone was quayd,
> And all his senses were with suddeine dread dismayd.
>
> So downe he fell before the cruell beast,
>> Who on his necke his bloudie clawes did seize,
>
> . . . .
>
>> No powre he had to stirre, nor will to rize.
> (I.viii.14–15)

Timias's sickness suggests that which is threatened by Saint Paul against those who abuse the Eucharist in 1 Corinthians 11:29–30:

29   For he that eateth and drinketh unworthily, eateth and drinketh his owne damnation, because he discerneth not the Lords body.
30   For this cause many are weake, and sicke among you, and many sleepe.

The text is echoed in Article 25 and in the Short Exhortation to Communion. Although by "unworthily" Saint Paul probably meant communicating while in a state of sin, Spenser here applies Paul's warning, as Calvin did, to communicating while holding a false, Romish view of the Eucharist.[48] Duessa's cup, too, is a "sacrament prophane in mystery of wine," a genuinely demonic parody of the true cup.

Duessa's cup by the symbolism of witchcraft, in that the Mass "bewitched those who became enamored of her" (*Duessa*, 104–6).

48. Calvin interprets the "punishment" literally as "pestilence . . . or . . . other kinds of disease . . . in consequence of that abuse of the Supper." He claims that Romanists profane the Eucharist: "We see, throughout the whole extent of Popery, not merely horrid profanations of the Supper, but even a sacrilegious abomination set up in its room. . . . *Fourthly*, there is there no explanation of the meaning of the sacrament, but a mumbling that would accord better with a magical incantation. . . . *Seventhly*, it is fitted to intoxicate miserable men with carnal confidence, while they . . . think that by this charm they drive off everything hurtful, and that without faith and repentance." *Commentaries on I and II Corinthians*, 390–91, on 1 Cor. 11:30.

Timias's plight can be seen not only as a punishment but as the doctrinal error that merits it. Arthur sees him in this state as "into such thralldome brought." Protestants often think of Catholics as in thralldom and servitude to the hierarchy—partly an intellectual thralldom of blind faith in unscriptural dogma. Now in this posture, Timias would remind Spenser's audience of victims of the Whore of Babylon, of the biblical "nations" and "Kings of the earth" who have become "drunken with the wine of her fornication" (my conflation of Rev. 17:2 and 18:3). Taking a cue from this, visual art represents kings kneeling before her, her beast, and her cup, for example, in the pictures of the Whore in Jan Van der Noot's *Theatre,* undoubtedly seen by Spenser; in John Bale's *Image of Both Churches;* and in Andrea Alciati's emblem "Ficta Religio." [49] We know that the kneeling posture of these figures identifies them as the wine-drunk "Kings" (Rev. 17:2; see also 18:9) and "nations" (Rev. 18:3) because Alciati labels the worshipers an "ebria turba." While Alciati and his commentator Mignault remain denominationally noncommittal, in Protestant exegesis the apocalyptic kings represent "Popysh princes" who defend the Roman church.[50] A drunkenness that makes one kneel must symbolize misdirected faith. Kneeling during the Eucharist was a practice that was considered Romanist by some because it was thought to imply transubstantiation—the doctrine that the elements had literally become Christ. If one accepts that Timias's collapse represents kneeling, then the wine with which he is sprinkled from the Whore's cup represents—as some critics have loosely conjectured that it does—not just the Mass but transubstantiation, that false doctrine which makes people kneel.[51] Duessa's "charmes and some enchauntments said" calls to mind, first, the words of consecration spoken by the priest, words that are alleged to work transubstantiation—a magical transformation of the wine to the blood of Christ. This suggests that Timias's "sin" is to believe in such magic and to express it by kneeling.

49. Van der Noot's *Theatre* , the work at least some of whose sonnets Spenser translated, sig. D4, illustrating the sonnet summarizing Rev. 17–18; reprinted in SPRT, 83, plate 6; also in Bale's *Image of Both Churches,* reprinted in King, *Tudor Royal Icongraphy,* plate 65. *Andreae Alciati . . . Emblemata* (Leiden, 1591), Emblem 6, pp. 58ff. This emblem came into *Emblemata* belatedly with the edition of Venice, 1546, still in plenty of time for Spenser to have seen it. Alciati was himself a Romanist.

50. See Brocard, *The Revelation of S. John reveled,* trans. James Sanford (London, Thomas Marshe, 1582=STC 3810)*, fol. 142v on 17:2, fol. 148v on 18:9.

51. On her cup as symbolizing all the evils "distributed aboute the Chalice," see Van der Noot, *Theatre,* fol. 45v. I have not found it interpreted specifically as transubstantiation until the seventeenth-century commentary of David Pareus (*Commentary,* 505 [*sic*], so misnumbered for 415). Spenser's contemporaries implied transubstantiation within more capacious interpretations—idolatry and false doctrine.

Now, the kings in Revelation and its illustrations have drunk of the Whore's cup deliberately; they have also fornicated with her deliberately. Another meaning of cups in the *distinctiones* is *voluptates,* and Red Cross has taken his pleasure with Duessa. This meaning is obvious in the cup of Excess and Genius's "mazer bowl"; they epitomize all the delights of the flesh which make one "drunke with drugs of deare voluptuous receipt" (II.v.34). This association of various lascivious cups is supported here by the metaphorical equation of drinking with linking in Revelation 17–18. Since Timias has only been sprinkled with her wine, he is not of course in any way responsible for what the Whore Duessa does to him; he is an oblique echo, a conditional parallel, of the kneeling, drinking, linking kings in iconography. Within the poem, as a victim of Duessa, Timias is a sort of double of, a conditional parallel to, Red Cross.[52]

Red Cross himself also stands in his own oblique relation to the Whore's kingly customers; he and Timias form the textual base of a triangle, the "Kings of the earth" the apex. Red Cross did not literally drink of his whore's cup either, nor was he sprinkled from it; but like the kings with the biblical whore, he did deliberately fornicate with her (I.vii.7). Then, with the help of a drink from the Well of the Lazy Nymph, Red Cross suffered an intoxication and an enervation similar to that now experienced by Timias. Both characters have yielded in one way or another to the deceptions of Rome, but Red Cross's yielding is voluntary and inexcusable, implying by parallel and contrast that Timias's yielding is involuntary and purely intellectual. Timias, by being sprinkled against his will, represents those misled by Rome, such as the Irish, described in similar imagery in Spenser's *Vewe:*

> Religion was generally corrupted with theire Popishe trumpery Therefore what other Coulde they learne then suche trashe as was taughte them And drinke of that Cupp of fornicacion with which the purple Harlott had then made all nacions drunken.

Spenser has hope of their salvation because their baptism was valid (Var. *Prose Works,* 137). Van der Noot avers that those deceived by the Whore include "the elect and chosen of God" (fol. 47v), who presumably will be delivered from their error. Similarly, Timias too recovers from his sickness; it was not unto death.

Now we are ready to answer two possible objections. The fact that Timias does not "sup" and "drink" the wine but is merely "sprinkled"

---

52. Cf. Waters's claim that Timias somehow *is* Red Cross: "the Squire's swoon before the witch's enchantments, viii.14" represents what goes on "in Red Crosse's heart" (*Duessa,* 104).

with it does not obviate the eucharistic meaning: sprinkling is a liturgical gesture; and being sprinkled by it is Spenser's symbol for drinking it involuntarily. The fact that a liquid can be sprinkled is one reason (besides its being the Whore's attribute) why Spenser chose to represent the Romanist Eucharist in terms of wine rather than bread, despite the recalcitrant fact (and this is the second objection) that in the Roman Mass of those days, only the bread was available to the laity. Communion "in both kinds" was evidently not an issue for Spenser.

The bad cup shows the Romish Eucharist to be bad by its effects and by the way it operates. Although so far my case has not required such specificity, I agree—because of Timias's kneeling and Duessa's magic—with those who say that what makes Duessa's cup bad is its embodiment of transubstantiation. The parallel and contrast with Fidelia in one way reinforces, in another way problematizes, this interpretation. The Romanist cupbearer is a "witch"; the good cupbearer is faith. Of course, the Romanists also portrayed faith as holding a cup, and they too would have said that faith intensified the effect of the sacrament, but not that it was a prerequisite for transubstantiation to take place. The sacrament is so powerful, in their view, that it affects unbelievers too; they can be healed by it or see the bread bleed when they mutilate it. In this context, Spenser's calling Duessa's cup "replete with magic arts" (I.viii.14) indicates that it works not only on the wine but also transitively, or *ex opere operato,* on the communicant regardless of his or her state of mind. This is another example of that ritualism which Protestants denigrated as magic in the Roman Mass. Spenser contrasts Duessa and Fidelia as magic and faith because the Thirty-nine Articles contrast transubstantiation and faith: "Transubstantiation (or the change of the substance of bread and wine) in the supper of the Lord" is not to be believed because "The body of Christ is given, taken, and eaten in the Supper, only after a heavenly and spiritual manner. And the mean whereby the body of Christ is received and eaten in the Supper is faith."[53] This much of the distinction of cups in terms of sorcery versus faith constitutes a typical example of what I call *distributio.*

But if this were Spenser's only point, he would not have made Fidelia's cup so unpleasant and so like Duessa's. He does so in order to unsettle the reader who thinks she knows what a true and a false Eucharist are. We saw that since Spenser condemns people who kneel to cups and their

53. Article 28. For further documentation on transubstantiation versus faith, see Rogers, *Catholic Doctrine,* on Article 28, Props. 3 and 4, in Parker Society 41:285–89; and Peter Martyr Vermigli, "Of the Masse," 133, and "A Disputation of the Eucharist," in "Another Collection," 220a, both treatises in his *Common Places.*

contents, he objects to transubstantiation. While Fidelia's cup is not kneeled to, while no charms are said over it, it does have Christ in it, as Romanists claimed for their Eucharist. We know this because Fidelia

> . . . in her right hand bore a cup of gold,
> With wine and water fild up to the hight,
> In which a Serpent did himselfe enfold,
> That horrour made to all, that did behold;
> But she no whit did change her constant mood.
> (I.x.13)

Her cup recalls imagistically Duessa's cup of "secret poyson"—a cup in which a serpent would be a more fitting inhabitant (for example, in iconography, a serpent in a cup symbolized the poison that Saint John the Evangelist drank off with impunity). As several critics have argued, this serpent must be *in bono* and must represent Christ crucified, echoing his image of himself in John 3:14 as the brazen serpent of Numbers 21:8–9.[54] This presence was later to be endorsed straightforwardly by Spenser in the HHL: "Even himselfe in his deare sacrament, / To feede our hungry soules unto us lent" (195–96, YSP). The "wine and water" which at certain periods of church history had been mingled in the eucharistic cup signifies the blood and water that flowed from Christ's side on the Cross (John 19:34); in Spenser's time the dilution had been dropped from the Prayer Book as too Romish, as implying a presence of Christ that was too physical and thus transubstantiation. The reader thought she had arrived at the *distinctio;* but the good cup which she expected to be only a symbol is more, provided the communicant believes it to be so.

The horror of the serpent is analogous to the frisson of awe attending the doctrines—shared by Rome and Canterbury—that God became an organism, that partakers somehow ingest him, and that if they do so wrongly, they may lose their salvation. That Spenser presented a good thing in this horrific way (in the style of baroque religious poetry such as Southwell's *Burning Babe*) relates to the topics of this chapter not only in providing a reptile *in bono,* but also in proving that Spenser values shock and other experiences of the first-time reader. Thus the reader is unsettled both by the imagistic similarity to Duessa's cup (serpent and poison) and by the thematic one (the contents being something potentially worshipable).

54. A. S. P. Woodhouse interprets the serpent as both the brazen serpent of Numbers 21:9 and "a symbol of menace doubtless with reference to I Cor. 12 [*sic,* for 11]:27–9," in "Nature and Grace," 589, n. 12.

These similarities make Fidelia's cup a correction not only of Duessa's cup, whose evil was clear from the outset, but also of the false notion of the norm which Duessa's cup implied. In her response to the shock, the reader must discriminate between uses and abuses of the Eucharist, specifically between true and false notions of how Christ is present in it. She must run through the warring contemporary views.[55] Some Protestants went to the extreme of saying that faith does everything in the Eucharist; it has no intrinsic power but functions psychologically in the mind and heart like any other token, any other physical stimulus—a candle or a holy picture. This extreme opposite of transubstantiation is the memorialism of Zwingli, and this is what Spenser seems in I.viii.14 to endorse when he condemns Duessa's cup as magic and as an object of worship and extols faith (I.x.13). At least the norm violated by Duessa's cup is valid insofar as it forewarns the reader not to interpret the serpent in *Fidelia's* cup as transubstantiation, as she might well have done if she had not previously encountered Duessa's. Other Protestants believed that faith, while necessary, only releases the power intrinsic to the sacrament. In that spirit, Fidelia's cup then nudges the reader away from her previous Zwinglian memorialism and toward the *via media*. The reader would see in the serpent present but not kneeled to and held by faith something more like the Establishment's mediating doctrine of the Real (but not physical) Presence. Claiming to have Christ in the communion cup is not idolatrous in itself, so long as the means of getting him there is correctly defined, and that is a means which does not require kneeling.

This exercise in readerly discrimination has religio-political relevance. Both the doctrine of the Real Presence and Zwinglian memorialism are somewhat incongruously enshrined in the inclusive (a cynic would say evasively heterogeneous) Words of Administration in the Elizabethan Book of Common Prayer—a heterogeneity that is biblical because found also in Christ's words of institution as reported by Paul in 1 Corinthians 11:24. In line with this verse, the Words of Administration contain two faintly Romish statements: "The body of our Lord Christ . . . preserve thy body and soul into everlasting life. . . . Feed on him in thy heart by faith with thanksgiving. . . .The blood of our Lord Jesus Christ . . . preserve thy body and soul into everlasting life." These conservative words existed in the first Edwardian Prayer Book of 1549 but were excised in the second Edwardian version of 1552, then reinserted in the Elizabethan version of 1559. This reinsertion was probably done, as Dom Gregory Dix

55. See Waters, *Duessa*, 111–12, for a helpful discrimination between the degrees of efficacy variously attributed to the Eucharist in Spenser's time.

conjectures, on the insistence "of the Queen herself," thus creating not so much a *via media* as an unstable mixture. The precisian part of the Words of Administration, inserted instead in 1552 and incongruously retained in tandem in 1559, is "Take and eat this in remembrance that Christ died for thee, etc. . . . drink this in remembrance . . ."; this part, also based on 1 Corinthians 11:24, does not require the Real Presence and sounds like that Zwinglian memorialism which Duessa's cup implies as the norm.[56] In I.viii.14 and I.x.13, Spenser, like the Words of Administration and their source, inscribes the warring views of his time and forces the reader to experience them and to join him in fine-tuning his definition of a good Eucharist. As for the effects of a good Eucharist, they are not explicitly shown in the House of Holiness but will be shown, first, in the presumably eucharistic Tree in the Dragon-Fight, and then, I will suggest, in Cambina's cup.

In Book III the adulterous lovers' "sacrament prophane in mystery of wine" is not exactly demonic parody so much as worldly travesty. This profanation extends not only to the Eucharist, of which they are not even thinking, but also to marriage, even though Hellenore's particular marriage from its inception was less than ideal. Harold Weatherby has established that Spenser believed marriage to be at least sacramental if not a sacrament.[57]

In Book IV we encounter a cup which reconciles combatants (IV.iv.42–49). It is wielded by another sorceress, a good one, Cambina, yielding a pattern of sorceresses *in bono et in malo*. Here magic acquires a favorable role, as it did in I.vii.33–36 and viii.19 (Arthur's shield), and in Books II (the Palmer's magic) and III (Britomart's spear); and, as with Arthur's magic shield, one of its possible meanings is divine grace. The cup represents, I propose, the Eucharist in its socially unifying effect, whereby participants reaffirm their mutually supportive roles as members of the body of Christ. Cambina's cup of nepenthe is only outwardly classical; by inducing forgetfulness of injuries, it allegorizes Christian forgiveness. As a cup of forgetfulness it forms a contrast *in bono* with the forgetfulness induced by Acrasia's intoxicating cocktails—presumably those administered in the cups of Genius and Excess (II.xii.49, 56)—which made Mor-

56. Parker Society, *Liturgical Services*, 195; both parts have been essentially retained up to the present day. On Elizabeth's role, see Dix, *Shape*, 674–75. On the vacillation of Cranmer (the author of the memorialistic Words of Consecration) as to whether Christ is present only in the hearts of the faithful or also somehow in the elements, see Hughes, *Theology*, 195–96, 364, versus Thompson, *Liturgies*, 236–44.

57. Contribution to panel, "Spenser and the Sacraments," Sixteenth Century Studies Conference, Toronto, October 23, 1998.

dant unable to recognize his wife (II.i.52, 55). According to Hugh, the Bible too contains cups of good and bad forgetfulness.[58]

The Eucharist is the principal sacrament which unites Christians. Article 28 of the Thirty-nine Articles asserts that brotherly love is symbolized and perhaps imparted by the Eucharist: "The supper of the Lord is . . . a sign of the love that Christians ought to have among themselves one to another." The effect of this cup—social bonding—parallels the previous action of a mother in uniting three brethren, first, by their upbringing in fraternal and punningly "brotherly" love, then with literal magic "into one body" successively as they die off (IV.ii.50–iii.22). Agape, the name of the mother—the boys' common origin and the arranger of this magical unification of them with one another—denotes this peculiarly Christian kind of love. *Agape* as a common noun also served in the early church as a synonym for a eucharistic celebration. The surviving brother shares an *agape* in this sense with his opponent, thus extending the bond of brotherly love to him; they will in fact become brothers-in-law. As to how Christian brotherly love could contravene death by inserting the soul of a dead brother into a living one, this much-maligned episode is a myth, in general, of the way in which all the dead survive inside their living loved ones, and in particular, of that special communion with the dead offered in the churches both of Rome and of England by their practice of praying for them. In late-medieval England, entire chantries did nothing but pray for the dead; such prayers form an integral part of every Sunday Mass, a part retained in the BCP up to the present day.[59] Thus, eucharistic doctrine gives religious rationale and relatedness to two episodes which at first seem separate and merely sentimental. Agape acts out the goal, her daughter and pupil Cambina the means; both allegorize the church.

As if in contrast, later in Book IV, Concord, another and a genuinely classical mother, unites her sons without cups or other magic by a force

58. See within Hugh's *distinctio* of "vinum," "Malae Oblivionis. Isa. 28.b. . . . Bonae oblivionis. Prov. 31.a," *Opera* 2, fol. 151r–v on Ps. 59 (so numbered in Vulgate; Protestant 60).

59. On the social utility of prayers for the dead, see Duffy, *Stripping of the Altars,* 124–25; on the communal character of late-medieval Christianity in general and the Mass and prayers for the dead in particular, see 121–54, and, indeed, the entire book. On the general Christian matrix of Cambina's cup, see Nesselhof, "Spenser's Book," 125–26 and n. 34, quoting Thomas Becon's Catechism on Agape as a common noun denoting the Eucharist. Nohrnberg devotes precisely two words—"or communion"—to the possibility of this interpretation of Cambina's cup (*Analogy,* 649); he also sees Christian brotherly love in the bond of the brothers (615–16), but without its reincarnational communion between the living and the dead. Intercession for the dead is based on 2 Macc. 12:42–46, 2 Maccabees being one of those deuterocanonical books to which the Establishment then granted a qualified acceptance.

that seems in its Lucretian context to be purely natural, the cohesiveness of certain atoms and bodies (IV.x.31–36; 44–47). Since Concord covers bonding in general, this contrast confirms that Cambina's cup must represent a special kind, the social benefit of the eucharist, an effect Spenser did not mention in connection with Fidelia's cup or the presumably eucharistic Tree of Life (I.xi). Book IV as a whole is about the multiplication of private friendships into that sense of community which subtends public virtue. Spenser here acknowledges that this sense of community is something the church has always provided. Spenser gives us four eucharistic cups: the true Eucharist, a demonic parody thereof, and a social Eucharist, all from the Bible, and a farcical sexual travesty of the true Eucharist.

Propaedeutics to Spenser's Method in the Preceding and Surrounding Culture

Objections to this filiation arise from Spenser's confessional allegiance and his humanist training. True, Spenser was a (moderate) Protestant, and in his time all *distinctiones* (either imagistic or thematic) were either medieval or Counter-Reformation Catholic; naturally, therefore, the *distinctiones* could not have contributed his anti-Catholic meanings. But his religious sentiments are often quite medieval and on the whole (if, indeed, they are coherent enough to summarize) less rabidly anti-Catholic than is currently imagined. Moreover, as Fowler generalizes, "Renaissance culture . . . developed within a medieval matrix that gave it life as well as confined it," and one of his examples is imitations of a biblical structure, that of the Psalms.[60]

Again, humanists like Spenser are reputed to be hostile to scholasticism. The *distinctiones* is indeed scholastic, as Jean Leclercq laments,[61] with its hair-splitting and its view of the Bible as a single God-authored book in which one can skip around without regard to differing genres, purposes, audiences, or historical periods. But *distinctiones* would not be as vulnerable as other scholastic genres to scholastic-bashing humanists because they focus at least as much on Scripture as on doctrine, if not more so. Arguments from cultural history cannot outweigh those from close reading. Any poet who encountered them, however anti-Catholic or anti-scholastic he might be, could still see *distinctiones* as a true per-

60. Fowler, *Time's Purpled Masquers*, 2–3.
61. Leclerq, *Love*, 95.

ception of how the Bible is organized, or at least as a model of how his own work might be organized. Even if Spenser devised images *in bono et in malo* on his own, his indubitable awareness that this device was also present in the Bible would have lent him confidence in its authority and its recognizability.

The habit of varying images *in bono et in malo,* then, derives ultimately from the Bible as constructed by the *distinctiones;* but it could conceivably have reached Spenser indirectly, through sermons based thereon or through other poems based on one or both of these intermediaries. Evidence for each can be adduced, and in each case from two directions, the intermediary's affinity on the one hand to the *distinctiones* and on the other hand to Spenser. Of the first, there are three trademarks: connecting related themes by biblical hook-words, varying them *in bono et in malo,* and allegorizing several traits in a natural object.

At least initially, the *distinctiones* made their way into poetry through the rhyming *divisiones* which preachers embedded in their sermons, as Siegfried Wenzel has shown. Since many of these sermons were in the vernacular, even people innocent of Latin were thereby exposed to *distinctiones.*[62] In the fifteenth and sixteenth centuries, as J. W. Blench says (2), all English preachers tried to imitate biblical poetics. They held the pre-Aquinian view that even the "verbal expression," including metaphoric images, of the Scriptures is divinely inspired; verbal expression can be imitated; therefore the Bible's style should be imitated by preachers. Spenser's own style is ornate; but this does not in itself keep it from being biblical. The Bible contains at least two styles, the plain and the eloquent. Some preachers (clearly exemplified in the authors of the two Books of Homilies) appealed to the plainer parts of the Bible as a model for sermons, others to the parts rich in schemes and tropes, both doubtless seeking to authorize their own taste and aesthetic principles.[63] Since Spenser demonstrably liked Psalms and Revelation, he would have liked the preachers who emphasized and imitated books of such eloquence, especially their imagery. Although the topical *distinctiones* such as Alexander Anglicus could have influenced, and probably did influence, all preachers throughout the sixteenth century, it would have been the older, imagistic *distinctiones* that furnished such preachers with outlines for a poetic and "metaphysical" type of sermon. I propose that the love of the Bible's repeated and varying images, probably fostered by imagistic *dis-*

62. Wenzel, *Preachers,* 4–5, 8–13, et passim.
63. On John Downame versus Donne, see Bush, *English Literature,* 310.

tinctiones, while declining after the first decades of the sixteenth century, also revived in the last decades.

Spenser's image-structures resemble those in the sermons of Fisher at the beginning of the century and Andrewes at the end; and for a poet, reading or hearing a *distinctio* in a sermon—except for the fact that the sermon would already have imparted to it some slant or other—would have functioned just like reading one in exegesis. Fisher he could have known in print; Andrewes he must have known in person. Somewhat like Spenser, Fisher distinguishes three holy mountains—Sinai, Sion, and Jerusalem. More important, he spells out the hermeneutical principle of repetition of images *in bono et in malo:*

> For one and the same thinge by a divers consideracion may be taken figuratively for two contraries. Somtime in holy scripture the lion signefieth Crist and sometime by the lion is signefied the devile, as in the epistle of Saint Peter. *Tanquam leo rugiens circuit* [1 Pet. 5:8]. It signefieth Crist as in the appocalypse. *Vicit leo de tribu Iuda* [Rev. 5:5].

The image that is Fisher's main subject here is Jonah, who is a type of Christ, but who can also, Fisher argues, be taken *in malo* as a typical sinner. Without ever employing the Latin terms, Fisher also explicates the four rivers of paradise *in bono et in malo.*[64] In the course of a sermon of 1508, Fisher employs a traditional yet vividly detailed *distinctio* of birds—the pelican, night raven (owl), and sparrow of Psalm 101 (Vul.):7–8, a Penitential Psalm. Being part of Fisher's series on all the Penitential Psalms, it would have held some interest for Spenser, and the series was printed twice.[65] Fisher's printed works, Romish though they were, were still available at Cambridge*. Moreover, in 1578, Spenser worked as secretary for John Young, in the line of Fisher's successors in the see of Rochester; Young must have inherited the works of his predecessors and harbored enough interest to read them or to have Spenser read and summarize them for him. Then in the 1520s, a preacher is still basing a bird distinction on these same verses—John Longland, confessor to Henry VIII and bishop of Lincoln (a town with which Spenser seems to have

64. *English Works,* pt. 1, quotation, 201; Sinai, 167; rivers of paradise, 34–35; see also Blench, *Preaching,* 11–12. On the lion, Fisher reflects a long line of *distinctiones:* as Stephen Barney kindly informs me, in about 1190, Peter the Chanter offers, among several others, the same meanings for it *in bono et in malo* using the same verses.

65. In 1509 and 1555. See Fisher, *English Works,* pt. 1, 151–54. Two additional sermons were issued in 1532.

had connections)[66]—indicating that bird imagery was as attractive to early sixteenth-century preachers as it was to Spenser. Longland, too, was printed. Another set of birds, those offered at Mary's Purification, inspires John Tayler in 1508 to draw another bird distinction; and he adds to Scripture a bird *in malo,* "a caren crow."[67] It is true that Elizabethan sermons by and large are not structured around *distinctiones* as medieval ones are; this means that most of the sermons Spenser actually heard could not have supplied global models for his structural image-patterns the way medieval sermons did for medieval poets such as Langland, though they could still transmit to him those individual local *distinctiones* which they still contain.

Closer to Spenser in time and place, the career of Lancelot Andrewes overlapped with that of Spenser at the Merchant Taylors' School. Andrewes then spent more than fifteen years (1571–1586) at Pembroke, first as a student, later as a don; his career at Pembroke overlapped with Spenser's from 1571, when Andrewes matriculated, to 1576, when Spenser graduated M.A. and left. Also graduating M.A. in 1576, Andrewes immediately became a Fellow there; he was ordained deacon in 1580 and both priest and Catechist of Pembroke in 1581, at which time he began to gain recognition; he moved away in 1586 but returned in 1589 to be master of Pembroke.[68] The sermons of this Pembroke man exhibit all three trademarks of *distinctiones:* concordantial composition, variation of images, and analysis of a natural object. Their concordantial organization has been described in terms that, on the one hand, perfectly describe the imagistic structure of the FQ as I see it and, on the other, have been used to describe the *distinctio* effect. Andrewes employs what Douglas Bush calls "sonorous and repeated key-words as welding rivets."[69] He selects "one or two words," says Debora Shuger,

> usually concrete nouns or verbs, from his lection and then connect[s] them with related terms or images, generally from other portions of the Bible. . . . The structure created by the recurrence of the same word in different contexts discloses the relationship between those contexts.

66. In a sermon preached in instalments in 1523–29 and published in 1532; on both sermons, see Blench, *Preaching,* 24.

67. MS. Harl. 131, fols. 4–7, summarized in Blench, *Preaching,* 8–9.

68. See Higham, *Lancelot Andrewes,* 11–13; and DNB.

69. Bush, *English Literature,* 305. He attributes the same strategy to Donne and blames our blindness to it on our reading "scraps of [their] sermons in anthologies," with the result that "we miss the order and clarity of the total design." Perhaps our reading in snippets also explains why we have not seen their pattern of images *in bono et in malo.*

In one of his sermons, Christ is a stone:

> In His Birth: Daniel's "Stone, cut forth without hands." 2. In His Passion: Zachary's Stone, graven and cut full of eyes, all over. 3. In His Resurrection: Esay's Stone, laid in Sion . . . "he that believeth in Him then, shall not be confounded," saith St. Peter, *Hic est Lapis.* He is the Stone of our faith, saith St. Peter, *Lapis erat Christus.* [4] And *Petra erat Christus* saith St. Paul. He is "the Stone" of our Sacraments; the Water of our baptism, and of our spiritual drink, both issue from Him.[70]

This passage happens to coincide in imagistic structure and at times almost verbatim with a classic example of a medieval sermon structured around a *distinctio*—Gilbert Foliot's on the same topic, as preserved in the report of an auditor.[71] I therefore propose, though I must leave the full argument to Andrewes scholars, that he was using the method of the *distinctiones.* Finally, on occasion Andrewes also varies images *in bono et in malo.* In his empathic sermon on Mary Magdalene, he contrasts her meeting the resurrected Christ in a garden with Eve bringing death to the race in the Garden of Eden; he contrasts her weeping on a misapprehension with our failure to weep for our sins. Andrewes occasionally extends a metaphor, in this case a natural object, to such a metaphysical length that it becomes allegory and thus resembles the FQ, as in his four-page allegory—loosely based on Ecclesiastes 12:6—of the body as a pot hanging by a silver cord over a well.[72] In this *distinctiones* manner, Spenser interprets the properties of the panther as an allegory of the lady in Am. 53.

In manifesting the three trademarks of *distinctiones,* Andrewes illustrates the shaping influence that *distinctiones,* however mediated, could have on writers of Spenser's generation. Andrewes may have imbibed this

---

70. Granted, this sermon was not preached until 1611, but it indicates the vitality of the tradition and may indicate Andrewes's long-established habits of reading and composition, probably derived in part from his own copy of the *distinctio*-rich Hugh of St. Cher and from the same Pembroke-owned *Distinctiones* which I have invoked for Spenser. Andrewes, *Works,* quotation, 274–75, elaborated, 275–78; quoted and discussed in Shuger, *Habits,* 58–59. Shuger does not mention *distinctiones* or repeating images *in bono et in malo.*

71. Foliot's "whole sermon was varied by certain *distinctiones.* . . . When Gilbert spoke of Christ as a stone, he brought forward the stone which the builders rejected, which is become the head of the corner, he brought forward the stone which Jacob set up for a pillar and on top of which he poured oil, he brought forward the stone that was cut out of the mountain without hands." The reporter is a late twelfth-century prior named Peter, who was so impressed that he compiled a *distinctiones* himself. The report is edited by R. W. Hunt, "English Learning in the Late Twelfth Century," *Transactions of the Royal Historical Society* 19 (1936):33–34, and quoted in Smalley, *Study,* 248.

72. *Works,* 90–93, introducing a sermon on Penitential Psalm 51.

influence while studying at Pembroke either directly from the various *distinctiones* there or mediated by local preachers who used them; additionally, if he absorbed it while at Pembroke, he may have encouraged his classmate the poet to do so, or vice versa. Even if Andrewes imbibed it later in life, Spenser is likely to have paid attention to the subsequent and stellar career of his fellow alumnus. Although Spenser was living in Ireland by 1580, he could have heard Andrewes preach on his periodic visits to England.

Imagistic *distinctiones* produce a development of images which anticipates metaphysical poetry. In their organization around images and their obvious use of a biblical concordance, Donne's divine poems, his sermons, and his *Devotions upon Emergent Occasions* often sound exactly like medieval sermons based on *distinctiones,* such as that of Gilbert Foliot on Christ as stone quoted above. Donne even employs images *in bono et in malo.*[73] Since his religious works come too late to serve as sources, since he could in fact have learned the technique from Spenser, I invoke them to manifest the continued vitality of the tradition in the seventeenth century and to encourage Donne scholars to investigate *distinctiones. Distinctiones* may have been as compelling a model for Elizabethan and Jacobean imagistic structure as was the Memory Theater extolled by Frances Yates.[74] Spenser could conceivably have derived his images *in bono et in malo* from previous poets, who in turn derived them from *distinctiones.* In the first place, *distinctiones* formally resemble poems in that they rhyme, as any poet who encountered them would notice. More broadly, Barney says in his conclusion of his study of Peter the Chanter's *distinctiones:*

> I would argue that the Chanter's handling of the flow of meaning in the articles, from concrete to abstract and the reverse, displays visibly the kind of thinking that an allegorist, a Jean de Meun or a Dante or a Langland, undertakes as he constructs his narrative. (103)

Dante and Langland frequently vary images *in bono et in malo,* though not much has been made of it. Their resemblances to Spenser, though not the reevaluation of images, have been explored by A. C. Hamilton and, in the latter case, Judith Anderson. We have almost certain evidence

73. For example, preaching on Isaiah 52:3, which in his Bible reads, "Ye have sold yourselves for nought, and ye shall be redeemed without money," he suddenly inverts "to sell yourselves" into a favorable sense (the martyrs), *Sermons,* no. 1, 1:157.

74. See Yates, *The Art of Memory.*

that Spenser knew Langland; he apparently refers to him as a model in the envoi to the *Shepheards Calender,* "the pilgrim that the ploughman playde a while," and he alludes to Langland's protagonist in the character Piers in "May."[75] There is no doubt whatever that Langland imitated the structures attributed to the Bible by *distinctiones.* "The influence of their structure" (i.e., that of the *distinctiones*) says Jill Mann, "is fundamental to his meditation on the many biblical texts which involve the ideas of eating and drinking, hunger and thirst." Another similarity is that Langland varies images *in bono et in malo,* though none of his critics, so far as I know, employs this particular phrase. Langland uses the image of sleep in this way: in the sense of spiritual torpor at the beginning of Passus I ("sleep and sleuþe seweþ hem evere," Prologue 45; all quotations from the B text) and in the sense of the quietness of contemplation at the beginning of Passus XVI; he is following a sevenfold *distinctio* on sleep in an anonymous *Allegoriae.*[76]

More important, Langland distinguishes, as J. A. Burrow shows, between "two manere of medes" or rewards, good and bad, and between good and evil minstrels (B text, Prologue 31–39 et passim). Burrow compares Langland's statement about "medes" to "the scholastic philosopher . . . with his *distinguo*"—"the kind of intellectually satisfying solution that Aquinas aimed at"—namely, through his proposition, objection, and resolution by a distinction. Aquinas' procedure did not die with the Middle Ages, for William Streat still uses it in 1654, as we shall see in Chapter 4. We can take Mann and Burrow one step further and state that Langland employs images *in bono et in malo* and infer that he derived this arrangement too from the *distinctiones.*

Building on E. Talbot Donaldson, Burrow distinguishes in *Piers Plowman* a satisfying versus an unsettling shift in evaluation of an image. About minstrels, Langland vacillates, gradually narrowing the repertory of the good minstrels to religious subjects and identifying himself as author with this class. Langland's treatment of minstrels in contrast to meeds represents an attempt, "not without difficulty, to sort out his mixed feelings." Burrow goes on: "It may be that the authorities differ among them-

75. Even though Langland is not well attested at Cambridge (nor for that matter is Spenser), he was printed by Grafton for Crowley in 1550, and powerful internal and external evidence for Spenser's knowledge of him is given in Hamilton, "Vision," and in Anderson, *Growth,* 2–3.

76. Mann, "Eating and Drinking," 36–37 et passim; Spearing, "Development," 252; Alford, "Biblical *Imitatio,*" 11, and "Role of the Quotations," 92. On *dormitio,* see PL 112:913, invoked by Robertson and Huppé, *Piers Plowman,* 5–6.

selves . . . ; or one's own experience may be confused and confusing; or reason itself may prompt conflicting arguments in the mind, *pro* and *contra, sic* and *non.*" [77]

Spenser could conceivably have learned to repeat his images and to vary them *in bono et in malo* from Dante. Although we have no certain evidence that Spenser read him, he certainly could read Italian, and he read authors who cite him—Van der Noot (fol. 54v), Sidney, and Tasso among others—and he certainly knew of him, for Adams lists an overwhelming sixty-six copies of the *Commedia* before 1590 in Cambridge libraries at large*. A. C. Hamilton has pointed out several similarities, for example, beginning in a dark wood and proceeding to a battle with a beast. [78] It is therefore significant that, as Judson Allen declares, "the distinctio . . . is the literal governing strategy, for Dante, of the whole, as well as of the most detailed of the parts, of the *Commedia.*" [79] Canto XI of the *Inferno* is at once a *distinctio* on the gravity of various sins and a map of Hell, as if the landscape rendered the *distinctio* three-dimensional. Dante's figure of Satan (*Inferno* 34), whose three heads parody the Trinity draws upon exegesis of the three-colored mulberry *in bono et in malo* to parody the crucified Christ. [80] Dante structured the *Purgatorio* around good and evil women; [81] and Spenser organized FQ Book I around good and evil women, one of whom, Una, resembles Dante's Beatrice.

On two occasions, Dante seeks out an honorable example of an unpleasant thing. After duly describing the suicides in Hell, Dante goes out of his way to portray a suicide *in bono*—Cato, the coastwarden of Purgatory (*Purgatorio,* 1–3). Dante employs the seven heads and ten horns of the apocalyptic beast with straightforwardly biblical loathing when their pullulation signals the corruption of the chariot of the church in *Purgatorio* 32.142–47. Earlier, however, he goes out of his way to employ them in a favorable context; he attributes them somewhat implausibly to the lovely lady the pristine church in *Inferno* 19.106–11. The heads-horns motif is unique to the Bible; it is repeated with a fair degree of consistency there, all four instances being *in malo:* three times in Revelation 12,

77. Burrow, *Langland's Fictions,* 28–29 and n. 1. Unlike Mann, Spearing, Alford, and Judson Allen, Donaldson and Burrow do not mention *distinctiones* as a genre. Quotation from *Piers Plowman,* B text, Passus 3, l. 231; the good meed turns out (for the moment) to be that which is bestowed by God in heaven.

78. Hamilton, *Structure of Allegory,* 30–43.

79. Allen, *Ethical Poetic,* 154.

80. Freccero, "Sign," 170–71.

81. See Hollander, "The Women of *Purgatorio:* Dreams, Voyages, Prophecies," chap. 4 of his *Allegory in Dante's Commedia,* 136–91.

13, and 17, with an anticipation in Daniel 7. Only the desire to imitate God's strategy of varying images *in bono et in malo* could have led Dante to use this grotesque image in a favorable sense, almost as if he were parodying the strategy.[82] Incidentally, Spenser duly renders this biblical image, always *in malo,* when he translates the Revelation sonnets (i.2 and ii.4–5) in the *Theatre;* moreover, he echoes the seven heads in Duessa's beast while wisely skipping the incommensurable horns (FQ I.vii.17–18; see also "Ruines of Time," 71; "Visions of Bellay," viii; x, *Complaints* version only). As we have seen, in his one good dragon, Spenser follows Dante's pattern of straining for a favorable instance of a monster.

Although many poets before Spenser had repeated images without knowing or without imitating the Bible, only Langland and Dante had organized their repeated images *in bono et in malo;* and they were deeply influenced by the Bible. Thus, even if derived from them, this organization of images remains biblical, either directly or indirectly. Of course Spenser's plot (a romance-epic) disguises this filiation because it is more entertaining, less obviously didactic, than that of the Bible, or of the *Commedia* (a travelogue of the otherworld with moments of bildungsroman), or of *Piers Plowman* (a typical medieval allegorical journey). Whereas Dante is the most relentless imitator of *distinctiones* in all their aspects, Spenser is the most relentless repeater of images *in bono et in malo* (my Appendix of Images shows many more than could possibly be found in Dante or Langland). Even if someone were to find a few images *in bono et in malo* in a secular author such as Horace, Spenser exhibits to a higher degree something that is characteristic of much literary style. His habit of carrying a practice to an extreme makes his style more analyzable than those of other poets; this in turn is what earned him the title "the poet's poet." Other poets can learn from him.

What Difference Does It Make?

When these biblical patterns are noticed by the concordantial reader, what difference does it make to the poetry? *Distinctiones* and the Bible as they portray it are exhaustive, covering all the possibilities. Erwin Panofsky found a common element—"totality (sufficient enumeration)"—

---

82. Stambler, *Dante's Other World,* notes in relation to the instance in *Purgatorio* 32 that *Inferno* 106–11 anticipates it "in a peculiarly altered fashion" (370, n. 6). A further reason for this grotesque but favorable instance is that there is an entire poetics of such undignified imagery for the divine. See Chapter 5.

running through scholastic thought, the *Commedia,* and medieval cathedrals.[83] This characteristic Jesse Gellrich sees in the *distinctiones,* especially when they distinguish *in bono et in malo.*[84] So does Judson Allen: he claims that they exhibit "all the possibilities," and, moreover, that certain writers of fiction—Dante and others—adopt the *distinctio* structure in order to be or to seem comprehensive.[85]

Spenser lays claim to an exhaustiveness rivaling that of the *distinctiones* in the Letter to Ralegh. He professes to portray the twelve moral virtues displayed by a gentle person in her private capacity and promises another twelve public and politic virtues. This is the classificatory zeal of the moral encyclopedias, the topical *distinctiones.* The idea that the Aristotelian moral virtues were twelve in number is scholastic. That Spenser's scheme later telescoped to three private and three public virtues does not make it less schematic, though the various ways in which it was (and was not) actualized sometimes do so. Similarly, according to the possibly fictional but undoubtedly Spenser-influenced *Dialogue of Civil Life* by Lodowick Briskett, the FQ is a substitute for, the fictional equivalent of, Aristotelian moral philosophy. Grandiose as this claim may seem, we can find or easily construct in the FQ not one overarching scholastic system, it is true, but at least several different systems by juxtaposing passages linked by repeated motifs. These organizing schemata could be said to constitute what Sidney in the *Defence* called "the fore-conceit, the *architektonike* of the poem."

Many exhaustive lists, reflecting the moral encyclopedias, occur in the allegorical tableaux: the House of Alma dramatizes a series of scientific distinctions; the House of Holiness, of moral and spiritual distinctions, including seven good deeds to balance Lucifera's seven deadly sins; the Masque of Busirane applies such a rational structure to love-psychology (especially III.xii.24). As I have said, the many characters clustered around the theme of glory and honor—the allies, associates, and antitypes of Arthur and Gloriana—seem to form a *distinctio* on glory: glory is *vera* when it is the testimony of a good conscience (FQ II.vii.2); it is *humana, mundana,* perhaps even *vana* when it is not truly eternal (Cleopolis); it is *vanissima* when it is not merited by birth or deed (Braggadocchio, "The scorne of knighthood and trew chevalrye, / To thinke without desert of gentle deed, / And noble worth to be advaunced hye: / Such

83. Panofsky, *Gothic Architecture,* 31, 44–45, and esp. 38–39.

84. Gellrich, *Idea,* 70–74, esp. 72. His example is "cathedra," "chair," from Bersuire's *Repertorium.*

85. Allen, "Malory's Diptych," 239. See also Allen's *Ethical Poetic* on the Wife of Bath, 136. Allen's theories and his background information are useful even though his literary examples are too remote from his point and his similarities too general to be susceptible of verification.

praise is shame; but honour vertues meed / Doth beare the fairest flowre in honorable seed" [II.iii.10]).

At the micro-level of rhetoric, in the dialogue between Belphoebe and the now unrecognizable Timias, Spenser makes elaborate use of the biblical figure *reditio* to flaunt his exhaustiveness: [86]

> Ah wofull man, what *heavens* hard disgrace,
> Or wrath of *cruell wight* on thee ywrake?
> Or *selfe disliked life* doth thee thus wretched make?
>
> If *heaven,* then none may it redresse or blame,
>
> . . . .
>
> If *wrathfull wight,* then fowle rebuke and shame
> Be theirs, . . .
> But if through inward griefe or *wilfull scorne*
> *Of life* it be . . .

Timias runs through the same causes yet again:

> Then have they all themselves against me bent:
> For *heaven,* first author of my languishment,
>
> . . . .
>
> Did closely with a *cruell one* consent,
> To cloud my daies in dolefull misery,
> And make *me loath this life,* still longing for to die.
> (IV.viii.14–16; emphasis mine).

Such exhaustive schemata constitute the paradigm across which the narratives play. They make the FQ at least look like the Bible as it was then presented through the *distinctiones* and moral encyclopedias.

Arrays seem exhaustive not only if they reach a mystic number but also if they include the peculiar, the liminal, and the perfunctory. Spenser's treatment of the theme of love includes what his culture would have considered peculiar: not just love of friends and of kin (see the *distinctio,* IV.ix.1–3) but of someone seen only in a vision (Gloriana by Arthur, Artegall by Britomart); voyeurism (II.v.34; VII.vi.46); rape (I.vi.5–6; in III.vii.37 a rape of a male by a female); adultery (III.ix–x); pedophilia (II.v.28.9); and both incest (father-daughter and brother-sister), and bestiality (III.ii.40–41; vii.47–49). The personifications in the procession that tortures Amoret at Busirane's house are said to include "a thousand monstrous formes" (III.xi.51). The sort of love that, as Blake says, "joys in another's loss of ease / and builds a hell in heaven's despite," as dra-

86. See Bullinger, *Figures,* 394–96.

matized in Busirane's entire treatment of Amoret, exemplifies what we now consider to be a separate "perversion," sadism. The complementary "perversion," masochism, is probably exemplified in Timias's persistent though unrequited love of Belphoebe and certainly in the half-humorous plea of the poet-lover of the *Amoretti,* "I will intreat / that for my faults ye will me gently beat" (24.8–9). Every Petrarchan to a greater or lesser extent laments yet enjoys the suffering that the beloved inflicts on him/her as well as her/his delight in inflicting it. Such arrays are also saved from being boringly predictable by the inclusion of the liminal. For example, friendship (the virtue of Book IV) is on the boundaries, first, between private and public virtue, and second, between virtue and fortune because it depends on an external circumstance, reciprocation.

The poet's distinction between the bad Genius at hand and some good Genius or Genii is exhaustive to a fault in that it mentions a good Genius, whom C. S. Lewis calls Genius Bb, "Who wondrous things concerning our welfare / Doth let us oft forsee" (II.xii.47), who never even appears in the plot.[87] This psychological benefit, otherwise perfunctory, is introduced here merely for the sake of contrast with the "guilefull semblaunts" induced by the bad psychological Genius at hand, who "secretly doth us procure to fall" (II.xii.48). The good Genius B in the Garden of Adonis, like everything else there, is part of the life cycle; if we extend the principle of contrast, it would seem that the bad Genius, like the rest of the Bower, is not. "Guilefull semblaunts" that entrap the soul yet do not promote the life cycle would be sexual fantasies used as a substitute for the act—yet another sexual "perversion." Another example of the perfunctory, not liminal this time but central, is the naming of Blandina, the wife of Turpine, as if she were a personification of flattery (Latin, *blandimentum*), even though in the plot her actions seem unimpeachable. In a Book of Courtesy, Spenser was compelled to include such courtesy *in malo* for the sake of completeness and the intellectual satisfaction it brings.

As we saw, Burrow distinguishes in *Piers Plowman* a satisfying versus an unsettling repetition of an image. Spearing, speaking in terms of audiences, classifies "the lewed" in Langland's audience as "aware only of repetitions," and the sophisticated as alert to the development of an image-chain because they were "familiar with elaborate sermons constructed with the aid of concordantiae and lists of *distinctiones.*"[88] Trans-

87. A Genius named Agdistes actually appears in III.vi.31–33, but he is purely generative, a Genius A. See Lewis, *Allegory of Love,* Appendix 1, "Genius and Genius," which incidentally itself represents a *distinctio* of the sort Spenser expects readers to assemble.

88. Spearing, "Development," 252.

ferring these responses into a single mind, we can say that almost any image that shifts is understood by the reader in three sequential moments: noting the repetition (reading concordantially); noting and wrestling with the variation; and, if possible, reconciling the diversity in a *distinctio* by explaining wherein one occurrence is good and the other evil.

The middle stage is unnecessary on the rare occasions when Spenser spells out part of the distinction for the reader at the outset: for example, that some Geniuses are good and some evil (see II.xii.47–49; III.vi.33). Only slightly less easy and satisfying to the reader are those distinctions that she anticipates from her experience of biblical distinctions ("the cup of the Lord and the cup of devils"); she jumps without any contestation straight from the first to the third or final stage of understanding: "Duessa's cup is bad because it is the cup of witches and heretics." Only its similarities to Fidelia's cup of the Lord necessitate the wrestling of the second stage. Whether anticipated or not, those shifts are also fairly quick and easy to explain which are between two different species of the image in question, a Manichaean cosmic symmetry, such as, again, the distinction between good and evil cups and Geniuses. False Florimell is the evil twin, the demonic parody, of the true (Books III.v–V.iii, passim): given that the reader is in on the ruse from the beginning and knows who is who, she can easily translate the situation into a distinction such as "some apparent beauty is not true beauty because it is purely material and not subtended by soul." I will henceforth specify such a satisfying scholastic *distinctio,* whether attained in the early stages (in the text or an obvious subtext) or in the third (in the reader) as a *distributio.*[89]

The reader satisfied with her final, exhaustive, unitive *distributio* should remember whether it came easily or with surprise and difficulty. A remembered difficulty often shows the reader how many control groups, how many borderline cases, the poet-speaker has considered for the sake of completeness.

In this chapter I have traced Spenser's peculiar structure of repeated images to the Bible by way of medieval and Renaissance concordance-makers, preachers, and exegetes who perceived such a structure there and expressed it in their *distinctiones.* Since repeated images were beloved of New Critics, this usage has also historicized the New Criticism as an approach to the literature of the Middle Ages and the Renaissance. A *distinctio* is a spotty *explication de texte,* yielding a *distributio* that imparts a

---

89. *Distributio* and *distinctio* are the terms employed in a similar classification by Rendall, *Distinguo,* in regard to Montaigne.

feeling of exhaustiveness. The same primary source material, however, provides the first coherent account of Spenser's shifts in evaluation of these repeated images, a strategy barely mentioned by the New Critics. They perceived the building blocks but not their alternating black and white colors. Unmentioned even by rhetorical manuals, the use of images *in bono et in malo* is not only the most medieval of the strategies I will be discussing but also the most distinctively biblical. Images that vary in this way, however, do not always—certainly never in the second, the agonistic, stage of perception—possess that "organic unity" or compose those static, timeless, simultaneous visual patterns into which the New Critics (and also numerological critics) arrange them. Most of Spenser's *distributiones*—those about glory or reptilians, for example—develop only gradually in the mind of the reader, thus inviting reader-response criticism. I see the cup of unity as half-empty, neither completely empty as the deconstructionists once saw it nor full—if often of paradoxes—as did the New Critics. External evidence plays a greater part in my argument than in any of theirs because of my overriding concern with intertextuality—with Spenser's imitation of another text, and one of peculiar status in his place and time.

CHAPTER THREE

IMAGES THAT CORRECT

THEIR PREDECESSORS

Some of Spenser's image-pairs *in bono et in malo* cannot be resolved into a *distributio;* the second statement denies the primary statement either totally or in part. Like Langland's pronouncements on minstrels, these conflicting pairs are, or at least initially appear to be, genuine vacillations. They form patterns whose initial effect on someone reading in chronological order yet concordantially is not harmonious or symmetrical but surprising, agonistic, and hermeneutically unsettling. Lack of foreshadowing or of a preformed *distinctio* inflicts a psychological shock that mingles with the logical. We have already seen an example in the way in which the Christ symbol in Fidelia's cup corrects the false norm of Zwinglian memorialism against which Duessa's cup at first seemed to be weighed and found wanting. The *distinctio* yielded by such a pattern is not "there are two kinds of A" but "A is bad, no, A is good when . . ." or vice versa.

Spenser reverses his evaluation of sexual pleasure in the second garden in the FQ. From the first garden, the Bower of Bliss (and, indeed, from most of Book II), the first-time reader derives the impression that sexual pleasure, at least in excess, is a vice; reading the first half of Book III, she notes a few expressions of sympathy with it; she then is surprised to find it celebrated in the otherwise similar Garden of Adonis. The norm against which it was weighed and found wanting in the Bower of Bliss was Stoicism, but this is now declared to be false. She surmises that there is, as C. S. Lewis discovered, a "deliberate differentiation" (*Allegory,* 326); in other words, she constructs a *distinctio* and tries to make it a comprehensive *distributio.* Battered and jerked around, she gradually accommodates the statements and examples in the two episodes into some sort of complex generalization containing an adversative, an "if" or a "when," such as, "Sexual pleasure is a vice, but good if it results in procreation and if it is according to nature and not prolonged by art." But she wonders why Spenser did not just say what he meant the first time, or present the two gardens successively side by side on a Pythagorean Y, as Ariosto presented Alcina's garden followed by the (differently) normative palace of Logistilla (*Orlando Furioso* X, sts. 43ff.); and Lewis has no answer.

One way of reading that takes account of propositional contradictions, and also, I think, by analogy, of reversals in the value of an image—my second aesthetic problem in the Introduction—is Stanley Fish's manifesto of affective stylistics, the appendix to *Self-Consuming Artifacts* titled "Literature in the Reader," still a classic in its own right, though it has been adapted by many in many directions. Some readers will protest about a poem, just as they do about the Bible, that if contradictions can be reconciled, they aren't contradictions; but Fish would answer that they must first be perceived as such. Does the second statement deny the first? Very well, Fish would say, mistakes "are part of the experience . . . and therefore part of . . . meaning."[1] For Maureen Quilligan, who applies such reader-response criticism to allegories in general, including FQ, meaning is not carried by allusions that one can look up in books but develops "horizontally," "by a gradual revelation."[2]

Thus, there are (at least) two different ways to read: statically versus temporally; simultaneously versus linearly; spatially versus kinetically; unitively versus "differently"; treating the work as a visual objet d'art, as C. S. Lewis, Frye, and the New Critics did, versus treating it as if it were a piece of music, as Fish does.[3] That Spenser intended his reader to read temporally and experience an initial surprise is indicated by his frequent appeal to another real yet transitory pleasure of temporal reading: suspense. The Bible too can be read in either way, and was so read by Christians with regard to the OT versus the NT, as we shall see.

Despite Fish's protestations to the contrary, the two ways of reading are not mutually exclusive. They are not simply the right way and the wrong way to read an unsettling text. As I explained at the end of the last chapter, one reads such a text temporally at first, then sees it whole. (The time Fish and I are talking about is not clock time, narrative time, or even, except in my heuristic fiction, the number of times the reader has to reread it, but readerly time, the stages required to rationalize the shift and reach the *distributio*.) In my treatment of images that are repeated *in bono et in malo* (Chapter 2), I have seen the work for the most part from

---

1. Fish, *Self-Consuming Artifacts,* 405; see also 387–88. Hereafter cited in text.
2. Quilligan, *Allegory,* 227.
3. Cf. Gilman, *Iconoclasm,* 23, 189–91.

a bird's-eye view, simultaneously and spatially; in the present chapter and Chapter 4, "Propositional Contradictions," especially my treatment of correction, I view the poem linearly, kinetically, and temporally.

If we read FQ in this way yet concordantially, we are rewarded by seeing that Spenser keeps reversing or otherwise correcting himself throughout Books II and following about sexual pleasure, gardens, and the superiority of nature over art. He does so in an intertwined chain reaction of contradictory words and images. Entwined with the linked gardens is a chain of explicit and contradictory references to "art" and "nature."

For example, Spenser's correction in the Garden of Adonis itself requires correction. It is so headlong that it goes to the opposite extreme of advocating untrammeled promiscuity ("franckly each paramour his lemman knows," 41) and rejecting art altogether ("not by art," III.vi.44). This overcorrection receives correction by the Temple of Venus. In the garden surrounding the Temple, lovers and same-sex friends walk and talk together, as A. Kent Hieatt puts it, in "a freely yielded and mutually willed spiritual friendship."[4] This element of communication corrects not only the sexual relationships in the Bower of Bliss, where it was prevented by Verdant's somnolence and the bestial inarticulateness of the transmogrified lovers, but also those in the Garden of Adonis, which by including the animals preclude conversation or declare it to be inessential—relationships that while good for the species are merely physical. Moreover, the same-sex friends are said to ground their desire in "chaste virtue" and to express their love in "bounteous deeds"—another element missing even from the Garden of Adonis and here supplied at last as a supplement to it. I do not think this means that the heterosexual lovers in both corrective gardens *aren't* virtuous, just that the same-sex friends focus on virtue, having, according to Spenser, no physical pleasure as a further or ulterior motive (down goes sexual pleasure again!), whereas in the Garden of Adonis, "all pleasure flowes" (III.vi.41); they thus isolate in pure culture an element, virtue, that deepens even the heterosexual human relationships. Though the "lives" of these pairs "decay'd, / Yet loves decayed never" (IV.x.27); intense and lasting love is a remedy for death. As such it compares and contrasts with a previously mentioned and also erotic remedy for death: procreation. Spenser's placing happy outdoor inhabitants of the Isle of Venus in a garden seems meant to recall and to correct or supplement the human relationships in the other two gardens.

The chain thickens with the theme of art versus nature. The Garden of

4. Hieatt, "Scudamour's Practice," 201, referring not to these lovers but to the ideal against which Amoret's and Scudamour's relationship is weighed and found wanting; see also the brief thematic discussion of the three gardens in his *Chaucer, Spenser*, 95–106.

Adonis was about as good as it gets, and it had no art. Art is condemned in the Bower of Bliss by the gold ivy with green paint over it, the grapes made out of jewels, and the nonfunctional ivory gate with verisimilar scenes from the life of Medea. Art would seem to be merely a seductive illusion. (The cautionary example of the House of Busirane, an unnatural place, a temple not a garden, also serves to condemn "art" as, among other things, illusory.) The Temple of Venus provides a mild correction to this false negative impression:

> For all that nature by her mother wit
> Could frame in earth, and forme of substance base,
> Was there, and all that nature did omit,
> Art playing second natures part, supplyed it.
> (IV.x.21)

From this the reader, after her initial surprise, derives the *distributio* that art is good when it supplements or complements nature. Good art is illustrated not in pictures but in a work of architecture: the bridge. That building bridges is a proper activity for artists is shown by the statement about one of the emperors of Faeryland, a land that, according to Thomas P. Roche, Jr., represents The City, the realm of politics and art:[5] "He built by art upon the glassy See / A bridge of bras, whose sound heavens thunder seem'd to bee" (II.x.73). Its decoration is "fram'd after the Doric guize," that is, in the simplest of the three major orders; but the mere mention of the orders, a technical topic, marks the bridge as a work of art. Architecture is an art almost as closely allied with nature as is gardening. One might think of a bridge as competing with nature in that it overcomes a natural obstacle. But it could be seen as supplementing nature's failure to make a causeway just here; and it is useful. All this is confirmed by a subsequent description of this bridge from the inside emphasizing the voluntary cooperation of nature with art:

> I . . . Past forth on foote, beholding all the way
> The goodly workes, and stones of rich assay,
> Cast into sundry shapes by wondrous skill,
> That like on earth no where I recken may:
> And underneath, the river rolling still
> With murmure soft, that seem'd to serve the workmans will.
> (IV.x.15)

Competing with nature is the fundamental flaw of the art in the Bower of Bliss (II.xii.42, 50, 58–59). Such art is not useful; because it is verisim-

5. Roche, *The Kindly Flame*, 34–38.

ilar, it could be summed up, as Albert Ascoli has suggested to me, as mimetic art. Not all art but only nonfunctional mimesis is a seductive illusion. This condemnation of mimesis and approval of utilitarian fabrications that the reader derives from comparing the Bower with the Isle of Venus corresponds exactly to Plato's view of art in the *Republic*. Spenser's correction here does not go very far in defense of art; it does not accommodate, for example, Aristotle's conciliatory doctrine that mimesis itself can be salutary. In their nonrepresentational realm, bridges are analogous to didactic allegory in that both are useful. Spenser's correction here accommodates the FQ itself, but only insofar as it is didactic; its mimesis is redeemed (as the Letter to Ralegh affirms) by its allegorical meaning. This instrumental view of art is the reigning medieval view (as exemplified, say, in Aquinas)—plausible though not exalted.

The final *locus amoenus*—Mount Acidale in VI.x—also dramatizes and comments on art and nature, offering a final and more satisfying round to the evolving discussion on art hitherto imaged in gardens. The hook-words "garden" and "art" are not mentioned, though art is clearly exemplified in the poet Colin and implied by its mentioned opposite, "nature." As in the Garden of Adonis, the beautiful setting is made entirely "by natures skill" (VI.x.5). Colin, Spenser's pastoral persona, by playing his pipe has worked an artistic theurgy: he has summoned not only his lady love, the subject of his song, but also the Three Graces and their hundred understudies, and by an epideictic miracle, he has apotheosized his lady "to be another grace" (VI.x.16). But when an intruder comes upon the scene, the whole corps de ballet vanishes, and Colin ruefully explains that "by no meanes thou canst recall [them] againe, / For being gone, none can them bring in place" (VI.x.20). Like the highest kind of courtesy, the highest art must be spontaneous, not "enforst with paine" (VI.ii.2), as architecture might be; the artist must be carried away.

While this elusiveness is unfortunate for the distracted poet, it represents the occupational hazard of an art that is above bricklaying: the phrase "but as they list" implies that artistic inspiration is the secular analogue of the Holy Spirit as described in John 3:8. In part, inspiration is defined negatively, by its departure. The intruder is Sir Calidore; in the judgment of his ladylove, Pastorella, Calidore's own love poetry falls short of "Colins carolings" (VI.ix.35); it must be for the lack of this *je ne sais quoi* in his own art—however present it is in his conduct (VI.ii.2)—that the Graces cannot abide him. Art must spring from inspiration (love, the Graces, and their understudies). This view of art as inspiration contrasts with that in the *Republic* and resembles that in Plato's *Phaedrus* and *Ion.* It clearly rejects purposeful effort; it transcends or mystifies nature's role, reminding us of Yeats's ecstatic query, "O body swayed to music, O brightening glance, / How can we know the dancer from the dance?"[6] Thus it provides a fitting conclusion to a far-flung debate about love, death, and art versus nature linked by the images of various *loci amoeni.*

Throughout the rest of this chapter I concentrate on pairs and short chains of images. The core of this group is ecclesiastical: it consists of fasting, abandoning shields, altars and their iconoclasm, beads, crosses, and holy water, with backward glances at cups in the preceding chapter. Somewhat similar to these in indeterminacy, as well as being biblical and complex, is another image-pair, cities. Certain patterns are shared by most of the group. Sometimes the variation happens quickly, sometimes within the same episode, as with cities and the blood on Ruddymane (to be considered in Chapter 5), or within the same book, as with fasting (I), beads (I), and abandoning shields (V). Sometimes it is both quick and punctuated typographically, as a *distinctio* often is in exegesis—in adjacent sonnets, as with the laurel leaf, or in adjacent cantos, as with abandoning shields. These divisions highlight both the parallel and the contrast. The contrast is heightened when the very same thing is reevaluated, as is sexual love in the *Fowre Hymnes,* the laurel leaf in the *Amoretti,* and in the FQ, fasting, beads, abandoning shields, and the blood on Ruddymane; this is not division but revision. Whereas the monk's repetitions of an image, according to Leclerq, are "not . . . necessarily referring to what he has already said,"[7] such adjacent repetitions of the very same thing are demonstrably self-echoing, and if self-echoing, then, because of the shift in evaluation, also self-contestatory. Three of these adjacent shifts in evaluation—those of the laurel leaf, cities, and the blood on Ruddymane—are also debated in the text; these debates employ characters both to call attention to the shifts and to model for the reader something of the *distinctio* Spenser wants her to think up. If adjacent corrections are agreed to be deliberate, then the far-flung corrections and those that are not debated in the text must be purposeful as well, with the formulation of the *distinctio* left up to the reader, not handed to her on a silver platter, as is the *distinctio* between Geniuses.

A brief correction has two steps and illustrates all these patterns: Amoretti 28 and 29 constitute a debate about hermeneutics—the symbolism of the laurel leaf which the poet-speaker has given the lady and which she

6. Yeats's metaphor is based on Plotinus, whom Spenser could have known in Ficino's translation.

7. Leclerq, *Love,* 91.

obligingly wears. First the poet-speaker interprets the laurel leaf as the poet (*in bono* for him in that it both symbolizes him and threatens her with Daphne's fate should she fail to accept him). Then in 29, the lady counters that it symbolizes her as the conqueror (*in malo* for him as implying her power over him). In the poet-speaker's rebuttal, also in 29, he volunteers to play the poet who sings the praises of the conqueror; he thus incorporates the symbolism both of his profession from 28 and of her dominance from 29; by virtue of this comprehensiveness, his interpretation can lay claim to being a synthesis and thus a correction. By thus incorporating her interpretation, the debate dramatizes a tense but ultimately harmonious friendship. More cynically, by this facility he demonstrates his ownership of language and thus his power as a poet, a power not to coerce but to interpret. This development of the laurel leaf illustrates another possible *distinctio*—another possible reason for a shift in evaluation of the same thing—a shift of perspective. A common shift, illustrated here, is from partial to comprehensive; another possible one, present in several shorter poems but rare in the FQ, is from materialistic to spiritual.

Fasting appears *in bono et in malo* in Spenser, in the Bible, and in the *distinctiones,* as we have seen. Being the very same thing, reevaluated in the same book, and by a more spiritual practitioner and teacher thereof, it illustrates all the aforementioned characteristics except that it is not debated in the text. (Of course an action, such as fasting or suicide, cannot be, as a physical object can, exactly the same each time it is repeated.) Fasting is the first of many images in which the shift in perspective is from Protestant to popish, or to irenic, or to ecumenical, the last two of which perspectives enjoy the merit of comprehensiveness. Seeking for what makes fasting good or bad lends significance to Corceca's error. Corceca's computation of its frequency (thrice three times) implies that she thinks it is intrinsically meritorious (I.iii.13–14). Then in Canto x, the Hermit explicitly uses it as a psychological exercise to reduce physical desires, and he enjoins it upon Red Cross to release the spirit. Corceca's fasting does not have this virtuous goal, or any goal beyond itself; she abuses fasting by treating it as meritorious, a standard Protestant accusation. Nothing is good or evil in itself, Spenser implies, as he declares about female beauty in the *Hymne of Beautie:*

> Yet nathemore is that faire beauties blame,
> But theirs that do abuse it unto ill:
> Nothing so good, but that through guilty shame
> May be corrupt.

(155–58)

Fasting per se is not papistical or unfruitful but permissible in its place. Other pairs will confirm that vice is to virtue as the abuse is to the proper use of a thing.

To rationalize the contradiction, the reader might first conjecture that the second, the affirmative instance of fasting, must be ironized, must represent a reprehensible transgression of the first categorical negative judgment. An instance of this ironic contradiction is the amenability to fornication displayed by Red Cross in I.vi.7—clearly a backsliding from his abhorrence of fornication in himself and others in I.i.47–ii.6; but this is to the best of my knowledge the only instance. Fornication is never portrayed *in bono.* Moreover, the fasting of the normative Hermit Contemplation is unlikely to represent a transgression; therefore it remains a correction which can be paraphrased "fasting in itself is neither good nor evil."

There is another good fasting which seems to be valuable in and for itself, not precisely as meritorious but at least as a propitiation to God for a "crime" (I.x.28); and to this extent the correction remains irreconcilable. Once accepted, this contradiction conveys a kind of relativism—a relativism that defies paraphrase, but that constitutes an attitude toward ecclesiastical practices which many Establishment leaders advocated.

The abandonment of one's shield is reevaluated quickly; it is one and the same thing insofar as an action can be; it provokes a debate; and the difference lies in the circumstances. In addition, viewing the leitmotif *in bono et in malo* as well as in its historical context reveals an important statement about the Irish Question. This contradiction has received little attention since R. E. Neil Dodge first pointed it out (Var. 5:264). Spenser seemingly reverses himself on whether or not a knight is permitted to abandon his shield in battle. The opinion that he should not do so is inscribed by examples from I.vii, I.xi, and V.xi.27. In Book I these examples are first cautionary, then exemplary. Red Cross abandons all of his armor when he disarms to fornicate with Duessa (I.vii.7–8), thus allowing Orgoglio to capture him "ere he could . . . get his shield" (I.vii.8); this represents the low point of his moral development and prepares the reader to suspect any disarming in an outdoor situation (I thus exclude Britomart's two indoor disarmings). The reader of the 1590 edition would have concluded from the Letter to Ralegh appended to it that the shield is "the shield of faith" from Ephesians 6:16. Its device is a red cross on a white field; another knight calls this device "the sacred badge of my Redeemers death" (Guyon; II.i.27). To abandon it, therefore, would symbolize abandoning one's religion. This clear symbolism will be repeated and then finally denied in Book V.

Sometimes a knight is tempted to abandon a shield when an antagonist is clinging to it, thereby threatening to drag him around or pull him
off his feet, that is, to rob him of control, of the ability to express his titular virtue. In I.xi.40–43, Red Cross keeps his grip on his shield after a
struggle. As I have argued elsewhere, the claws of "that old Dragon," or
the devil, sticking in the shield of faith must allegorize doubts, a religious
threat with which it is forbidden to compromise, at least in one's actions.
With his "sword of the Spirit, which is the word of God" (so glossed in
the aforementioned Eph. 6:17), Red Cross forces one of the paws to let
go, that is, he refutes some doubts with the aid of the Bible and the Holy
Spirit. The Letter's definitions are unquestionably applicable to the second day of the battle, because on that day Red Cross is indubitably a
Christian. Yet for all this divine panoply, Red Cross cannot dislodge the
other paw from his "shield of faith," but can only sever it from the dragon's
body, thus regaining his freedom of action, symbolizing that some doubts
cannot be refuted and have to be lived with, just not acted upon.

In Book V, Arthur, in his battle in Geryoneo's chapel, holds onto his
shield with typical chivalric tenacity even though Geryoneo's Monster has
fixed her grip on it. Although Arthur's device is not religious, religion is
again at stake here, since the Monster represents the Spanish Inquisition
(V.xi.27). So tenacious is this antagonist that Arthur finally has to cut off
both her paws.

Then in V.xi.57–65, Artegall reluctantly and condescendingly helps
a knight, Sir Burbon, who has done the unthinkable and relinquished
his shield in battle in order to win a lady (V.xi.46–56). Artegall earnestly
admonishes the knight that the shield should have been preserved at all
costs:

> Hard is the case [the noun from which "casuistry" is derived], ...
> Yet not so hard (for nought so hard may light,
> That it to such a streight mote you constraine)
> As to abandon, that which doth containe
> Your honours style, that is your warlike shield.
> (V.xi.55)

We know religion is at stake—although Artegall does not mention it—
because this shield is connected imagistically to that of Red Cross. It is a
gift from him and contains a miniature duplicate of its device "upon the
bosse," called "His deare Redeemers badge" (V.xi.53), as if Sir Burbon
were a Platonic emanation or low-grade version of Red Cross. Since, for
Red Cross, to abandon his shield is to renounce the "true" Protestant

faith, Sir Burbon's same act must symbolize the same breach of faith. It is for this reason that although he receives aid, Sir Burbon is scorned not only by Artegall but also by the narrator (V.xi Arg.; 46; xii.2). Sir Burbon's real-life counterpart was Henri de Navarre, Duc de Bourbon, King of Navarre, who switched from Protestant to Catholic in order to win Flourdelis, that is, to become King Henry IV of France. Sir Burbon offers the defense:

> . . . when time doth serve,
> My former shield I may resume againe:
> To temporize is not from truth to swerve,
> Ne for advantage terme to entertaine,[8]
> When as necessitie doth it constraine.
> (V.xi.56.1–5; see also 46)

This casuistry alludes to the controversial principle that the end justifies the means. It smacks of the duplicity both of Machiavelli (whose alleged justification for insincere actions, *necessità,* seems echoed here, and whose *Discorsi* is invoked in the *Vewe*) and of the outwardly conforming Romanists in late Elizabethan England.[9] Religious temporizing was then an issue at Cambridge: Spenser's friend Gabriel Harvey pilloried as a "chameleon" the notorious Andrew Perne (1519–89), master of Peterhouse, and in 1574 vice chancellor of the university. Perne had switched from outspokenly Protestant to outspokenly Catholic when Mary acceded to the throne, then back again upon the accession of Elizabeth.[10]

But Artegall himself, in his own battle in the very next canto, as if in contradiction of his previous uncompromising stance,[11] and as if in imitation of the contemptible Sir Burbon, relinquishes his shield to his opponent Grantorto and wins thereby (V.xii.21–23). First, Grantorto's axe gets stuck in Artegall's shield:

---

8. I.e., to accept conditions, as A. C. Hamilton explains.

9. On the casuistry of Catholics in Elizabethan England, with some applications to Spenser, but not this one, see Gallacher, *Medusa's Gaze,* 63–93.

10. See Stern, *Gabriel Harvey,* 38, quoting *Pierces Supererogation* (1593), Sig. Ddi.

11. The contradiction is pointed out in Hamilton's note at xii.22. Kenneth Borris recognizes it, though he tries to minimize it by saying that "the opportunistic Burbon wholly abandons" his shield, whereas "Artegall tactically gives up his shield the better to maintain its values . . . (V.xii.21–23)," appealing to V.xii.19; but Burbon lays claim to the same tactical motive; see V.xi.56.1–5, quoted above. Borris suggests vaguely that Artegall's abandoning his shield "may well express the pragmatic value of religious tolerance for Protestants in conflicts involving religion, and perhaps also that of some political flexibility" (*Spenser's Poetics,* 66).

> Long while he tug'd and strove, to get it out,
> And all his powre applyed thereunto,
> That he therewith the knight drew all about:
> Nathlesse, for all that ever he could doe,
> His axe he could not from his shield undoe.
> Which *Artegall* perceiving, strooke no more,
> But loosing soone his shield, did it forgoe,
> And whiles he combred was therewith so sore,
> He gan at him let drive more fiercely then afore.
> (V.xii.22)

Although the narrator does not comment on this undignified maneuver, he explicitly praises another undignified maneuver of Artegall's on grounds of its result: "No shame to stoupe, ones head more high to reare, / And much to gaine, a litle for to yield" (V.xii.19; see also VI.xi.6.9). This comment can be considered a rebuttal of Artegall's earlier intransigent stance on abandoning one's shield: although stooping is a compromise with heroism—an aesthetic standard, not a moral or legal standard— still it models one sort of compromise, one sort of temporizing; it also prepares us to see his imminent abandonment of his shield in a positive light.

Now, Artegall's shield—whichever of the two he may currently be wearing—has no religious meaning, though it may partake of his titular virtue of justice. At Artegall's first appearance in Venus' looking glass, his shield is that of Achilles, whose device is said to be an ermine crowned— an obvious allusion to Queen Elizabeth—on an azure field (III.ii.25). His second is that of a "salvage" man (taken up in IV.iv.39 and never explicitly relinquished). Since Spenser does not specify which shield he is currently carrying, it must not matter; it is the shield of the knight of justice and that is all we need to know. Neither is the villain, I believe, religious. Although Grantorto represents Catholic Spain in the Burbon episode (see V.xi.50.3), and thus could have a religious dimension here too, that role seems to have been shunted over to the intervening villain Geryoneo, so that in the episode as a whole, religion is not prominent. Spenser juxtaposed these contrary assessments of one and the same gesture in adjacent cantos in order to shock and confuse the reader; and he succeeded beyond his hopes with Dodge, who calls this "one of the grosser inconsistencies" and can explain it only in terms of mode: "Burbon's shield has a meaning, Arthegall's not" (Var. 5:264). But I claim that Artegall's shield is left superficially indeterminate (I will suggest a meaning below) precisely to symbolize something indeterminate: all other values but the religious. Spenser contradicts himself not ineptly, as Dodge believed, but in a biblical pattern of *in malo* and *in bono*.

As T. K. Dunseath argued, the battle allegorizes a law case.[12] Abandoning one's shield suggests some kind of flexibility, as Kenneth Borris perceived—given the legal context, a rhetorical concession or plea bargaining. So long as religion is not involved, Spenser seems to be saying, temporizing is permissible; the end does justify the means, even if they include abandoning one's titular virtue. Presumably, as in Machiavelli, this end would not be just one's private good but some real or fancied public good, such as both Burbon's and Artegall's are (becoming a king, "liberating" a realm). Not every cause is worthy of martyrdom, nor need one submit to being dragged about, that is, imprisoned or otherwise taken advantage of, in order to maintain one's political or moral beliefs, only one's religious beliefs. The first, the idealistic assessment of abandoning one's shield, inscribes the discourse of strict Protestantism with its zeal for martyrdom and its scorn for Jesuitical casuistry, saying with Artegall, "Knights ought be true, and truth is one in all" (V.xi.56); the second assessment inscribes a worldly wisdom associated with such Romanists. Spenser here softens the rigid Protestantism of his own day; he may be anticipating that Protestant casuistry which William Perkins was later to formulate, but we obscure the timeliness and courage of Spenser's criticism of his own society if we merely use Perkins to gloss him.[13] Perhaps inspired by Machiavelli, Spenser thus takes a step not only toward Perkins's casuistry but also toward Lord Halifax's "Character of a Trimmer" (1682). He modifies an oversimple choice between good and evil into a distinction between religious and nonreligious circumstances and values. It is in order to jar the reader into some moral flexibility that Spenser contradicts himself about shields.

A literal example of compromise with the truth which is condoned because it is both secular and necessary to avoid the fate worse than death occurs in Book VI, where Pastorella while imprisoned by the brigands pretends to reciprocate the captain's affections in order to protect herself from being raped or sold as a slave. The narrator comments approvingly: "A little well is lent, that gaineth more withall" (VI.xi.6). Besides expressing a flexible personal morality, Pastorella's authorized coquettishness may allude in the political matrix to the notorious coquettishness of

---

12. Dunseath, *Spenser's Allegory*, 227ff.

13. Most people felt that justification by faith made casuistry unimportant; see Davies, *Worship and Theology*, 19.

Queen Elizabeth and may condone it when it protected the interests of England.

When we bring these biblical and textual precedents to bear on the names and allegorical significance of the characters in Artegall's battle against Grantorto, we arrive at a more focused and determinate interpretation of Artegall's nonreligious temporizing. Irena, the beneficiary of Artegall's battle, represents Ireland; thus Spenser's *Vewe of the Present State of Ireland* is relevant. Given the bias of that book, she probably represents the Anglo-Irish, and among these probably only the New English, not the Old. Conversely, with colonialist doublethink, traits of the native Irish are reinscribed onto the invader Grantorto. For example, as Elizabeth Heale points out, a contemporary MS gloss on the poem identifies him as the leader of the Desmond Rebellion,[14] and his equipment is that of the Irish gallowglass; Heale sums him up as the "the combined threats of rebellion and Roman Catholic aggression in contemporary France and Ireland" (SE). Grantorto created the situation in which Sir Burbon abandoned his shield; now he does the same for Artegall.

I agree with Dunseath that here the "tort" in his name ascends to prominence, and thus that the frame of reference is legal. This is the more credible because in medieval reality, and at any period in chivalric romance, combat itself may be judicial. Artegall claims that he is "trying" Irena's "cause"—in the plot, as her "champion," but given his titular virtue, also as the judge (V.xii.8.9). On all these grounds, I propose that his shield represents justice itself or its embodiment in English Common Law, which Ciaran Brady considers to be central to the *Vewe*.[15] Spenser argues that in Ireland, justice should bend and compromise:

> Iren. . . . . [T]he same Lawes me semes Cane ill fitt with theire disposicion or worke that reformacion that is wished: for lawes oughte to be fashioned unto the manners and Condicion of the people to whom they are mente and not to be imposed unto them accordinge to the simple rule of righte.[16]

Looking closely at the vicissitudes of the battle, we can find a gradually emerging allegory of a complaint about English Common Law voiced in the *Vewe*, a specific reason why it must bend and compromise and in which direction. Grantorto, by means of his axe sticking in Artegall's

---

14. Anonymous, "MS Notes," 513.
15. Brady, "Road." See also Brady's *Chief Governors,* xii, 141.
16. *Prose Works* (Var. 9), 54, hereafter cited in text.

shield, "the knight drew all about" (V.xii.22.3)—a vicissitude risked but never experienced by previous knights with their embattled shields. This dragging could allegorize the way in which the native Irish manipulate trial by jury:

> *Iren.* The Comon Lawe appointeth that all trialls as well of Crymes as titles and rightes shalbe made by a verdite of A Jurye Chosen out of the honestest and moste substantiall frehoulders / Nowe all the ffrehoulders of that realme are Irishe which when the cause shall fall betwene an Inglisheman and an Irishe, or betwene the Quene and anye ffrehoulder of that Countrye they make no scruple to passe against the Inglishman or the Quene thoughe it be to straine theire oathes. (66)

Such behavior, whatever the motive, "has come to be known as jury nullification, the exercise of jury discretion in favor of a defendant whom the jury nonetheless believes to have committed the act with which he is charged."[17] It happened for various reasons on scattered occasions in England, too, and once in the similarly situated Welsh Marches, a region marginalized by and once independent of England.[18] Just as Artegall "did it forgoe" (V.xii.22), so Spenser recommends that in Ireland, English Common Law be modified or abandoned: "it is good reason that either that course of the lawe for trialls be altered or other provision for Juries be made" (66). This passage is but one of three ambivalent comments on law (for the other two, see above and Chapters 4 and 5) which assert that although "the lawe [is] of it selfe / (as I said good) and the firste institucion theareof beinge given to all Inglishemen verye rightefull" (66), nevertheless it "Cane ill fitt with their disposicion [that of the Irish] or worke that reformacion that is wished" (54–55, quoted in part above). As to what changes Spenser had in mind, "other provision for Juries" means allowing the New English to sit on or even dominate them. One way of altering "the course of the lawe for trialls" which was coming into use in England at the time was the practice of plea bargaining, by which a judge could keep a case from ever coming before a jury at all.[19] Although David

17. Green, *Verdict,* xiii.

18. "Historically, some instances of nullification reflect the jury's view that the act in question is not unlawful, while in other cases the jury does not quarrel with the law but believes that the prescribed sanction is too severe" (ibid., xiii). "It must also be noted that juries nullified the law in many instances not out of mercy but out of fear . . . , or for political favor, or even, perhaps, for monetary gain" (xx). In the Welsh Marches, a statute of 1534 complains, "Divers murderers, friends and kinfolk to such offenders have . . . suborned [jurors] to acquit [offenders]," which jurors were themselves accordingly punished for perjury, i.e., straining their oath (114, n. 24).

19. Ibid., 150–52, n. 179.

Edwards argues convincingly on other grounds that Spenser favored the substitution of martial for English Common Law,[20] this passage does not go so far.

Another possible relativization of justice which might be hovering in the background, though it corresponds less neatly to the details of the story of Artegall and Grantorto, is that *ius politicum* which demands punishing the mere thought in the case of someone who plans to kill the sovereign. Ordinarily, and rightly so, the law punishes the deed, not the thought. But, as Irenius pragmatically claims, in this case the harm that could result to the entire body politic if the state waited for this particular thought to be put into act justifies the small injustice of punishing someone for thoughts alone (65). Here the "Gran-" in Grantorto's name ascends to prominence. In these two instances, Spenser agrees with Sir Burbon that "to temporize is not from truth to swerve . . . [w]hen as necessitie doth it constraine" (V.xi.56). Whatever the symbolism, comparison of the contradictory evaluations forces the reader to append a "yes, but . . ." to the first, the idealistic one, to limit its applicability.

As we see, Spenser in the *Vewe* bends the law away from mercy and democracy and toward the power of the English conquerors. Spenser's earlier statement, that "the lawes ought to be fashioned unto the manners and Condicion of the people," may sound conciliatory toward the native Irish, but it is not. The supposedly overriding end of law and order to which justice is sacrificed is diminished by the fact that the Anglo-Irish planters had what we today consider an insufficient warrant for being there (conquest, the invitation of one clan, and the gift of a pope). This tempts one to construct a simpler, postcolonialist reading of these adjacent episodes. Certainly Artegall becomes morally repellent in the subsequent denouement when he punishes with "heavy pain" all who rebelled against Irena's rule "That . . . Not one was left, that durst her once have disobayd" (V.xii.25). Artegall's inconsistency about temporizing could be seen as backsliding like Red Cross's about fornication; his idealistic speech to Sir Burbon could be seen as condemning his subsequent actions out of his own mouth. Artegall's backsliding here mirrors Spenser's self-serving exploitation of a compromised colonial situation—or so a postcolonialist critic might say.[21] By ironizing the subsequent approval, this interpretation would preserve unchanged the initial condemnation.

An opposite interpretation of Artegall's final tolerance of temporizing

20. Edwards, "Beyond Reform," 21.
21. This interpretation was suggested in class by Richard Weldgen of Cornell University, though the formulation is my own.

has been suggested by Anne Lake Prescott in a discussion following her lecture "Protecting Knights Who Throw Away Their Shields,"[22] namely, that it is the norm, illustrating Christ's maxim "Judge not, that ye be not judged." While recognizing a genuine shift in evaluation, this interpretation would favor the second statement at the expense of the first, rendering it a drastic correction. Granted, in Book V so far, Artegall has not been perfect; nevertheless, "Judge not" is an unlikely caveat for a knight of Justice. Moreover, against both of these interpretations, I have shown that in the FQ, inconsistency is not a crime; a reevaluation of an image or an action cannot in itself count as a black mark against a character or the poet-speaker because virtuous characters and the poet-speaker himself have indulged in it dozens of times before. To the postcolonialist, I would add that usually the first statement is not the standard by which the second statement is weighed and found wanting; rather it is corrected by the last word, which is the more reasoned, comprehensive, and practical. But I am not so concerned to nail down one particular interpretation as to celebrate the richness of these corrective shifts of evaluation, the explanatory power of an approach that looks for them.

We must therefore praise "sage and serious Spenser" for ethical complexity and for candor in admitting, if my connection to the *Vewe* is convincing, that his program for Ireland is not completely just, while we deplore that program as a whole. Spenser's concession of the necessity of temporizing is, as it were, the momentary intrusion of the voice of the embattled New English planter who wrote the *Vewe* into this otherwise idealistic poem.

Thus, awareness of Spenser's biblical repetition of images *in malo* and *in bono* has narrowed the meaning both of retaining and of abandoning one's shield, revealed a complex political allegory, and steered us away from a postcolonialist misinterpretation. Spenser's cynical endorsement of timeserving here may be an instance of the recently noted cynicism of Books V and VI at large. The relation of the paired images of abandoning shields *in bono et in malo* warn us that the idealism of the first three books, like that of Artegall's speech to Sir Burbon, is not thereby canceled, put under erasure, or even palinodically retracted, as if Spenser had either lost his innocence or conveyed no message at all; it is merely qualified, or, at most, problematized, pluralistically bracketed as just one perspective, one imbued (in the first two of the three books) with religion.

Almost the same pattern can be seen in altars and their iconoclasts, and it is precisely Arthur the shield-gripper who smashes the bad altar. This

22. Kathleen Williams Lecture, Kalamazoo, May, 1996.

justifies their inclusion here even though they are not reevaluated quickly or debated in the text. The good literal altar in *Epithalamion* (215, 223, and 230) represents a correction of the idolatrous metaphorical altar in *Amoretti* 22. This pattern of altars *in malo et in bono* is also found in the FQ, and one of these altars corrects another. The approximately two dozen altars in the FQ at first give the impression that altars are either neutral or bad, but the very last "altars" in the poem, although still associated with Romanism, are good (VI.xii.25). Unlike the examples above, altars are neither debated nor reevaluated quickly; but the second instances are approximately the same object and action, so that the reversal is fairly pointed. The last bad one is destroyed, an act of iconoclasm, and so is the final unsettling and self-contestatory good one.

Geryoneo's altar in V.xi shares a common background in Revelation 6 with Orgoglio's well-known bad altar in I.viii, illustrating the way in which Book V often picks up images from Book I. Both are encountered by Arthur; both, like their apocalyptic model, are associated with martyrdoms (I.viii.36; V.xi.19–20). Although Arthur kills Orgoglio, he commits no iconoclasm; he does nothing about his altar. In Book V he encounters a similar altar; along with killing its owner and its monster guardian, he destroys it. It is almost as if Arthur went back to the same altar in Book I to finish what he started; he must extract the full penalty in accordance with the titular virtue of Book V. This altar of carved ivory in a "Chappell" (V.x.28) is a prime target for Arthur's iconoclasm because on it rests an "Idole" (V.x.28.4; 29.2) representing its maker's father, now declared a god (V.x.8). It is at this altar, we learn, that the sons of Belge and all those who fail to pass the Sphinxlike "inquisition" (V.x.27–28; V.xi.25) of the Monster who lives under the Altar are eaten by her (V.xi.21.7; V.xi.22.4) and are thereby offered "to him [the idol] in sinful sacrifice" (V.x.28). When Arthur "did all to peeces breake and foyle / In filthy durt" the idol (V.xi.33), we may presume that he also destroyed the altar upon which it sat.

Now for the allegory. Both of the bad altars can be explained quite simply as Romanism in general, and the martyrs slain thereon as Protestant martyrs slain for refusing allegiance to the Roman church. Protestant exegetes such as Brocard* interpreted the martyrs in Revelation 6 as Protestant martyrs, particularly victims of the Saint Bartholomew's Day Massacre. Like other commentators, Brocard sees the altar as their own attribute, namely, the true worship of Christ, which does not fit Spenser's story, where the killer owns the altar (fol. 84v). But Lauretus, after expounding many good altars, including that in Revelation 6, interprets the *arae* of the heathen as "the errors of heretics" (s.v. "Altare, ara"). Reading Spenser's altar in the light of this meaning, a Protestant might recall the Romanist "error," highlighted, for example, by Luther in "The Pagan Servitude of the Church," that the Mass is a sacrifice, an error that some precisians saw to be implied in celebrating at an "altar" rather than at a mere "table." This religio-political overtone supports existing interpretations (Hamilton's, for example) of the altar in Book V as specifically the Romanist "Sacrament of the Altar," refusal to endorse and partake of which had provided grounds for the martyrdom of Cranmer and many others. Spenser caters to precisian prejudice here; but he plans to shock the precisians in Book VI with the occurrence of a Romanist altar that is good.

Arthur fighting for Belge represents something between myth and actuality: a displaced political version of his Christlike fight to liberate Red Cross in I.viii.19; 39–40, and an idealized version of Leicester defending the Protestant faith against the Spanish Catholic tyrants in the Netherlands. Although no one destroys the bad biblical altar in Revelation 6, another biblical model exists for Arthur's iconoclasm. His smashing and defiling the idol, and by implication the bad altar on which it stands (V.xi.33), parallels King Josiah's smashing and defiling heathen statues and altars (2 Kings 23:8, 12, 15–17, 20). Children had been sacrificed to one of these statues, Moloch (2 Kings 23:10; see also 16:3), as were Belge's children to Geryoneo's idol (V.x.8; xi.19), indicating that Spenser did have King Josiah's iconoclasm in mind.

Spenser's good altar is that in the monastery destroyed by the major villain of Book VI, the Blatant Beast: he "altars fould and blasphemy spoke." A bad iconoclast who committed this sin appeared in Lucifera's dungeon back in I.v.47—Antiochus Epiphanes, who "on his [God's] altars daunst" (see Hamilton's note *ad loc*); Spenser adapts him from 2 Maccabees 6:5, from a deuterocanonical book that was considered a part of the Bible by the Church of England. Because of the different valences of the altars they destroy, Josiah is virtuous and Antiochus evil. Similarly, the monastic altar is stained with no martyr's blood; while "Images" or statues are associated with it, their destruction is likewise lamented, so that they too are *in bono,* perhaps because they are not resting on it and therefore are not worshipped and hence not abused (VI.xii.25).

Spenser has gone out of his way to create a pattern, not only of altars *in malo et in bono* but also of iconoclasts *in bono et in malo,* in which last he is also correcting anti-Catholicism. Although one could object that it is not so much the altar that is good in VI.xii as the Beast's motive for destroying it that is evil, namely spite, the altar is given a positive valence when the Beast's evil is summed up as "Regarding nought religion, nor their holy heast" (VI.xii.24). This neat pair of incidents involving bad and good altars and good and bad iconoclasm must have been suggested by the Bible as it was then read, for example, by Byard and Lauretus, in terms of images *in bono et in malo;* the specific meanings, however, come from Spenser's religio-political milieu. His inflection renders the shift a correction of the precisian belief that for a Christian all altars are bad and all iconoclasm good. Instead, in moving from the confusion of Stage Two to a *distributio,* the chastened reader finally limits the semantic field of the bad altar and its good iconoclasm in V to a specifically abused Romanist altar; she reserves a rightful place for those altars that are not abused by idolatry and autos-da-fé.

Another pair of images reveals the ecclesiastical principle underlying several of these shifts in evaluation. In Book I, the images of beads are employed in a particularly contradictory way as attributes of both bad and good characters. As with fasting, the primary statement comes in the first canto, the reversal in the tenth. The reversal is sharp; it is not debated or even commented on. In the primary statement, beads are satirized even more clearly than is fasting: Archimago the hypocritical hermit (I.i.30; Arg. ii) and Corceca (Blind-heart, or, as the Argument has it, Blind Devotion) use them to record their numbers of "Pater Nosters" and "Aves" (I.iii Arg. and 13–14). Worse still, the female is presumably Latinless and unable to understand her own prayers; this repetitive approach to devotion was originally adopted partly for use by illiterates.[23] In the House of Holiness, however, as noted by Virgil Whitaker, D. Douglas Waters, and Beatrice Ricks, we find to our surprise that beads are now good. Dame Coelia, the mistress, spends "All night . . . in bidding of her bedes" (I.x.3.8–9); in fact, until she finishes bidding them, she keeps her guests waiting (I.x.8.3–4).[24] Both Artegall's abandonment of his shield and Coelia's nightlong bidding of her beads are as hermeneutically unsettling as is the pagan suicide Cato's serving as coastwarden of Dante's Purgatory.

In order to resolve the contradiction, the puzzled reader notices that Coelia's prayers, though presumably traditional and repetitive, are not numbered, and that she, unlike Corceca, intersperses good works: she spends "all the day in doing good and godly deedes" (I.x.3). The abuse is wasting the day on them, the time for action. Spenser apparently feels that the rosary is proper for a certain time, namely, at night, the time for contemplation, for abandonment to supernatural forces. A typically Protestant condemnation of a Catholic ritual is succeeded by an ideal that

23. *New Catholic Encyclopedia,* s.v. "Rosary."

24. See Whitaker, *Religious Basis,* 27 (page numbers are those that begin and end with Whitaker's piece; see Bibliography); Ricks, "Catholic Sacramentals," 328; Waters, *Duessa,* 106–7; King, SPRT, 61; Gless, *Interpretation,* 87–89.

turns out to be not its opposite but a sort of *via media,* like that advocated by Medina in II.ii.38. To adopt Swift's imagery in *A Tale of a Tub,* that model of a self-contestatory work, the condemnation of beads in I.iii.13 expresses the viewpoint of Jack, "Rip all the accretions off the coat," whereas the endorsement in I.x.8 expresses the viewpoint of Martin, "Granted it's an accretion, let's leave it on for fear of rending the coat itself." Martin's principle of the *via media* was just barely (how barely is not realized by Whitaker and Waters) starting to be voiced at this time: although it originated in practical ad hoc temporizing on the part of Queen Elizabeth, it was beginning to be hailed as the crowning glory of the English church, for example, by Jewel in his Apology.[25]

Note that the good beads are still physical, not a mere metaphor. True, E.K.'s gloss on "Bidde her god day" in "September" in the *Shepheardes Calender* interprets "to bidde his beades" as the equivalent of "to saye his prayers." We cannot, however, use this gloss to allegorize away the good beads of Dame Coelia: Corceca's beads were clearly material ones; and if Spenser had wished to avoid such popish overtones, he would have found a word for Coelia's prayer that did not remind us "too much of Roman Catholic ignorance and asceticism as symbolized by Spenser's own Dame Corceca."[26]

It is on the model of the Bible as portrayed by the *distinctiones* that Spenser went out of his way to portray a good use of such reprehensible and popish things as temporizing and the rosary. *Distinctiones* account for the process of writing and reading, though not, in these cases, for the Protestant content. When Dame Coelia uses beads, then, Spenser first shocks the reader with the contradiction of his own previous portrayal. The reversal is not of symbolism, as it is with shields, as it usually is when a biblical image (e.g., the lion) changes value, for beads mean rosaries in both episodes, but one of evaluation alone. The most the reader could say of Coelia's beads to cushion the shock of the contradiction is that, by being in complementary distribution with good deeds, they have become a synecdoche for the entire contemplative life, a life that Protestants endorsed so long as it alternates with good works. In any case, Spenser leads the puzzled reader to smooth down the contradiction into a fine distinction. She might say, for example, "Beads are evil when the bidder thinks

25. This has been reaffirmed by a scholar usually skeptical of conventional wisdom, Peter Lake, *Anglicans and Puritans?* chap. 1, esp. 24 and 67, n. 46. So far, my argument resembles the interpretation of Whitaker and Waters. But Whitaker and Waters are too facile; they fail to discuss either the hermeneutic problem of why the poet did not say what he meant the first time or the historical problem of reconciling Romanist beads to a generally Calvinist religious climate.

26. Waters, *Duessa,* 106.

her action is meritorious and devotes all her time to them, but good when she alternates them with good works." This *distributio* between use and abuse of the same thing is chiefly one of timing. Since the *distinctiones,* according to Barney, frequently vary meanings according to "quando," they fostered this process of reading.

In giving beads even this endorsement qualified by previous condemnation, Spenser became so reactionary that he risked not only shocking the reader but incurring accusations of papistry as well. Admittedly my approach has led me to an interpretation that on historical grounds seems incredible, pushing text-centered interpretation to the limit. If we look to Elizabethan actuality, we find that rosaries were universally rejected as among the filthiest rags of popery.[27] True, some Henrician and Edwardian reformers such as Latimer redefined rosaries, retaining some of the Romanist "bidding the beads" in the service of Holy Communion, a vestige of which ritual was to survive into the BCP as the "bidding prayers" or intercessions;[28] but the physical "beads" had dropped out long before Spenser, and even this analogue does not explain Dame Coelia's bidding beads in private and taking all night about it. But the fact that this favorable image defies the culture is no reason to explain it away, for example, by denying its physicality. Rather than impose a change of meaning, we should explain it by resistant elements in the culture and/or relate it to the culture in a way other than by straightforward didacticism.

Unless he is a Henrician Protestant, which seems historically unlikely, Spenser cannot really be straightforwardly didactic here; his recommendation of rosaries is first of all an overstatement in order to shock, then a hypothetical one illustrating a religious principle, something like, "Why even bidding beads could conceivably be all right under certain circumstances, for example, as a psychological exercise, provided it does not interfere with good works."

Readerly thought processes can be contextualized by relating them to

27. Relevant Elizabethan and Edwardian injunctions are quoted or summarized in Aston, *England's Iconoclasts,* 1:306–12. Cranmer assailed as "Papisticall superstitions and abuses" all "Beads, . . . Rosaries, . . . halowed Beades," in the third part of his "Homilie or sermon, of good workes annexed unto faith," in Book of Homilies, quoted in SPRT, 19. See also criticisms by Grindal in York Injunctions; Tyndale in "Obedience of a Christian Man"; and J. Rhodes in "An Answere to a Romish Rime," all in Parker Society, locatable through its index, s.v. "Beads." Rhodes merely belittles them as trivial compared to good works.

28. In *Visitation Articles,* see Latimer's injunctions for Worcester diocese, 1537, no. 11, 2:17; Frere describes the redeeming change which "the king ordains" (2:17, n. 1), namely, replacing the prayers for the pope accompanying the rosary with prayers for the king as head of the church; also Latimer, like Spenser and Rhodes, wants to allot less time to the rosary. See also Shaxton's injunctions for Salisbury, 1538, no. 3, 2:54; and Royal Articles of Edward VI, no. 45, 2:109.

thought processes in the religion of the poet's time, especially if the subject matter is the same. This one illustrates adiaphorism, a doctrine that is scripturalist yet not legalistic and that is expressed in hermeneutically unsettling reevaluations of images in the Bible: Christ attaching no intrinsic value to fasting or observing the Sabbath; Paul attaching no intrinsic value to celibacy or circumcision or disvalue to meat that has been offered to idols.[29] Although Paul preferred celibacy and advocated marriage only as a compromise with man's sexual nature, most Protestants tended to level out this choice—a leveling expressed by Spenser in his bifurcation of chastity into virginal and marital. Circumcision changes its value according to circumstances, even to the point of evoking contradictory behavior: for example, Paul circumcised Timothy but not Titus (Acts 16:3; Gal. 2:3). Refuting the taboo attached to eating meat that had been offered to idols led Saint Paul to codify Christian adiaphorism: "Unto the pure are al things pure" (Titus 1:15), and "All things are lawful unto me, but all things are not profitable" (1 Cor. 6:12). To "al things," the Geneva adds the important gloss: "Whatsoever: but this generall word must be restrained to things that are indifferent" (gloss g; see also 6:8; 10:14–33). A thing is defined as "indifferent," or as an *adiaphoron,* either (1) if it is specifically designated in Scripture as neither intrinsically sinful nor necessary for salvation, or (2) if it is just not mentioned there. Toward such things the Christian has what Saint Paul calls "liberty." They are not morally neutral, to be sure (though this is the meaning of the term in some philosophies), since the individual must still choose or reject them on moral and other grounds; but one's beliefs about them do not determine one's salvation or damnation. This quality of "indifference" was conferred upon some Catholic objects, practices, and beliefs by Erasmus, Melanchthon, and Hooker, by the Royal Injunctions of Kings Henry VIII and Edward VI, and injunctions and other influence of Queen Elizabeth I.[30] Adiaphorism formed the cornerstone of Anglicanism, says Patrick Collinson, and was important in Lutheranism as well.[31]

Adiaphorists may take either a negative or a positive stance. Negative

29. Bryan Berry first labeled beads "a thing indifferent" in an MLA paper, "Spenser's Rhetorical and Semiotic Strategies amid Sixteenth-Century Religious Controversies," summarized in *Spenser Newsletter* 23.1 (1992): 20.

30. See Verkamp, *Indifferent Mean,* on Erasmus and his many English followers on this point, 24–40, 82–83, 94–97 et passim; on Melanchthon, 24, 26, 28, 34 (n. 72), 107, 114 (n. 84), 132–33, 142; on Latimer, one of the Erastian condoners of rosaries, see xv, 36; on Peter Martyr, 79; on the injunctions, 37–38, 101, 145. For Elizabeth, see Aston, *English Iconoclasts,* 299, 320–25. For the extreme adiaphorism of Sebastian Franck, who will become important later in this study, see Verkamp, *Indifferent Mean,* 79–83.

31. Collinson, *Elizabethan Puritan Movement,* 27–28.

adiaphorists or biblical reductionists want nothing that is not commanded in Scripture; they formed the "precisian" or Puritan wing in the
Elizabethan church; "liberty" for them meant freedom from the practice,
not freedom of choice. This negative adiaphorism led the aforementioned Elizabethan and Edwardian injunctions to condemn rosaries, and
to do so, as Spenser limits them, in favor of good works, which are commanded in Scripture. But when unqualified, the term usually means positive adiaphorism. Positive adiaphorists freely debate the merits of an indifferent religious object, practice, or belief on the many other possible
grounds aside from the missing divine revelation, be it tradition (especially the Creeds), its repugnance to or harmony with the spirit of either
Scripture or tradition, its reasonableness, its having been commanded or
prohibited by the sovereign,[32] or the fear of giving offense to ignorant
laymen. In general, adiaphorism forms a necessary foundation for the
doctrines of use versus abuse and the *via media.* I know of no one who
specifically justified rosaries as adiaphora; but Latimer both condoned
rosaries, as we have already seen, and is listed by Bernard Verkamp as an
adiaphorist, albeit a fairly negative one (xv, xviii, n. 5, and 36).[33] Adiaphorism is doctrinal flexibility; it is a step toward religious tolerance and
even pluralism; indeed, it was distrusted by some Englishmen for this
very reason.

Spenser's self-correcting ecclesiastical images — rosaries, statues (as I
have explained elsewhere), altars, fasting, and temporizing — resemble
Saint Paul's adiaphora because they fall under the same rubric, church
discipline. Therefore they express adiaphorism — or rather, they elicit it
from the reader.

One reason why critics have not previously recognized this evidence
for adiaphorism is their expectation that Spenser will simply announce
a generalization all in one place. Spenser expresses adiaphorism not co-
herently but by an epanorthotic style, one that continually violates the
reader's expectations, leaving her to explain the contradictory evaluations
by formulating a generalization or *distributio* such as the one I formulated
about rosaries. Spenser may well have employed this style and evoked this
thought process to train the reader in the discrimination of adiaphora.

32. As the injunctions concerning the rosary indicate, in practice, the sovereign as the
head of the church tended to claim jurisdiction over whatever was indifferent and thus to
close down debate and repress individual choice. See ibid., 27–28, 71; Verkamp, *Indifferent
Mean,* 142–43, 171–72; and Kahn, "Revising the History," 526–61.

33. See Verkamp's *Indifferent Mean,* 96–99, on transubstantiation, held to be an adiaphoron by a "few" Englishmen, and Purgatory, "repeatedly" called an adiaphoron. Usually
adiaphora were practices, like saying the rosary, not beliefs.

Some features of this style and process of thought are recognized by Stephen Gilman and John King. In a refreshing and provocative extension of my idea of images *in bono et in malo* as it was first presented in a conference paper, they have related such reversals to another religious thought process, iconoclasm—a sample of which Spenser could have witnessed at Cambridge in 1572—which made him anxious about painterly poetry.[34] Their extension of the term is metaphoric, for they presuppose three things: first, that iconomachy included suspicion of verbal as well as visual art; second, that it attacked not just popish objects in art and literature but the very faculty of the imagination itself and therefore all poetic imagery; and third, that the anxious poet performed iconoclasm on his own preceding passages in the same work. They do not document these assumptions.

Let me begin by agreeing that the prevailing censoriousness, of which iconoclasm is one example, must indeed have worried all artists and have caused some of them, obviously including Spenser, to employ various self-corrective strategies—strategies such as the punishment of the bad poet Malfont (V.i.25–26)—to avoid being pinned down. These critics could also have argued that Spenser performs a mild internal self-iconoclasm on two popish objects: holy water and crosses. Applying holy water to objects is praised in Book I (xi.36.2; xii.37.3–5). The next and remaining use is ironic because amatory and presumably delusory: in Busirane's pageant, Hope carries "An holy water Sprinckle" with which she "sprinckled favours manifold" (III.xii.13). This disapproval is Protestant, exemplified in the Edwardian injunction against "casting holy water upon his bed . . . and other dead things."[35] The cross is engraved ("scored") on Red Cross's breastplate and shield, and it is efficacious: in the words of one of Red Cross's frustrated enemies, it is "that Crosse . . . that keepes thy body from the bitter fit" (I.ii.18; see also I.iv.50.5–7). In III.iii.38, Spenser adds to his sources (See Hamilton's note *ad loc.*) that at Heavenfield a band of angels won the battle for King Oswald by holding up crosses. "A religious object which is productive as an instrument of spiritual good, is a peculiarly Catholic application," declares Beatrice Ricks.[36] But then when Archimago disguises himself as Red Cross, his "vainely crossed shield" fails to protect him (I.iii.35). Now, as Ricks

34. For the 1572 iconoclasm, see Greenblatt, *Renaissance Self-Fashioning*, 188 and n. 64; King, SPRT, 68 and n. 56; Gilman, *Iconoclasm*, 81.

35. *Visitation Articles*, no. 27, 1:126.

36. Ricks, "Catholic Sacraments," 326. See also, on the cross and related issues, Nelan, *Catholic Doctrines*, 11.

points out, these objects fall into the category that Catholics call not "sacraments" but "sacramentals." The abuses lead the reader to formulate a *distinctio* inscribing what even Romanists say about them: they are sacramentals. Unlike baptism or the Eucharist, they do not work *ex opere operato* but depend for their efficacy on "the disposition of the user" (Ricks, 330). A sacramental is similar to but not the same as an adiaphoron: both put the responsibility on the user—a sacramental to cultivate the mental disposition necessary to make it effective and an adiaphoron to distinguish between use and abuse. This doctrine also explains what is wrong with the holy water of a nonreligious or superstitious Hope. Thus, two popish practices are first set up *in bono* and then their superstitious abuse is "broken" or discredited because of a circumstance—the evil or frivolous nature of their users. These disapproving self-corrections could have been invoked by King and Gilman as internal poetic iconoclasm. But even these corrections are mild; the good element is still Romanist, the bad element extrinsic, and the contradiction easily resolved into a *distributio.*

As we have seen, however, Spenser had doubts about iconoclasm, so that he would have been unlikely to model his poetry on it. Moreover, Reformation iconoclasm as historically defined is directed against popish images. Before any critic looks for an iconoclastic mindset in Spenser's secular images, she must begin by proving—as King, Gilman, and Stephen Greenblatt have not done—that Spenser handles in an iconoclastic way his obviously popish images: fasting, cups, hermits, a lifetime vowed to celibacy and contemplation, beads and beadsmen, statues, casuistry, flagellation, material crosses, and holy water. Except for the last two, I do not think he does.

An iconoclastic treatment would be a symmetry of intrinsic, absolute good and evil and a resulting polarization of images and their demonic parodies. Polarization exists, especially in Book I, but, with the possible exception of cups, it is not the historical objects of iconoclasm, the rags of popery, which are so polarized but persons—the good and bad Geniuses and the true and false Unas, Red Crosses, and Florimells. Toward these pairs of persons, Spenser's attitude is as black and white as is that of an iconoclast; he distinguishes them for the reader by a simple *distributio.* But what justifies the altars in Book VI, for example, is not that they are essential to salvation the way Una, Fidelia, and her good cup are, but that they are simply an adiaphoron, good or bad according to circumstances, as altars indeed were to Queen Elizabeth I and to many of her clergymen.

Again, Gilman asserts, as Fish does about other authors, that the reversals are so violent as to cancel out both image and meaning.[37] The propositional reversal in the *Fowre Hymnes*—the correction of sexual love by Christian love—is indeed self-canceling. But the bad popish objects are not totally rejected. The reader can eventually sort out the favorable and unfavorable instances into a *distinctio,* even an exhaustive *distributio* (insofar as one can paraphrase any literary effect). When she does so, their correction is too mild for iconoclasm: it reaffirms much in them that is papistical; Spenser first implies anti-Catholicism as the norm and then corrects the norm rather than the Catholicism. The political motive for Spenser's surprisingly mild shift is tangential to the present study; it could be shown to be the same as I have elsewhere documented with regard to statues (hence my omission of statues here) and other popish objects and practices: Elizabeth's personal adiaphorism.[38]

In addition, to uncover an iconoclastic poetics, strictly speaking, these critics would have had to cite a shift that is negative, an image-pattern strictly *in bono et in malo,* setting the image up and then breaking it, ending, not beginning, with a disapproving gesture. Gilman is so vague and so short on examples that it is difficult to come to grips with him, for which reason I will engage King. King's example of the culture's imagery of the Virgin Mary for Elizabeth (SPRT, 148–52) does not make Spenser iconoclastic, since Spenser, unlike the culture, never "breaks" the imagery of the Virgin Mary: he never employs it *in malo.*

Most of Spenser's reevaluated images vary *in malo et in bono,* so that they are not "broken" but reinstated. As Fowler says: "We may almost formulate a natural law of Spenser's Fairyland: At least one corresponding evil image precedes a virtuous image."[39] Fowler's explanation of this progression—a Neoplatonic ascent to the idea—represents a better theory; it accounts for the mildness of the correction. But it does not save all the phenomena: the Hermit Contemplation's fasting is not the Platonic idea of which Corceca's fasting is a false copy, but differs merely in the circumstances as use to abuse. The virtuous altars, temporizing, and mitres (those worn by Isis' priests, V.vii.13), are not the Platonic idea of which Geryoneo's altar, Burbon's religious temporizing, and Duessa's mitre (I.ii.13) are the material and imperfect copy; they are on the same ontological level, as is usually the case in Scripture. From these image-pairs, the deducible ethics is neither iconoclastic nor Platonic; it is situational.

---

37. Gilman, *Iconoclasm,* 81; Fish, *Self-Consuming Artifacts,* 397, 401.
38. Kaske, "Audiences," 15–35.
39. Fowler, "Neoplatonic Order," 71.

King does engage Spenser's positive self-corrections; he compares them to the way in which a real-life iconoclast would sometimes "redefine" an image, that is, set up a better image in place of the one destroyed (SPRT, 57 and n. 53). But since in Spenser this redefinition occurs almost invariably, it must belong to the essence of the thought process. The more positive thought process to which both destruction and redefinition is analogous is adiaphorism.

I also question the historicity of King's term "redefinition": the "better" image set up by a real-life Elizabethan iconoclast was not precisely Protestantized so much as politically co-opted, as when he tore the crucifix down off the rood-loft and substituted the arms of the monarch, or, in the realm of words, when he allowed rosaries so long as they included prayers for the monarch. The FQ does indeed reflect this political redefinition of temporizing: it is evil when the accommodation is to popery but necessary to civilize the Irish. Dame Coelia, however, is not said to be praying for a monarch any more than Corceca is. The corrective cup and altar are not more royalist than their predecessors; indeed, the corrective altar (Book VI) is less so. On mature consideration, the term "adiaphorism" seems more appropriate to the many mild and minimal redefinitions of popish images.

Finally, there are two pairs of images that yield contrasts that are significant but not black and white, ethically or in any other way. One pair, Cleopolis and the New Jerusalem, bears some resemblance to the adiaphoristic group of ecclesiastical images insofar as its members appear close together; their incompatible claims on their citizens are debated; something—the interpretation, not the image—is corrected; and the contradiction between the two images is "reconciled" by a normative speaker in terms resembling use and abuse. Now, Cleopolis is the poem's most important city, the city of Gloriana, the Faerie Queen. It is described in I.x.59, II.x.72, and III.ix.51. In the first and most interesting passage, it is contrasted in detail with the New Jerusalem, yet surprisingly endorsed.

The idea of portraying the New Jerusalem, and pairing it with an earthly city, is unquestionably biblical. The New Jerusalem appears not only in Hebrews 12, examined in the preceding chapter, but also in Revelation, especially in Chapters 21–22:5 (also 3:12); it is contrasted with Babylon, the bad earthly city, which is portrayed in Chapters 17–19:3. Each of these cities is metaphorically a woman: the New Jerusalem is "the bride, the Lamb's wife," and Babylon is a whore. Red Cross longs to go to the New Jerusalem and he longs to marry Una. Applying the biblical city = woman equation to FQ I explains the surprising deferral of Red

Cross's wedding (I.xii.18): it reveals (1) that return to the Faerie Queen represents a return to her city Cleopolis, with the aforementioned implications; (2) that Una as the bride of a Christlike Red Cross symbolizes the same thing as does Spenser's New Jerusalem; and thus (3) that marrying Una (I.xii.19) symbolizes the same thing as returning to the New Jerusalem (I.x.61, 63–64), namely, the "spiritual marriage" of perfect and endless contemplation, a state that is possible, as the Hermit says, only after a successful earthly career and, by implication, only in old age or at death. Una's father implies this when he refers to this marriage as an "everlasting rest" (I.xii.17).

Spenser's earthly city has no interest in God, but unlike the biblical Babylon it is not portrayed *in malo;* it is all right in its proper time. Although the two Spenserian cities are somewhat analogous—a ruler with a tower grants "grace" of one kind or another to a social circle (I.x.55–58; 60; 62)—the means of attaining grace in them are diametrically opposed. In social structure, the New Jerusalem is egalitarian: "Now are they Saints all in that citie sam," that is, "now are they all saints together in that city," and even the superior angels visit them "As commonly [that is, casually, without distinction of rank] as friend does with his frend" (I.x.56–57.8). Its entire ethos, being predestinarian, is grace-centered, although the term is not used. Anybody can receive sainthood in the New Jerusalem, not by achievement but by being "chosen" and "purg'd from sinfull guilt" (I.x.57) through Christ's self-sacrifice. Cleopolis is hierarchical—a hierarchy based on deeds, a meritocracy.

Cleopolis means "fame-city," and its inhabitants live for fame (I.x.59), which by definition cannot be shared equally across the board. A knight must earn it as a "guerdon" for specific achievements. The term "her grace" here equivocates on the theological sense, but since it is earned by "service" (60.3), the relationship must, at least for a Protestant, be more of a contrast than an analogy (for a ruler's purely secular "grace" to those who earn it, see also FQ I.i.3 and MHT 717–93).[40] Fame is not even socialized, as in MHT, the *Aeneid, Beowulf,* the *Divine Comedy,* or the *Morte Darthur,* as a reward for serving the common good or contributing to the glory of the nation; it is a reward for serving Glori-ana, fame for the sake of fame.

This contrast between meritocracy and egalitarianism is also drawn by the ensuing debate concerning how and when to go to the New Jerusalem. First, in his Pauline mood, the Hermit teaches Red Cross the egalitarianism of the New Jerusalem. Red Cross asks, "How dare I thinke such

---

40. Cf. Hamilton's note relating I.x.60.2 to 62.1.

glory to attain?" (I.x.62)—meaning *gloria verissima,* the glory of being a saint and his nation's patron in the New Jerusalem. "You can't, nobody can," replies the Hermit in effect, for "Those that have it attaind, were in like cace / (Quoth he) as wretched, and liv'd in like paine," that is, as he said earlier (I.x.61.5), they were simply "ordaind," or predestined, for it. That Red Cross expected the answer to be "by deeds" is evidenced by his next question, "But deeds of armes must I at last be faine / . . . to leave . . . ?" The Hermit dismisses them—"What need of armes?"(I.x.62). Deeds, especially warlike ones, get you to Cleopolis, they even win you "glory" there, *gloria humana,* but Cleopolis is not even on the "path" to the New Jerusalem. Thus Red Cross is corrected even if neither city is. Going to the opposite extreme, he then begs either to die and go to the New Jerusalem immediately or to remain forever on the Mount of Contemplation with the Hermit, and the reader too wonders why he should not. In terms of character, this reversal is biblical: in his need for correction, his spluttering tergiversations, and his desire to remain on the Mount of Contemplation, Red Cross parallels Saint Peter at the Transfiguration (whose gauchery on that occasion is referred to, incidentally, in VII.vii.7). The Hermit replies that he must return to the world; he must not only do a good deed for Una—which would accord well enough with a Christian active life (63)—but also hang his shield "high emongst all knights" in Cleopolis (I.x.60), with no particular goal beyond fame itself. Although the dichotomy between the active and the contemplative lives—always conflicted but seldom irresolvable—certainly underlies Cleopolis and the New Jerusalem, the centrality of fame renders Cleopolis irreconcilable with Christianity.

The towers are beautiful, but not equally so: "this bright Angels towre quite dims that towre of glas" (I.x.58). Being on a higher ontological level, the angels' tower could indeed be seen as the Platonic ideal of which all the other towers are an imperfect copy. The Hermit surprisingly rejoins, "Yet is Cleopolis, for earthly frame, / The fairest peece, that eye beholden can" (59). By relating something to its heavenly counterpart not as bad but as merely earthly or human, in this one place, the Hermit speaks the language of Neoplatonic scalarism. The exegetes too had invented terms for this sort of pairing—*gloria verior et verissima* or *humana et celestialis.*

A faint and mostly structural parallel to Cleopolis can be found in the Bible. There is another earthly city besides the execrable Babylon (from which Cleopolis borrows nothing) which is contrasted with the New Jerusalem—the old or earthly Jerusalem, "Hierusalem which nowe is" (Gal. 4:25). The old Jerusalem is mentioned in Revelation 11:2, 8, and 13, but more as a setting than a symbol. In a highly allegorical passage, Gala-tians 4:25–26, Paul employs the full city = woman = mountain equa-tion to contrast two "testaments," two covenants, two codes of behavior, gospel and law, which were real-life alternatives for Paul's immediate ad-dressees.[41] The heavenly woman-city is "free" (Gal. 4:26, 30, 31) and at-tained by a "promise" (4:23, 28), that is, by predestination, like Spenser's New Jerusalem; the old or earthly Jerusalem represents "works of the law" such as circumcision (Gal. 3:5, 10), a faint parallel to the activism of Cleopolis, its ethos of effort. Spenser has slotted Cleopolis into the bib-lical two-cities pattern in place of the earthly Jerusalem. Thus these paired biblical cities represent a contrast of codes or covenants along somewhat the same lines as Spenser's cities. Paul does warn that the code of works which obtains in the earthly Jerusalem is antithetical to salvation by Christ (Gal. 5:1–2), which is what his New Jerusalem symbolized. Thus Paul's cities fall into patterns of *in bono et in malo.*

Another unusual feature of this episode as a whole is the assignment of speeches: the biblical *contemptus mundi* to the youthful knight but the praise of the earthly city and the easygoing acceptance of contraries to the recluse. Red Cross is the limited disciple figure in this dialogue, a figure for the reader, a choral character, and his inconsistencies are gently ironized. The Hermit himself slips into an ascetic mood that accords with his Pauline soteriology when he says of combat, "Bloud can nought but sin and wars but sorrowes yield" (I.x.60). Red Cross has learned from past images *in bono et in malo*—good and bad hermits and women—to see the world, as young people often do, only in black and white; he therefore tries to form a *distinctio* of cities *in bono et in malo.* Fasting and beads have already been disparaged and then reinstated in an adiaphoris-tic way, but Red Cross does not adopt an adiaphoristic distinction be-cause he is not acquainted with this more tolerant relationship; he has seen only the valid, not the unfruitful versions (I.iii.14). The heavenly city inspires him to reject the earthly city for another reason: he is a new convert or returner to the fold, and as such he wants to renounce some-thing, to make an either/or choice. Spenser is gently ironizing a mindset that he himself has inculcated by previous image-pairs, thus dramatizing its limitations.

The praise of Cleopolis is assigned to the Hermit because of his au-thority, to assure us that it is not being ironized or corrected, to insist that both cities are truly good. In terms of intellectual history, we can say that

---

41. The city = mountain equation (Heb. 12:22–23) was discussed in Chapter 2. Undis-cussed references to heaven as a city include Hebrews 11:10 and 13:14.

Red Cross in his momentary renunciation of Cleopolis (x.63) voices the Augustinian assumption that an earthly city must be of the devil, whereas the Hermit's inconsistent praise of it represents "the sixteenth-century innovation of entertaining belief in an ideal earthly city."[42]

If the way in which Spenser relates the New Jerusalem and Cleopolis is not *in bono et in malo,* then what is it? Some would describe it as one of participation in a Neoplatonic and syncretistic hierarchy—heavenly idea and imperfect earthly copy—and I agree with regard to the towers. Moreover, Gloriana is analogous to God: each city's monarch is said to bestow "glory" in a wordplay that could be called Neoplatonic (I.x.59.8, 62.2). Gloriana has the right to bestow this "glory" because "she is heavenly borne," which could imply that her glory too is heavenly. Some have therefore believed that she promotes to heaven, others, more recently and cogently, that she pulls heaven down to earth, equating fame with salvation. But "heaven" and its derivatives are cheap compliments in Spenser's works; "heavenly borne" (I.x.59) in particular is expended not only on Queen Elizabeth and her surrogates in the FQ but also on one hundred nymphs of her court (CCCHA 256) and even on a horse (FQ II.xi.19). The analogies are not equations, nor are they sufficient to explain everything: the fact that Cleopolis and the New Jerusalem are attained by contradictory means stretches correspondence to the breaking point.[43] Also, had Spenser intended to convey a unitary message in a Platonic hierarchical progression, he would have put Cleopolis first and arranged for it to be mildly corrected by the New Jerusalem.

Like an adiaphorist, the Hermit refuses to evaluate the cities except with a temporal "when." Each is permissible at a certain stage in an individual's life. In his epistemologically unsettling but morally bland *distributio,* the Hermit voices a situational ethic, a historical relativism, a principle voiced in Ecclesiastes (3:1) and applied to biblical hermeneutics by T. Grashop: "Consider the course of times and ages, with such things as belong unto them." This is a *distributio* of sorts. To say that something ostensibly evil (as is the earthly city in the Bible, as is fame in most Christian discourse) is really good in its place or time is to reapply the biblical principle of positive adiaphorism; it resembles the reader's conclusions that fasting, beads, and temporizing, though practiced by Romanists, are permissible when used properly. The analogy with adiaphorism is especially close when the motif is Cleopolitan chivalry, since one Establish-

42. Paster, "Cities," SE.

43. For the background of Cleopolis and its "heavenly borne" queen, see Bergvall, "Between Eusebius and Augustine," 5–20.

ment justification for adopting an ecclesiastical adiaphoron was its having been commanded by the sovereign.

The New Jerusalem and Cleopolis can be nonjudgmentally and anthropologically distinguished as respectively a guilt-culture and a shame-culture.[44] Just as guilt-cultures threaten people with guilt before the gods, so the New Jerusalem contains "people purg'd from sinfull guilt" (I.x.57), whereas Cleopolis pays no attention to guilt. In the same vein, cultures could also be distinguished by their positive values—some cultures promise people fame, honor, and glory among men; others promise them the favor of God or the gods, sometimes, as here, in heaven—yielding guilt-heaven cultures and shame-fame cultures. The guilt-heaven city looks to eternity, the shame-fame city looks only to posterity; it "eternizes" not personally but only metaphorically. In these respects, the two cities are distinguished merely as different—different in an undecidable and pluralistic way.

Their undecidable relationship is also akin to Bakhtinian dialogism because it is not just between two things but between two discourses. The New Jerusalem is described in the God-centered egalitarian discourse of Protestant piety—"Now are they Saints all" because they are "chosen" (I.x.57)—whereas Cleopolis is described in the discourse of an elitist call to arms, either courtly-chivalric or classical: "And well beseemes all knights of noble name, / That covet in th'immortall booke of fame / To be eternized, that same to haunt" (I.x.59). Though one could give the relationship a philosophical label, say, for example, "double truth," as in Pomponazzi, the indeterminacy seems also to be of a Bakhtinian sort because the discourses can be aligned with two genres—religious discourse and chivalric romance—and with two social groups: godly Protestants and the court as it was constructed by romances, courtesy books, and many classical texts. The discourse of the court is like that of Don Quixote; and Cervantes, like Spenser, will refuse to decide whether or not it is preferable to its counterdiscourse (which in Cervantes will be the proverbial and populist discourse of the squire Sancho Panza). Thus Spenser relates a biblical image-pair—cities—which in the Bible is related *in bono et in malo* in a way that is more congenial to postmodern taste.

In II.x the poem parallels and contrasts not the capitals but the chronicles of the Britons and of the Faeries; it expresses no opinion as to which race, Briton or Faerie, one should want to belong to. This may be be-

44. Hugh MacLachlan invokes the distinction between shame-culture and guilt-culture to explain Guyon's preoccupation with shame ("The Death of Guyon," 113, n. 12).

cause, as I have argued in "Spenser's Pluralistic Universe," Spenser was genuinely attracted to the classical ethics represented by the Faerie race and its capital but could not completely reconcile it with Christianity;[45] or the dichotomy may represent that inevitable difference between the various worlds, such as young (Cleopolis) and old (Jerusalem), public and private, which any individual inhabits. However that may be, this dichotomy between the chronicles also exemplifies Bakhtinian dialogism not only on grounds of their incompatible worldviews but also because they inscribe two different discourses, genres, and cultures—Galfridian chronicle history (Christian by accident of time) and classical and humanist panegyric both of dynasties and of cities.[46] Both pairs involve the Faerie race. On the races, the reader remains stalled at Stage Two.

In the majority of the image-pairs, Spenser opposes the either/or thinking of the iconoclast. Just as the poet-speaker incorporates in his final interpretation of the laurel leaf both his own first interpretation and the lady's, so Spenser's adiaphoristic corrections of the reader's first interpretations of cups, fasting, temporizing, beads, and altars and their iconoclasts and of Red Cross's first interpretation of Cleopolis incorporate them into his nuanced if not entirely consistent situational ethics. The ecclesiastical images have the social purpose of promoting religious toleration.

45. Kaske, "Spenser's Pluralistic Universe," 127–30 and nn. 7–9 on 231; 144–46 and nn. 23–24 on 233.

46. On the chronicles as a whole, see Harry Berger's chapter "Intellectual History: The Chronicles," in *Allegorical Temper.* Panegyrics on dynasties are exemplified in *Aeneid* VI and its imitators. Concerning the panegyrics on cities that are sources for Cleopolis, see Rathborne, *Meaning,* chap. 1, "The Glory of This World."

PROPOSITIONAL CONTRADICTIONS
AND THEIR RESOLUTIONS

We have seen that when Spenser reevaluates an image or action, the paraphrase or *distinctio* he elicits from the second-stage reader (before she
smooths it out into a *distributio*) is a propositional contradiction: "beads
are bad, no, good, when . . . etc." This prepares us to consider a more radical and unsettling kind of variation: contradiction of an explicit statement
in the text. On the rare occasions when I merely infer a statement from
turns of plot, it will be an obviously didactic one whose distinctness marks
it as intentional. After laying down some background, this chapter begins
with formal contradictions resolvable either as tropes or by the distinction
between the contrasting halves of a work; it ends with authentic and substantive contradictions about free will and justification.

These two sections of the present chapter reflect the two degrees of
skepticism current in the Renaissance, generally summed up as Academic
and Pyrrhonistic. Victoria Kahn defines them in terms of their use of
contradictions. At least a moderate skepticism was imparted in the Renaissance by the training given in universities and secondary schools to
argue *in utramque partem,* that is, on alternating sides of a contested issue. The typical skeptic of Quattrocento Italy, an Academic, when he argued *in utramque partem,* felt obliged to reconcile contradictions into
such a degree of consensus as would be, if not logically coherent, at least
sufficiently homogeneous to instigate action in society.[1] Such *distinctiones*
are elicited by the first Spenserian contradictions to be examined.

1. Kahn, *Rhetoric,* 20–21, 183–84; for Spenser, see 188; see also Eden, *Hermeneutics,* chap. 1
et passim. Altman assesses the effect of this training on sixteenth-century English writers, dis-
covering a genre less overtly didactic than most, a genre he calls explorative, in *The Tudor Play.*

The radical skeptic, the Pyrrhonist, wears self-contradiction as a badge. Pyrrhonism and self-contradiction appeared in extreme form in Montaigne, who wrote, in his admittedly self-indulgent style:

This is a record of . . . irresolute and, when it so befalls, contradictory ideas: whether I am different myself, or whether I take hold of my subjects in different circumstances and aspects. So, all in all, I may indeed contradict myself now and then; but truth, as Demades said, I do not contradict.[2]

Victoria Kahn finds that by Montaigne's time, the later Renaissance, "the exchange of contradictory opinion" has become simply a self-reflexive substitute for action, the questioning of the very possibility of forming an opinion. It has been said, "While the opposite of a fact is a falsehood, the opposite of one profound truth may well be another profound truth." The statements "God is omnipotent" and "Man has free will" may both be profound truths despite being contradictory.

The two main sections of the present chapter also reflect the two degrees of skepticism that critics are willing to see in Spenser's contradictions. Some critics, especially devotees of organic unity and Christian humanism, or those riding one or another confessional thesis, do not recognize them at all; they sweep them under the rug by selective quotation or by discussing them in terms so vague that they are reconcilable. But Spenser's many tergiversations have long demanded special treatment. For the past two decades or so, more and more critics have been accepting and even celebrating Spenser's self-contestation rather than treating it as a problem to be explained away. Nevertheless, because of the proems, epigraphs, and moralizing first stanzas of cantos, because of the inclusion of the Letter to Ralegh in the first instalment, and following various precedents in the work of a diverse body of Spenserians, I believe that Spenser constructed most of his contradictions for some admittedly oblique didactic purpose such as is reflected in the qualified *distinctiones* hitherto discussed. This accords with the moderate, early Italian Academic skeptics who still aimed to influence action in society.

In recent years, however, certain Spenserians have gone too far in a new direction: they have admitted that substantive, self-canceling contradictions are present, but have claimed that they are neither intended nor distinctive; rather, they are a function of allegory, language, or representation itself, of rhetoric, of narrative, of a masculinist outlook, or of certain ill-defined and delusory "virtues." I admit the existence of such inherent

2. "Of Repentance," 3.2, in *Complete Essays*, 611.

contradictions, but they are few. Some of them are a function of certain necessarily ill-defined though nonetheless important doctrines. Free will and predestination are inherently contentious concepts, so that it is hard for anyone (except a Milton; see PL III, 98–128) to treat them consistently; the same is true of justification. In a chivalric romance, even one with religious overtones, Spenser could have avoided them, and his obvious decision to treat them shows their deliberateness and distinctiveness. Nothing compelled Spenser to treat them inconsistently. His treatment of free will and justification represents Pyrrhonistic skepticism, not, I will argue, as a self-reflexive substitute for action, but as a cautionary restraint upon action.

We saw that the moral codes of Cleopolis and of the New Jerusalem are equally irreconcilable yet equally authorized—practical only insofar as they remind the reader that not all values are compatible and force her to make her own choice between them. Spenser's treatment of gynecocracy is equally Pyrrhonistic but beyond the scope of this study. Some Renaissance Pyrrhonists employed their contradictions to drive the reader to faith, which in turn supplied the grounds for action; but I do not see this effect in Spenser's contradictions, since some are between two revealed truths and thus undermine faith, at least initially. Two similar degrees of skepticism can be found in the two degrees of contradiction, the apparent and the real, that Renaissance exegetes were willing to see in the Bible; but that is getting ahead of our story.

My first interpretive task is to prove what I have up to now simply asserted: that Spenser does indeed contradict himself, sometimes merely formally, sometimes substantively. To begin with formal contradictions, Spenser wrote thirteen poetic dialogues. Some of these—CCCHA and, in the SC, "February," "May," "July," and "October"—consist largely of debates (see Beverley Sherry, "Dialogue, Poetic," in SE). He composed one such dialogue in prose, the *Vewe of the Present State of Ireland;* he probably translated another, the *Axiochus* (John Day, "Dialogue, Prose" in SE). In his other fictions, he also stages debates, private or forensic, between characters. In the FQ alone, we encounter these among others: Arthur versus Una (I.vii.41); Red Cross and Una versus Despaire (I.ix.28–54); Red Cross versus the Palmer (II.i.32–33); Guyon versus the Palmer (II.i.57–59; II.ii.4, 5–10); Guyon versus Mammon (II.vii); the trial of Duessa (V.ix–x); and that of Mutability versus the Goddess Nature and the poet-speaker (VII.vi.13–viii.2). Some of these formal and apparent debates are left unresolved, which could indicate that their contradictions are authentic and substantive.

The following sets of statements are obviously if sometimes only formally contradictory. The poet-speaker says of Artegall's relation to Rade-gund: "So was he overcome, not overcome / But to her yielded of his own accord" (V.v.17). The poet-speaker of the *Amoretti* goes back and forth as to whether the lady should look down on him or up to him. In the *Fowre Hymnes* the entire structure, as previously noted, is a large-scale contra-diction, the first two extolling human beauty and sexual pleasure and the second two repudiating it. In the FQ, finally, normative speakers contra-dict one another as to whether someone like Duessa deserves punish-ment, whether "bloud is no blemish" (VI.i.26) or yields "nought but sin" (I.x.60) and whether change is intrinsically bad or just the downward part of a cycle. All such formal contradictions are constructed to evoke, at least initially, the heterogeneity of experience.

Other contradictions are less obvious but nonetheless real and sub-stantive. Robin Headlam Wells and James Schiavoni have established that Spenser contradicts himself about free will.[3] A hitherto unnoticed but substantive contradiction exists on the closely related theological issue of justification (which in turn is inseparable from questions of merit and predestination). I explicate it here as an introductory example. The com-mon element in the confessionally differing definitions of justification is obtaining heaven—a topic to which Spenser devotes some attention. The primary statement is Una's rebuke to the suicidal Red Cross in I.ix.53. Red Cross's guilt coupled with Despair's reminder of God's justice has convinced him that he is headed for hell, a conviction that drives him, in a kind of vertigo, to attempt suicide. Una intervenes with the comfort (a standard Calvinist prescription for such cases) that he will not go to hell no matter what he does because he is "chosen;" in this she agrees with the Hermit Contemplation that predestination alone qualifies one for the New Jerusalem (I.x.57). Spenser does not go so far as the corollary doctrine of predestination unto damnation, a doctrine that had, through Calvin and Luther, become Protestant orthodoxy; but he does, through Una, characterize God's love as arbitrary; he does not claim that it is for those who show love. The predestinarian I.ix.53 is a corollary of the no-toriously grace-centered I.x.1. Separated by only one stanza of narrative, the two stanzas constitute a "Calvinist manifesto."

Una's Protestant advice is contradicted, however, by a number of pas-sages in Canto x, most obviously the one describing the Seven Corporal Works of Mercy as part of "the way, his sinfulle soul to save" (I.x.51; to be addressed in more detail below). Conversely, God hates and damns the souls of those who are full of "wrath, and hatred" (I.x.33). Regarding the

---

3. Wells, "Christian Knight"; Schiavoni, "Predestination"; both hereafter cited in text.

fifth beadsman, whose workplace amid the dying and the desperate recalls the suicide scene in I.ix, the poet-speaker inscribes a soteriology
quite different from Una's; he comforts

> . . . those, in point of death which lay;
> For them most needeth comfort in the end,
> When sin, and hell, and death do most dismay
> The feeble soule departing hence away.
> All is but lost, that living we bestow,
> If not well ended at our dying day.
> O man have mind of that last bitter throw;
> For as the tree does fall, so lies it ever low.
> (I.x.41)

That is, unless one is in the proper frame of mind on one's deathbed, one
can fall from grace totally and finally, incurring the danger of going to
hell. Sometimes Spenser's God plays favorites; sometimes he keeps score.
And however much of a reconciliation theological traditions and their
textual and cultural contexts might provide, these assertions were obviously constructed to sound contradictory, indicating that Spenser's contradictions are indeed worthy of extended treatment as a group. In Section I of this chapter I supply background; in Section Two, where my
interpretation really begins, I discuss those contradictions that yield, at
least in large part, to mainline Protestant treatment; and in Section 3, those
on free will that remain, like those on justification, above, unresolved.

Background: The Views of Exegetes and of Spenser
about Contradictions in Scripture

I propose that Spenser's contradictions, especially those on religious or
moral subjects, derive from the Bible. When educated laymen read the
Bible, the whole Bible, and nothing but the Bible, and, wherever possible,
read it literally, as Spenser and his cohorts were encouraged to do, they
uncovered fissures which medieval exegetes had papered over, first by allegoresis and then by metaphysics. The Reformers who encouraged this
mode of reading did not of course intend this result; indeed, they hoped
that this common foundation in the work of a single divine author would
bring the confessions into unity.

Even within individual books, however, contradictions exist. For example, in one of the Proverbs, the contradiction comes between adjacent
verses:

4   Answere not a foole according to his foolishnes, least thou also be like him.

5   Answere a foole according to his foolishnes, least he be wise in his owne conceite (Prov. 26:4–5)

The contradiction is rhetorically heightened by keeping as many words as possible the same; the reconciliations, if any, between the two verses reside in the various glosses and in the mind of the reader. TJ rightly call it an antithesis, but it is more hermeneutically unsettling than that. Looking for a moral message, TJ plausibly aver that the contradiction advocates "prudence" and, in effect, situational ethics; it leads the reader to see that answering a fool is an adiaphoron, that it can be construed *in malo* or *in bono* according to the circumstances of "what, when, and how." But the poet-speaker may also be self-reflexively dramatizing that same contradictory nature of proverbs about which Don Quixote warns Sancho. Similarly, the author of the First Epistle of John first says, "If we say we have no sin, we make him a liar . . ." (1:10), then turns around and denies that the regenerate ever sin (3:9; 5:18). These two contradictions were recognized as contradictions by a seventeenth-century exegete, William Streat.[4]

Unsurprisingly, the various human authors also contradict one another. Job contradicts a corollary of retributive justice—that if you are suffering, you must have sinned—a doctrine that is paradigmatic to most of the Hebrew Bible. The deuterocanonical, but still included, Ecclesiasticus contradicts Paul both on free will and on merit. James contradicts Paul by name on whether faith without works can save, thus lending to the NT a dialogic or symposium structure on the subject of justification by works (contrast James 2:14–26 with Romans 4:3–25 and Galatians 3:10). That James and Paul could not easily be reconciled is indicated by the Pauline Luther's doubt as to James's canonicity (see his Preface to his translation of this Epistle). In the FQ, alongside the fifty-six references to the eleven Epistles traditionally ascribed to Saint Paul, Shaheen lists fourteen references—six undoubted and eight possible—to the Epistle of James alone. The most blatant contradictions arise from Christianity's troubled relationship to its parent religion, making its Bible a radically self-contestatory text; the New Testament supplements, com-

4. *Dividing of the Hooff*. . . (London, 1654), a work to be discussed later in this chapter. Proverbs 26:4–5 makes up Contradiction 158, on which Streat's reconciliation is similar to TJ's; 1 John 1:10 versus 3:9 supplies Contradiction 294, which he resolves by a "distinction" of sins in terms of degrees of gravity and voluntariness. The Geneva Bible drew the same distinction, calling it not a resolution of a contradiction but a "taking away of an objection"; see glosses on 1 John 5:16 and 17.

plements, revises, abrogates, and even contradicts the Old on topics as specific as divorce, cursing, work on the Sabbath, attitudes toward enemies and the wicked, and the importance of good and bad fortune. Witness these selections from Matthew 5:21–48, now significantly called "the Antitheses":

27 Ye have heard that it was said to them of olde time, Thou shalt not commit adulterie.
28 But I say unto you, that whosoever looketh on a woman to lust after her, hath committed adulterie with her already in his heart. . . .
38 Ye have heard that it hath bene said, An eye for an eye, and a tooth for a tooth.
39 But I say unto you, Resist not evill: but whosoever shall smite thee on the right cheeke, turne to him the other also. . . .
43 Ye have heard that it hath bene said, Thou shalt love thy neighbour, and hate thine enemie [Lam. 5:12].
44 But I say unto you, Love your enemies: blesse them that curse you: doe good to them that hate you, and pray for them which hurt you, and persecute you.

Although this set of contradictions was toned down by Beza and by the Geneva glosses which often echo him, the Lutherans Althamer and Flacius nevertheless maintain that parts of it such as "turn the other cheek" genuinely contradict the law. In this place and to these exegetes, the New Testament is in every sense a mirror image of the Old Testament.

Apparent contradictions were a widely recognized feature of the Bible's literary surface; and this alone is enough to justify including them as part of biblical poetics. They occur in discussions of inherently contradictory topics such as free will, but also on other topics such as bloodshed. Of course, exegetes medieval, Renaissance, and modern exert themselves to reconcile these contradictions because they preclude the establishment of creeds and unsettle both the didactic purpose of Scripture and the dogma of biblical inspiration. Gillian Evans speaks easily of "the long-running task of reconciling the Bible's apparent contradictions."[5] This task was the chief raison d'être both of scholasticism and of classical forensic oratory—a tradition that merged with biblical interpretation in humanist exegetes such as Erasmus and Melanchthon.[6] Protestant exegetes who

5. Evans, *Language . . . Reformation*, 40; this work and *Language . . . Middle Ages* hereafter cited in text. The medievals also argued *in utramque partem*, but they sought an intellectual solution in logical distinctions, *distributiones*, or compromises, whereas the early Italian skeptic of the Renaissance sought both less and more: he could rest content with two contradictory truths so long as he attained a basis for civic action.

6. See Eden, *Hermeneutics*, 7–11, 22–24 et passim. She deals equally and interchangeably with exegesis and forensic oratory, demonstrating the analogies between them.

found contradictions in the Bible include a few thinkers, such as Althamer and Flacius, who saw a few genuine contradictions. Many thinkers
saw many apparent ones; Erasmus in his *Diatribe* (though not in his *Ratio*) and Franck in his *Paradoxa* declare even the genuine ones to be
many. Any exegete who affirms one or more genuine contradictions or
who dwells on the pervasiveness of apparent ones I will label a "splitter."
Most of the splitters were associated, in one way or another, with Lutheranism. Although "Lutheran" was a term of reproach in England (see
below), Spenser could have read and believed Lutheran biblical poetics
(and even, on many issues, Lutheran theology) and still remained loyal
in practice to the Established Church, as it was vaguely defined by the
Book of Common Prayer.

Erasmus' stance on free will epitomizes the views of the medieval
church and early modern Romanists on the Bible in general. Both he and
they gladly acknowledged the apparent contradictions in Scripture because these contradictions evidenced the need for a divinely inspired
magisterial church to interpret Scripture for the laity. More broadly, the
exposition of Scripture was one of the principal professions for which
universities equipped students. To such students, problematic aspects
were held up as intellectual challenges. Particularly in the later Middle
Ages, says Evans, there was a "flair and enthusiasm for debate in the
framework of formal disputation arising out of the study of Scripture"
(*Language . . . Reformation,* 108). In these quodlibetical questions, although the Bible was not the sole, or even the chief, sourcebook, texts
from Scripture were still brought in as one kind of supporting evidence
(109). The catch was that, because of the scholastic method of marshal-
ing arguments both for and against—as, for example, "John 14.6 to show
that since God is truth the existence of God is self-evident; Psalm 52.1 to
show that it cannot be self-evident since the Fool was able to say in his
heart that there is no God [Aquinas, ST Ia Q. 2.a.1]"—the Bible came to
appear contradictory. Evans reports Wyclif as lamenting that "the habit
of using Scriptural proofs both for and against had by a process of re-
bound a striking effect in encouraging some serious questioning of the
Bible's truth" and its logical validity (110–11). Abelard's *Sic et Non* (not
printed until the nineteenth century) is a collection of contradictions,
partly from Scripture, which reflect such disputations; in addition, the
text left them unresolved, presumably as "exercises in reconciliation . . .
for the classroom" (*Language . . . Middle Ages,* 136).

For all his hatred of contentiousness and of scholasticism, Erasmus,
too, urged the study of biblical contradictions in general upon professional expounders of Holy Scripture. In the *Ratio seu methodus . . . ad veram theologiam,* a manual for theological students (widely available at

Cambridge* and not to be confused with its early sketch, whose title begins simply *Methodus*), Erasmus challenges them to resolve "pugnantia" in the Bible—"things which at first glance seem to conflict with each other . . . and not to cohere with each other." Calling Christ a veritable Proteus, he suggests a long list of contradictions which vary in kind and importance. He does not mention free will here; but he mentions those similar aporias which arise if we say either that Christ is wholly God or that he is wholly man. Erasmus recommends that would-be ecclesiastics "philosophize and scrutinize with pious curiosity the mystery of the divine counsel."[7]

Despite his insistence that the Bible is clear about free will and predestination (see below), which insistence excludes him from the ranks of splitters, even Luther occasionally admits the existence both of some apparent contradictions in Scripture and even of one substantive one. He is led to an unsettling admission by a contradiction of a sort which in general does not interest me—that between two narratives of the same event:

> It is the custom of Scripture to appear at odds with itself, not in one place but in many, if they are compared. . . . Scripture appears to be written in sections and broken up, as it were, just as though all the works of God were varied and, as it were, all mixed up; nevertheless, they are most orderly, even though it does not appear so.[8]

Moreover, in Genesis, God commanded Abraham to sacrifice his miraculously conceived, and only legitimate, child, seemingly aborting his promise to make of him a great nation. Luther comments:

> Here God is clearly contradicting Himself; for how do these statements agree: "Through Isaac shall your descendants be named" (Gen. 21:12) and "Take your son, and sacrifice him"? . . . There is a contradiction with which God contradicts Himself. It is impossible for the flesh to understand this; for it inevitably concludes either that God is lying—and this is blasphemy—or that God hates me—and this leads to despair. Accordingly, this passage cannot be explained in a manner commensurate with the importance of the subject matter. . . . I am unable to resolve this contradiction.[9]

7. *Ratio seu methodus compendia perveniendi ad veram theologiam*, in *Opera*, vol. 5, cols. 75–138 inclusive; contradictions and my quotation are on cols. 93–94, Christ's two natures, col. 94 d–f. BCI lists eighteen copies of the *Ratio verae theologiae* [sic] printed separately and five of a collection that featured it, hence my total of twenty-three.

8. *Works*, 9:17, n. 7, *Lectures on Deuteronomy*, editor's note drawing on notes recording Luther's oral treatment of the subject.

9. Ibid., vol. 4, *Lectures on Genesis*, 92–93, on Gen. 22:1–2.

This incoherent outburst indicates that Luther takes Abraham personally as a model for the Christian reader who is plagued by the substantive contradiction in the Bible between general promises of salvation and the possibility of predestined damnation, the latter pole of which he privileged in *De servo arbitrio*. Here, Luther sounds less like the pugilist of the *De servo arbitrio* and more like Ochino or Melanchthon (see below); and if even Luther wavers as to the Bible's consistency, we need not find it implausible that Spenser should manifest inconsistency regarding biblical issues. Without mentioning any of these passages, Gillian Evans places Luther in her history of those who wrestled with contradictions. She recounts how, in Luther's *Table Talk,* people enjoyed confronting him with biblical contradictions, thus proving that in the Reformation, such contradictions remained an intellectual challenge to the theologian and a chief concern of the pastor (*Language . . . Reformation,* 113). I quote one such exchange below.

Sebastian Franck and William Streat, like the nominally Catholic Erasmus, say that the Bible, in general, contradicts itself, and this totalization, coupled with their admission of genuine contradictions on one topic (either free will or the ceremonial law), earns them my title of "splitters." Sebastian Franck (1499–1542) may once have been a Catholic priest; he showed some sympathy with Lutheranism before finally becoming an independent spiritualist. He translated Althamer's *Dialogues* into German; and he devoted a work of his own to the problem of the Bible's self-contradictions (*Verbuthschiert der sieben siegelte buch . . .*), which, however, is very rare and not attested to at Cambridge. He touches on the Bible's contradictions from time to time in another work, *Paradoxa.* Cambridge libraries possessed one copy of this work* and copies of several other works of his. He assembles 280 "Paradoxes" (in German, with Latin subtitles) about the Christian faith from scriptural, proverbial, and classical sources. They are paradoxes in that they conflict either with common sense or with one another; in the latter category we find, for example, "55 The law of God is both easy and difficult. 56 The word of God is both life and death. 57 All things have two appearances" (104–5). He warned:

> God intentionally shaped the letter of Scripture in such a discordant way . . . that . . . we should . . . not make an idol of it which we might then consult in all matters of faith. Instead, we are to address him about it . . . so that we always need him.

Like the Romanists, Franck sniffs out contradictions, not to reconcile them but to motivate them by way of a radical dualism, a Christian palinode.[10] Over this problematized Bible, Franck privileges not the magisterium but the inner light. Formally, this strategy resembles Abelard's practice of leaving contradictions unreconciled for theology classes to solve. The fact that the Bible contradicts itself in order to throw responsibility on the reader for the solution (whether the theology class, the magisterium, or the individual spiritualist) makes it a model of the calculated indeterminacy which a poet could cultivate.[11]

Finally, after Spenser, an English pastor and M.A., William Streat, produced a book with the quaint and wistful title *Dividing the Hoof: OR, Seeming-Contradictions Throughout Sacred Scriptures, Distinguish'd, Resolv'd, and Apply'd . . . To bring the Soule . . . into more familiar acquaintance with the LORD JESUS, the onely DAVIDS-Key, to unlock the Cabinet of JACOBS GOD, to fetch out that Secret, why he should lay his hands thus crosse when he gave his Children this Blessing?* Unlike Luther and like Franck, Streat boldly ascribes apparent scriptural contradictions to its divine author, as he indicates both in the title and in the first dedicatory epistle addressed "To God." He imagines the contradictions as the nuts in God's garden (Song of Solomon 6:11); with God's help, he will crack them. He adds in the introductory epistle "To the Christian Reader" that of course such contradictions must be reconcilable, as indeed most of Spenser's are.

The work's date (1654) precludes its having been a model for Spenser and his readers, and of course the idea of pervasive contradiction in the Bible is scandalous to the naively devout; but because the work was printed in England, we are assured that the subject was not too hot to handle, even in the vernacular. In this introduction, Streat acknowledges that "Divines in foreign parts" have already produced "reconcilings of the word," and these have always sufficed for those who had Latin; his work is "necessary heer . . . to such English Preachers that know no Latine" ("Epistle," fol. bv). This is one more testimony to my claim in the Introduction that cutting-edge scholarship on the Bible was still being done solely in Latin. Most important for our purposes, as his title announces, in each chapter he resolves one "seeming Antilogie" (e.g., 1 John 1:10 *contra* 1 John 3:9 and 5:18). He walks the reader through hermeneutical steps which are labeled in the margin "Oppos[ition]," "Doubt," "Distinction," and "Resolution." The first two correspond to my second stage of reading and the last two to my third or final stage, thus confirming the historicity of my hermeneutics. In general, the existence of splitters such

10. "To the Reader," in *280 Paradoxes,* quotation, 4–5.

11. This model lends historical credibility to the similar purposes that Quilligan and Gless have proposed for Spenser's contradictions.

as Erasmus, Franck, Streat, and sometimes Luther testifies to the existence of a dialectical hermeneutics in the Renaissance and thus of a small but distinct group who would appreciate the contradictions that we know to be present in Spenser.

This exegesis is compatible with what Spenser, or his *raisonneurs,* say about the Bible. Although Spenser never claims in so many words that the Bible is contradictory, he lays the groundwork for such a statement. While he affirms the importance of the Bible, he never affirms it to be the sole guide to salvation (the strong interpretation of the motto *sola scriptura;* see Chapter 1). Furthermore, he does warn that the Bible, in general, is not clear. The "sacred Booke with bloud ywrit" out of which Fidelia teaches "Of God, of grace, of justice, of free will" (I.x.19) contains "darke things . . . hard to be understood" (I.x.13). In saying this, Spenser widens "Peter's" lament in the Bible that there are "some things" in the Pauline Epistles that are "hard to be understood" (2 Peter 3:16). This statement hints that Spenser's own imitation of the Bible is self-contradictory. From all these sources (2 Peter 3:16 and the splitters), Spenser may have imbibed tolerance for divergent interpretations of the Bible and thus inscribed more than one standpoint on certain topics in his major poem.

In addition, Spenser shows familiarity with the Romanist warnings, as well as those of Elizabeth in her suppression of the "prophesyings," against letting the minor clergy read and expound the Bible, lest disagreements result which would break the church into splinter groups. He gives these arguments a voice—ironized, to be sure—in the formal priest's prissy objection to reading, a category that obviously includes Bible reading:

> . . . read he could not evidence, nor will,
>
> . . . .
>
> Of such deep learning little had he neede,
> Ne yet of Latine, ne of Greeke, that breede
> Doubts mongst Divines, and difference of texts,
> From whence arise diversitie of sects,
> And hatefull heresies, of God abhor'd.
> (MHT 382–89, YSP)

Despite the formal priest's insincerity, Spenser could conceivably agree with him about the danger that Bible reading would lead to fragmentation of the Body of Christ.[12] As Franck complains, without the divine inspiration that he claimed to have, Protestant literal readers of Scripture

---

12. See Imbrie, "Playing Legerdemaine," 142–55.

derived from it the basis for new sects.[13] The fragmentation of Protestantism proves to us, as it proved to some observers at the time, that its sole authority, Scripture, is contradictory on certain points.

Besides being hard to understand, Spenser says, Scripture can kill—Scripture in the mouth not only of Despair but of Fidelia as well. Although the Red Cross Knight gives Arthur "his Saveours testament" (I.ix.19) as a parting gift, Scripture is a two-edged sword in more senses than one: when Fidelia teaches him "heavenly documents" out of her book "with bloud ywrit," Red Cross, for the second time, wishes to die because of his past sins (I.x.21, cf. ix.50). This seems to act out the meaning of the assertion that "she was able, with her words to kill, / And raise againe to life the hart, that she did thrill" (I.x.19). "The word of God," said Franck, "is both life and death" (Paradox 56). We seem to have even the Bible *in bono et in malo.* Within the Bible, it is the law that is responsible for the killing. In I.x.53, as we saw, the Law given to Moses on Mount Sinai is characterized as "The bitter doome of death and balefull mone," the Pauline "letter which killeth." The Romanist answer to these difficulties—reserving to authorized churchmen the task of interpreting the Scriptures—does not seem to have been offered by Spenser, for no one personifying the church actually does this. Only Una clearly personifies the church as a whole, and she does not interpret the Scriptures. The only one who does is Fidelia or faith—a quality in an individual, as her sisters Speranza and Charissa clearly are, not the collective wisdom of the church.[14] That Fidelia's murders can be salutary if they receive the right supplement (on which see below) does not obviate the negativity of the portrayal of the Bible here.

The foregoing history has shown that the Renaissance Bible as a whole would have provided a poet with an authoritative model of a self-contestatory, agonistic text. In the sixteenth century, before the higher criticism, Bible readers privileged its single divine author, and therefore believed, as Luther complained, and as William Streat mused wistfully in his title, that God built the contradictions into it for some purpose or other. Thus a poet might see them as an ideal to be imitated along with the rest of its literary surface.[15]

13. *280 Paradoxes,* 5. In the Counter-Reformation, according to Evans, *Language . . . Reformation,* Bellarmine distrusted the laity's ability to read the Bible because they could read only literally; thus they would never get at the true meaning of the Old Law (40, 43); and they would then splinter off into sects (32)—which last charge Tyndale denied (35).

14. I no longer believe what I wrote in "Bible," SE, that Scripture kills "unless it is interpreted by the church."

15. Lewalski records the belief that God authored the tropes and figures of Scripture and noses out such biblical tropes and figures in sermons and divine poems, thus demonstrating

Contradictions That Mainline Protestants
Could Reconcile as Tropes

Contradictions existed, then, in both Spenser and the Bible, and the biblical contradictions were sometimes perceived. If their contradictions are on the same topics, then they are probably imitated from the Bible, and if so, then those on other topics are probably constructed on an analogous pattern. Let us focus on the hermeneutics of resolution or motives for irresolution, for here I am proposing that Spenser expects the reader to resolve these contradictions, and non-biblical ones as well, by the same hermeneutic strategies exegetes use to resolve those in the Bible.

Equivocation

Before proceeding to the resolutions of the overt contradictions in both texts, let us pause to look at a somewhat different compositional strategy we find there, a way of papering over a contradiction already established, particularly a blurring of the distinction between heavenly and earthly. Spenser equivocates on man's moral strength when he equivocates on "his"—the knight's or God's?—in I.xi.55, "That had atchiev'd so great a conquest by his might" (see Phil. 2:12–13). This equivocation refers, Darryl Gless discovered, to a mystical solution to the problem that has just been allegorically dramatized: Red Cross's mystical "participation" or "incorporation" with Christ, caused by the balm dripping from the Tree of Life and enabling him to kill cosmic evil and rescue Adam and Eve.[16]

Similarly, patristic, medieval, and sixteenth-century exegetes frequently harmonize a biblical contradiction, according to Kathy Eden, by explaining away one pole as an equivocation.[17]

The ever-popular Latin Father Cassiodorus noticed equivocation in the Bible at large in his *Expositio Psalmorum,* his biblical poetics. Like repetition *in bono et in malo,* it is a species of "bilinguitas":

> The main force of eloquence in the scriptures . . . frequently recounts certain things yet is often explaining matters greatly different from the words heard. This is a simplicity which is at two levels [*bilinguitas*], a guileless

---

a poetics of biblical imitation (*Protestant Poetics,* 83 et passim). Streat and Luther claim that God authored contradictions; therefore contradictions too would be a model for poets.

16. Gless's background chapter mentions this incorporation in *Interpretation,* 34; and Weatherby stresses Red Cross's "deification" in this episode in *Mirrors,* 35–43 et passim.

17. Eden usually calls them ambiguities and includes in them literal versus figurative; for example, *Hermeneutics,* 93, n. 7, quoting Flacius.

form of double speaking. . . . The device is not adopted in the interests of deception, but to achieve a most useful effect. It employs the Hebrew language to intimate the deepest of issues.

John Wyclif "puts the knowledge of the signification of terms and their equivocation . . . high among the tasks of the commentator"; for him, too, as Evans says, "Scripture's own equivocations are entirely good and helpful." For example, "There is a true mercy, appropriate to God and his angels, and there is the mercy we ourselves feel, which is a sensation of compassion compelling us to help the afflicted." [18]

Spenser employs equivocations, I will argue, primarily, to imitate Scripture, but also deliberately to obscure a contradiction giving an appearance of harmony by resolving it at the purely verbal level, and perhaps to allow diverse audiences to read into it their various beliefs. In both the Bible and the FQ, for example, the word "glory" is ambiguous. In Psalm 73 (Vulg. 72), verse 24, "Thou wilt guide me by thy counsell, and afterward receive me to glory," "glory" was read by Jews as earthly honor, by Christians as glory in heaven; for instance, it is glossed succinctly as "Eterna" by the Interlinear Gloss of the *Glossa Ordinaria.* (This Christian meaning lacks philological foundation in the Hebrew Bible; but I am here concerned only with the literal surface, not with correctness.) Similarly, while the "glory" that Gloriana dispenses to achievers in Cleopolis is the reward of effort (I.x.59.1–8) whereas the "glory" of being "Saint George of mery England" is not attained but simply "ordaind" (I.x.61), Spenser momentarily equates the two glories by equivocation when he gratuitously adds that the Faerie Queen can give glory because she "is heavenly borne, and heaven may justly vaunt" (I.x.59), constructing the monarch as sacred and adding sacred overtones to the competition for preferment. Spenser may well have viewed this equivocation on "glory" as good and helpful, as intimating an intuition of the Platonic translucence of heavenly glory in the earthly. God's glory and the world's have a bit more in common than do God's grace and the sovereign's.

Spenser not only reconciles to but sets at odds with each other the divine and the human causes of justification, as appears from my opening explication of I.ix.53 versus I.x.41. There are nine statements in I.ix and x that treat "mercy," divine or human, and its parts and synonyms as salvific: Una's Calvinist Manifesto; Epigraph x; x.33 (charity); 34.6–8; 34.9; 38 (feeding the hungry); 51.3–4; 51.7–9; and 67.4. Only one presents a

18. Cassiodorus, *Expositio,* Preface xv, 20; trans. P. G. Walsh, *Cassiodorus . . . Psalms,* 39; Wyclif paraphrased by Evans, *Language . . . Reformation,* 115.

compromise (34.6–8); the rest either contradict Una or are themselves equivocal. Just before the House of Holiness, in I.ix.53, Una has used "mercy" unequivocally for God's election to assure Red Cross that he will not go to hell despite his sins: "In heavenly mercies hast thou not a part? / Why shouldst thou then despeire that chosen art?"

The second unequivocal instance, however, traces salvation to human mercy. It is the long passage (with 38 inside it) devoted to Mercy's seven beadsmen in the House of Holiness in the very next canto (x.35–45). The beadsmen as a group dramatize the Seven Corporal Works of Mercy, which can only refer to human actions. Yet they are salvific, for they are represented as an unpacking of the personification Mercy's teaching about "to heaven . . . the ready path" (33.9), "the way, his sinfull soule to save" (51.3), and "the way to heaven" (51.4). "Way" in 51.3 clearly denotes "means." Mercy's salvific function in 51.3 can in the final analysis be attributed to her only in her role as human mercy because God's mercy is not "the way, his sinfull soule to save," in the active voice; it is the way for the soul to *be* saved. The Works were hardly ever even mentioned by Protestants, Schiavoni tells us (181), precisely because such classification implies they are meritorious.[19] Spenser's locating these two unambiguous voluntaristic statements in the very next canto after the predestinarian one (I.ix.53) sets the contradiction in high relief. (I employ "voluntarist" as the opposite of "predestinarian" or "grace-centered," not as the opposite of "intellectualist.")

To say as Spenser does that this septenary actively leads one to heaven and saves his soul is uniquely papistical, as most critics agree, whether grudgingly or enthusiastically. It accords fairly well, however, with the ethos of knighthood and of Cleopolis. Indeed, in the cantos to come, as I have argued elsewhere,[20] the knights Red Cross and Guyon between them perform most of the seven works and are told that thereby they have earned or may earn heaven (see below). Romanist voluntarism is more heroic than is Calvinist predestinarianism.

A hitherto unnoticed biblical source for the generally works-righteous coloring of the bulk of Canto x is Ecclesiasticus. Ecclesiasticus was in all Protestant Bibles of the time and is still in the lectionary. It is pervaded by what the New Oxford Annotated Apocrypha at 3:1–16 calls "the Jewish doctrine that the observance of the Mosaic law is meritorious. . . . contrast the teaching in Lk. 17:10."

---

19. Here, at least, Schiavoni's generalization, echoing Whitaker, is true: "Spenser provides clear statements on the value of good works for salvation" ("Predestination," 182).

20. See Kaske, "Religious Reuerence."

The second beadsman goes to an unequivocally papistical extreme which is supported by Ecclesiasticus (and not by Protestants, as illustrated by the Oxford Annotated Bible, above):

> The second [work of Mercy] was as Almner of the place,
> . . . .
> The grace of God he laid up still in store,
> Which as a stocke he left unto his seede.
> (I.x.38)

This stanza states that grace can be not only stored up against one's own final judgment but also even transferred to others like money, as the Roman Church transfers the supererogatory merits of the saints. To appreciate the full rationale for stanza 38 and the full extent of the influence of Ecclesiasticus here we have to consider the voluntaristic meaning of another and a partly equivocal statement about mercy, stanza 34.

This self-contradiction Spenser papers over by two truly ambiguous uses of the word "mercy"—I.x.34.9 and I.x.51.7–9—that leave it uncertain whether the mercy is God's or man's. Their ambiguity is modeled on the mild play on "mercy" in a popish-sounding Beatitude: "Blessed are the mercifull: for they shall obteine [God's] mercy" (Matt. 5:7), as is evident from Spenser's parallel repetition of the noun "Mercy":

> To whom [Mercy] the carefull charge of him she gave,
> To lead aright, that he should never fall
> In all his wayes through this wide worldes wave,
> That Mercy in the end his righteous soule might save.
> (I.x.34.6–9)

The terms in which all actions of Mercy are described here are voluntaristic and anti-Calvinist to the extent that, first, Red Cross is not saved already, as I.ix.53 and the predestinarians would claim he was;[21] second, one can fall from grace; and third, if he should fall, he might not finally be saved in the end, contrary to Una and agreeing with I.x.41. Romanist readers would read the works of mercy as actively and directly preserving one in a state of grace now and earning salvation in the end. Stanza 34 echoes not only part of the Sermon on the Mount, which is voluntaristic and works-righteous throughout, but also, by way of a commentary on this Sermon, Ecclesiasticus 17:20, a favorite verse of the Romanists and a stumbling block to Protestants. On Matthew 6:3–4, "when thou doest thine almes, . . . thy Father that seeth in secret, hee will rewarde

---

21. See Peter Lake's summary of William Whitaker on this point in *Moderate Puritans,* 100.

thee openly," Hugh of St. Cher, whose commentary was well represented at Cambridge,* constructs a tabular *distinctio* of the twelve rewards or fruits of almsgiving, almost all of which he borrows from Ecclesiasticus and two of which are in turn echoed by Spenser—the first in 34 and 38, the second in 51. Almsgiving (*eleemosyna*) is one kind of mercy (*misericordia*) and covers most of the Works of Mercy. One fruit is that almsgiving "preserves grace, Eccl[us.] 17.c" (= 17:18 in the Vulgate and TJ, 17:20 in the Geneva). To preserve one's grace is to keep oneself from falling, as in x.34.6–8.

Ecclesiasticus 17:20 also confirms that stanza 38 is Romanist. In Hugh's pre-Clementine Vulgate the verse reads, "The almsdeeds of a man are with him like his purse [Lat. *sacculus*] and will conserve the grace of a man as the pupil of his eye" (my translation). The almsgiver's preserving grace, papistically reified and commodified like money, in this "purse"— or, more vaguely, "the almes of a man, is as a thing sealed up before him [God?], and he [God] keepeth the good deeds of man as the apple of the eye" (Geneva)—suggests the second beadsman's reward: by giving away even more than he could afford, "The grace of God he layd up still in store" (I.x.38).[22] The Geneva translation, here oddly works-righteous, adds to the verse the idea of bequeathing grace to "his seede" (I.x.38): ". . . and giveth repentance to their sonnes, and daughters." Ecclesiasticus 17:20 is thus the source not only for the general idea that good works preserve grace, that is, keep one from falling from grace (I.x.34), but also for this particular image of the second beadsman storing up grace for his posterity (38). The text of Ecclesiasticus 17:20 and its medieval annotations both add a works-righteous meaning to stanza 34 and confirm that such is the only meaning in 38.

What is irenic is that this human Mercy directs Red Cross's steps "that he should never fall [i.e., from grace] (I.x.34.7). Certain Protestants could also agree with this clause because, according to this particular description of Mercy (as opposed to that of her deputies), she always directs his steps away from something (falling). A Phillipist Lutheran could interpret one's own works of mercy as preserving one in grace—that is, preserving faith and the presence of the Holy Spirit—indirectly in a negative and psychological way. Thus, expanding upon Melanchthon's Augsburg Confession, the framers of the Formula of Concord said in 1577:

> Do good works so that you remain in your heavenly calling, lest you fall away and lose the Spirit and his gifts, . . . which you retain through faith.

22. This reward is rightly labeled as Romanist by Whitaker (*Religious Basis,* 46) and Schiavoni ("Predestination," 182).

Faith, however, does not remain in those who lead a wicked life . . . and reject repentance.[23]

While Spenser vacillates, as we have seen, regarding whether one can merit heaven by works, he believes, as Melanchthon also did, that one can forfeit heaven in the end by serious vices:

> She [Charissa] . . . Gan him instruct in every good behest,
>
> . . . .
>
> And wrath, and hatred warely to shonne,
> That drew on men Gods hatred, and his wrath,
> And many soules in dolours had fordonne.
> (I.x.33)

If one persists in doing good, one will have less time and energy to hate and thus to lose one's salvation. As Melanchthon and his followers said, one will then maintain one's baptismal communion with the Holy Spirit, whose presence is salvific. This integrates works, not, to be sure, with the predestination invoked by Una (to which psychology is irrelevant), but with her own salvific presence. By his negative phrasing, akin to equivocation, Spenser has allowed for not just a Romanist but a Melanchthonian interpretation of I.x.34.6–8.

It is the second "Mercy" in stanza 34, that in line 9, which represents our first fully equivocal use: Mercy guides the knight "That Mercy [his own or God's?] in the end his righteous soule might save." Here Gless is right to maintain that Mercy is "Janus-faced," readable as either divine or human, in either a predestinarian or a voluntarist light.[24] Spenser performs a doctrinal balancing act, embodying simultaneously both of his conflicting theories about how we obtain heaven.

The other clearly ambiguous use of Mercy is I.x.51.7–9:

> Thou [Mercy] doest the prayers of the righteous sead
> Present before the majestie divine,
> And his avenging wrath to clemencie incline.

This could be read in the Protestant (if somewhat tautological) sense that God answers our prayers and refrains from punishing our bad deeds because of his own mercy. Alternatively, it could be read with Schiavoni in

---

23. Formula of Concord, Art. IV.33, expanding on "Apology of the Augsburg Confession," XX.13, both in *The Book of Concord,* 228 and 556.

24. Gless, *Interpretation,* 156–57.

the human and Romanist sense, that our good Works of Mercy can make satisfaction to God for our bad deeds so that he forgives us and withholds punishment (182). In the Sermon on the Mount, this divine quid pro quo is implied by the Lord's Prayer: "Forgive us our debts as we forgive our debtors" and Christ's expansion of it (Matt. 6:9–15). That this petition is works-righteous is acknowledged even by the Protestant glosses, their reluctance to do so by an anxious note to verse 1 denying that the scholastic doctrine of merit can be deduced therefrom (Geneva gloss a; Beza gloss b). This Romanist sense of I.x.51.7–9 also echoes the first fruit of almsdeeds in Hugh of St. Cher's distinction, "It procures forgiveness for past sins," and his cited authority, Ecclesiasticus 3: "For the good intreatie of thy father [because one has been good to him] shal not be forgotten, but it shall be a fortresse for thee against sinnes. . . . [T]hy sinnes also shal melt away as the ice in the faire weather" (vv. 3, 15–16). I.x.34.9 and I.x.51.7–9 are the two truly ambiguous uses of the word "mercy."

Spenser could find models of similar ambiguities about justification even in Ecclesiasticus 17:20—a verse he imitated in its straightforward papistical sense in I.x.38—if he read a tendentious Protestant gloss on it. In TJ's translation, "almsgiving" becomes the ambiguous "mercy," and mercy and grace migrate from man to God.[25] This drift is confirmed by TJ's gloss on it:

> Mercy] All that follows, on which we won't comment, confirms that the following is the faithful interpretation of this verse: it means that *God* possesses, sealed up in his secret counsel [i.e., predestination], *his* mercy by which he *will* accept *his own into grace and will preserve them* as the pupil of his eye. (translation and emphasis mine)

A predestinarian reader of I.x.34.7–9, though unable to admit the possibility it holds out of falling totally and finally, could impose on it a Protestant meaning of mercy just as TJ did on Ecclesiasticus 17:20: that God's mercy not only will save her in the end, as we have seen that she could gather from the text alone, but even, contrary to what we gathered from Ecclesiasticus 17:20 alone, that it is God's mercy that prevents her fall simply by preventing serious sin and thus divinely guaranteeing her unconditional perseverance (see Rom. 8:29–30). This second and pre-

---

25. Hugh's version has "The alms *of* a man is as a purse and will conserve the grace *of* a man as if it were the pupil of his eye"; see *Opera . . . In Evangelia* on Matt. 6:4. The TJ version has "For mercy *on* a man is as a thing sealed up [*sigillum*] before him, and it [meaning "mercy," or "he," meaning "God"; the subject is unexpressed] conserves grace *towards* a man as the pupil of his eye" (emphasis mine).

destinarian sense of "that he should never fall" harmonizes it with Una's "heavenly mercies."

Spenser's self-contestation about "mercy" and the divine and human causes of justification and his wordplay which blurs or dramatizes it are confirmed by the disagreements among Spenserians about the doctrine of Canto x.[26] By echoing such works-righteous Scriptures as well as predestinarian ones, Spenser obeys Melanchthon's principle of echoing the Bible even where it contradicts itself, thus making contradiction part of biblical poetics.

Spenser's both/and equivocations on "his," "glory," and "mercy," exemplify the "equivocal predication" which Heather Asals finds in Herbert's poetic treatment of the sacraments.[27] In Spenser as in Herbert, the alternatives can be read as both/and or as either/or, blurring together notions of human and divine agency or dramatizing their conflict. As Fish said of Herbert, "reading these lines is like looking at a gestalt figure in which first one and then another pattern emerge from the same physical (here verbal) components . . . until finally there is only one pattern made up of two declarations which, if they were laid side by side, would be perceived as mutually contradictory" (188). Unlike the ambiguity of Spenser's "his" (see below), those of "glory" and "mercy" are never sorted out. These last equivocations may instantiate what Thomas Greene calls the "blurriness" of Spenser.[28] Another feature of this episode—the way in which Spenser adopts a voluntaristic and works-righteous viewpoint for the entire House of Holiness proper but begins and intermittently intersperses it (I.x.1 and 57, 60–62) with a predestinarian one—may have prompted Empson to speak of Spenser's various systems floating side by side without ever touching.[29] The dialogues and debates, the contradic-

---

26. Whitaker, *Religious Basis* (e.g., 46), and Schiavoni take this septenary in the obvious voluntaristic sense; Daniel Doerksen, with the momentary endorsement of King (SPRT 216, but see 65), wrests them to the general sixteenth-century predestinarian doctrine that God's mercy leads one to heaven and saves one's soul; see "'All the Good is Gods,'" 11–18. In Gless's unifying mode, in which everything springs from "Reformed" theology, he imposes upon the House-of-Holiness episode the Protestant notions of imputed righteousness (*Interpretation* 157), of justification by faith (153), and above all of works as signs of faith and election (e.g., 146, 151–53, 156), none of which is mentioned here. Spenser pictures faith not as salvific but as an intellectual first step, the way James does. In all his works, Spenser never refers to justification by faith or to good works as signs of faith and election; he does refer to imputed righteousness once, but not in the FQ (HHL 148–50). Gless thinks imputed righteousness is implied in any reference to God's mercy, but God's mercy could mean forgiveness of sins, which just brings the beneficiary back to zero.

27. Asals, *Equivocal Predication*, esp. 4–8 et passim.

28. Greene, *Descent from Heaven*, 332, 329–30.

29. Empson, *Seven Types*, 41–42.

tions and compromises listed elsewhere in this chapter, however, resist either of these soft and fuzzy images; on the subjects of free will versus grace and predestination versus achievement of heaven, Spenser states contradictory propositions using the same or synonymous terms—so that if put side by side they neither blur nor float independently but fight each other.

By realizing that the word "saint" is equivocal, we can resolve another contradiction about justification. Through two ecclesiastics, Spenser predicates of saints denominationally contradictory things: they are arbitrarily chosen and they are self-made. The Hermit Contemplation first declares that everyone in the New Jerusalem is equally a saint; all are there because they have been "chosen" and washed in the blood of the Lamb, in other words, predestined and justified (I.x.57). The Bible and its commentaries display a somewhat similar ambiguity. "Saints" could mean the whole body of believers; this general sense of the word existed in the Middle Ages and was privileged by Protestants. But "saints" could also mean individuals who had been formally canonized, which is to say, recognized for their extraordinary virtue or holiness, and precisians resisted this elitism. Spenser employs and expands this ambiguity, thus showing he is not a precisian. The Hermit predicts that Red Cross will end up, first, "emongst those Saints whom thou doest see" (I.x.61), referring to all the inhabitants of the New Jerusalem, the Protestant sense, and, second, promoted to super-saint, "thine owne nations frend / And Patron: . . . Saint George of mery England, the signe of victoree" (I.x.61), a canonized exemplar. One has to be a saint in the broad sense before one can be a saint in the narrow sense.

While the two sainthoods can be theoretically reconciled as stages, Spenser creates an apparent contradiction in stating the two methods by which sainthood is obtained. To Red Cross's question on this head, the Hermit replies that all saints, including canonized ones, were "wretched" at the start (I.x.62), and implies that their special sainthood too is just "ordaind" (61); similarly, when he tells Red Cross to go back down the mountain and save Una's parents, it is for the sake of duty and fidelity, not to earn his sainthood.

The concordantial reader is startled when in the next book another elderly ecclesiastic, speaking about the same person, Red Cross, specifies a second and quite different method by which to become a saint. Guyon's Palmer tells Red Cross that he "a Saint with Saints your seat have wonne" by dint of "late most hard atchiev'ment by you donne" (II.i.32); since neither grace nor predestination is mentioned, this accords with the works-righteous statements in I.x and contradicts I.ix.53, and I.x.57 and 60–62.

Seeking a *distinctio,* the reader recalls the two senses of "saint" meaning either any believer or a canonized saint. This contradiction about saint-hood parallels that about heaven noticed in the Bible by Melanchthon between Luke 6:23, "your reward is great in heaven," and Romans 6:23, "the gift of God is eternall life." Is heaven/eternal life a reward or a gift? Melanchthon writes, "If these passages seem to our opponents [the Ro-manists] to be in conflict, let them see to it."[30] Later, in a more helpful mood, he explains the contradiction: "Though justification and eternal life belong to faith [in I.ix.53 and x.57, Spenser has said, to predestina-tion, a Calvinist nuance, but each salvific thing constitutes a gift], still good works merit other rewards, both bodily and spiritual . . . I Cor. 3:8," and presumably, since Melanchthon needs this to explain the contradic-tion, both in earth and in heaven.[31] Thus Melanchthon resolves a con-tradiction about how heaven is attained by distinguishing heaven as eter-nal life or salvation from rewards *in* heaven. Spenser could not have found this notion in the egalitarian eschatology of Luther or Calvin because they either rejected rewards completely or asserted them to be predes-tined with the same arbitrariness as is salvation.

By defining the sainthood attained by effort not as salvation but as heavenly rewards, Spenser's contradiction between the Calvinist Mani-festo and II.i.32 can be similarly resolved. The Palmer's subsequent words, "For which [his "atchiev'ment"] enrolled is your glorious name / In heavenly Registers above the Sunne" clearly refers not to salvation but to heavenly fame. The image of "heavenly registers" parallels and con-trasts with Gloriana's social register, her "immortall booke of fame" (I.x.59). As Milton makes Apollo say to the mourner in *Lycidas,* "all judg-ing Jove . . . pronounces lastly on each deed, / Of so much fame in Heav'n expect thy meed." This is not salvation but a bonus. Like the Her-mit Contemplation, the Palmer plays dizzyingly on "saint" in the broad sense of any regenerate and/or godly person and "saint" in the narrow sense of a canonized or canonizable person; only the second is the direct object of "have won": "Where you a Saint [i.e., being a saint already in the broad sense by virtue of election, as in I.x.57], with Saints your seat [your canonized title, as in I.x.60 – 62] have wonne" for your "atchiev'-ment." The first "saint" would have been redundant if it had meant the same thing as the second.

Although neither Luther nor Calvin would have endorsed II.i.32, it be-comes sufficiently compatible with Spenser's own Calvinist Manifesto

---

30. Apology of the Augsburg Confession, Art. IV, section 356–57, *Book of Concord,* 161.
31. Ibid., IV.366; see also 367.

once its play on "saint" is untangled by referring the first "Saint" to pre-destination and the second "Saint" to heavenly rewards. To quote Fish on Herbert again, "The experience of these [plays on words] is a succession of double takes" (188). Like an exegete reconciling a contradiction in Scripture, we can usually see one pole of a contradiction as equivocal; Spenser created such equivocations to paper over contradictions.

Correction

Correction is more unsettling than is equivocation because it involves a genuine contradiction, at least a partial one; nevertheless, insofar as it rejects something, it offers more closure. The majority of the contradictions that we will be considering represent self-corrections. For corrections, Spenser had two principal models: on the one hand the rhetorical figure *correctio* and on the other hand, I propose, the Bible. Corrections may be adjacent or far apart and involve either images (considered in Chapter 3) or propositions. (In the rhetorical manuals, *correctio* concerns only adjacent propositions.) Although I once claimed that the far-flung corrections are nothing but the rhetorical figure writ large, I now think the Bible provides a more exact model and a sufficient source for them, though of course the sources are not mutually exclusive.

Spenser, like other Elizabethans, frequently employs the rhetorical device *epanorthosis* or *correctio*. This is often a kind of contradiction. It is often introduced by the words "nay"/"not" or "or rather," and usually punctuated as a parenthesis: "And was arayd, or rather, disarayd" (II.xii.77). In the famous first lines of the FQ, the two "yet"s mark *correctiones* (i.1.6, 2.9). "So was he overcome, not overcome, / But to her yeelded of his owne accord" (V.v.17.1–2) was adduced by Alexander Gill under "epanorthosis or correctio" in his *Logonomia Anglicana* (1619) and quoted from there by Herbert David Rix in his monograph *Rhetoric in Spenser's Poetry*. Strictly speaking, it is the radical and contradictory ones that are covered by the term *correctio*. The term *epanorthosis* will not be used as being too broad, for it also embraces phrases such as, in "November," "Why doe we longer live, (ah why live we so long)" (73), which I would call intensive rather than corrective. About this line Spenser's mysterious commentator E.K. exults, "an elegant Epanorthosis," thus showing that some form of the device was known and favored by Spenser's circle. In this same eclogue, Colin's song about the death of one Dido contains one of Spenser's most revealing corrective contradictions, a classical example of *correctio* except that the two poles are a hundred lines apart: Colin suddenly reverses his position from "dead shee is" ("November," 57–59; see also 37) to "Dido nis dead, but into heaven hent" (169). The contradiction results from a shift in discourse or viewpoint from the "lower" to the "higher," the physical to the spiritual; realizing this resolves the contradiction by limiting the applicability of "dead shee is" to the valid but limited discourse of materialism. If corrections can be a hundred lines apart, then corrections five books apart become more credible.

A few striking parallels to Spenser's textbook examples of *correctio* can be found in the Bible, some on the same themes.[32] Christ's prayer in Gethsemane (Matt. 26:39), "O my Father, if it be possible, let this cup passe from me: nevertheles, not as I will, but as thou wilt," is labeled a *correctio* by Beza, and it is from a more spiritual viewpoint.[33] Paul's claim, "I laboured more aboundantly then they all: yet not I, but the grace of God which is with me" (1 Cor. 15:10) is pointed out as a *correctio* by Erasmus in his *Diatribe on Free Will:*

> "Yet not I, but the grace of God within me" (I Corinthians 15, 10). If Paul had done nothing, why did he state before that he has done something? Not only that, he even said: "In fact I labored more than many of them" (I Corinthians 15, 10). If it is true what he says, why does he correct this, as if he had spoken incorrectly? The correction obviously does not intend that one should think he had done nothing, but he wanted to avoid the appearance of having attributed to his own strength what he had accomplished with the help of divine grace. The correction aimed at the suspicion of insolence and not at the possibility of co-operation in action.

This correction too is from a more spiritual viewpoint. Erasmus adds, as is sometimes true in Spenser, that the second statement does not completely cancel out the primary statement but shifts the point of view, in this case, so Erasmus believes, from the theological to the moral and the purely rhetorical (*Erasmus-Luther,* 73–74). Thus Spenser would have found *correctio* in the Bible, and on his favorite topic of free will and grace. On the combined model of Spenser and the Bible, Milton chose to express free will and grace in a temporarily unsettling propositional *correctio:* "Man shall not quite be lost, but sav'd who will, / Yet not of will in him, but grace in me" (PL III.173–74).

The fact that Spenser employs textbook examples of the rhetorical

---

32. Bullinger, *Figures,* 909–11.

33. *Domini nostri Jesu Christi testamentum novum . . .* (Geneva, 1590), hereafter cited in text, gloss h.

figure *correctio* does not prove that the Bible is a source, but it lays the foundation for such a case: it confirms the validity of my wider applications of the term "correction" to images (adjacent and widely separated) and to distant contradictions. Still adjacent and quite obviously corrective are the contradiction of *Amoretti* 58 by 59, the first two of the *Fowre Hymnes* by the second two, and the Goddess Nature by the poet-speaker. In all three examples the reversal is highlighted by a formal distinction of parts. A special rubric links the two sonnets, a rubric seemingly attached to 58 because it appears between the number and its sonnet, but which governs 59 as well because 59 continues the same subject and uses the same key phrase. The subject reevaluated is pride, self-reliance, independence:

58

By [i.e., with reference to] *her that is most assured to her selfe.*
Weake is th'assurance that weake flesh reposeth
In her owne powre and scorneth others aide. . . .

59

Thrise happie she, that is so well assured
Unto her selfe. . . .

because not being desperate for a mate, if she chooses him, it will be for his unique qualities so that she will remain true to him. (Although it is not necessary to my case, I agree with those who regard this answer as spoken by the lady or as representing her voice, her point of view—a clear break with the tradition of Petrarchan solipsism.) It is hard to choose between them. While 58 has scriptural warrant, 59 has stoic grandeur, especially in the parallelistic lines 7–8. Sonnet 59 ends with a hint of future union: "but he most happy who such one loves best." I say "hint" because the line is equivocal: I have been presuming that "such one" is the subject of "loves." Since this hint is fulfilled in the sequence (62 and following), it retrospectively invests 59 with more authority than 58 (cf. 28–29). This example shows that contradiction and correction constitute a pattern that can be extended to non-biblical images and concepts.

The strongest intellectual correction is of course a palinode, and strongest of all when this is from a "higher perspective." The *Fowre Hymnes* inscribe contradictory discourses: the "Hymne of Love" inscribes erotic hedonism and idolatry and the "Hymne of Heavenlie Love" inscribes a narrow and otherworldly Christianity; it renounces sex on religious grounds—renounces, indeed, all the pleasures of this world. I have appealed to them so often up to now because the contradiction is self-evident. The opening stanzas of the *Hymne of Heavenly Love* warn against reading the first two hymns of earthly love, thus canceling them out:

> Many lewd layes (ah woe is me the more) . . .
> I have in th'heat of youth made heretofore,
> . . . And ye that wont with greedy vaine desire
> To reade my fault, . . .
> . . . quench my blame,
>
> . . . .
>
> For who my passed follies now pursewes,
> Beginnes his owne, and my old fault renewes.
> (stanzas 2–3, YSP).

Whatever reconciliations the appeal to convention may provide, the hymns are made to look like a self-consuming artifact. The dedication puzzlingly expresses the same otherworldliness yet attributes also the earthly love to the dedicatees; it claims that the last two hymns "by way of retractation, . . . reforme" the first two. The failure of decades of critical attempts to reconcile the hymns confirms this reader's impression that no *distinctio* is possible here, that Spenser regarded this work not as a vehicle of doctrine but as a site of internal contestation, an unresolved debate, like Abelard's *Sic et Non;* and if this work, why not certain topics in the FQ? Only a limited synthesis based on the beauty of nature yokes the syncretic hymns, HB and HHB—a syncretism based on Florentine Neoplatonism. Neither sexual love nor human beauty is reinstated.

Similarly, in FQ VII or the Mutabilitie Cantos, *correctio* functions as a structuring principle between two units which are formally distinct. The Titaness Mutabilitie claims she dominates the world. First, the goddess Nature corrects her; in a sublime synthesis, she answers that change is indeed omnipresent but not dominant because every change serves to bring out the subject's essential nature.

> . . . yet being rightly wayd
> They are not changed from their first estate;
> But by their change their being doe dilate:
> And turning to themselves at length againe,
> Doe worke their owne perfection so by fate:
> Then over them Change doth not rule and reign;
> But they raigne over change, and doe their states maintaine.
> (VII.vii.58)

The poet's answer to both goddesses is marked off from Nature's answer by the rubric "Canto VIII":

> Me seemes, that though she [Mutabilitie] all unworthy were
> Of the Heav'ns Rule [the celestial world, the visible
> heavens]; yet very sooth to say,
> In all things else she beares the greatest sway.
> Which makes me loath this state of life. . . .
>   (VII.viii.1)

Here the poet-speaker endorses Nature's correction of Mutabilitie but corrects Nature as well, not by synthesizing (Nature has done all that can be done in that direction, and critics who attempt more only distort the text), but by pointing out that her answer of cyclical immortality applies to heavenly bodies, not to individuals like himself. Only the heavenly bodies sink and rise the same; about individuals, he admits Mutabilitie's accuracy and simply reverses her value judgment. The poet-speaker thus restores a distinction that has been mentioned in the poem but that Nature has recently confounded—the distinction between the terrestrial and the celestial worlds.

After this negation, the correction then moves on to an affirmation, from what some would call a higher perspective, of the absolute stasis of eternity. Whereas Nature has issued an adiaphoristic correction of Mutabilitie—she is really all right in her place—this is a palinode, a radical, so to speak, an iconoclastic, correction of both Mutabilitie and Nature from a theological viewpoint:

> . . . no more Change . . .
> But stedfast rest of all things firmely stayd
> Upon the pillours of Eternity,
> That is contrayr to *Mutabilitie:*
>
> .   .   .   .
> With Him that is the God of Sabbaoth hight.
>   (VII.viii.2)

This stanza represents a final snippet of theological discourse, a rare and final glimpse at the realm of grace, appropriate as a proleptic conclusion to the foreshortened twelve-book poem. In the *Fowre Hymnes,* too, the poet-speaker issues his correction from a religious viewpoint. To a sixteenth-century reader this would rule out the possibility that the poet-speaker represents just one more perspective, like the contrasting cities, or just an addition to the primary statement, as in *distributio;* it renders the correction a palinode and gives a certain closure. The correction of profane by sacred love is iconoclastic; but on the topics of female independence and of change the corrections are milder: both poles of the contradiction have some validity as a kind of double truth. For Spenser, self-correction is not just a rhetorical device but a habit of mind.

Widely separated contradictions can be seen in the Bible, too. They are corrections because a certain evolutionary paradigm privileges the last word—for example, Job versus Deuteronomy, and, most of all, for Christians, the New Testament versus the Old. Within this, the fundamental correction is gospel versus law. A sweeping abrogation of the entire Mosaic law is expressed in the Epistle to the Hebrews:

> But nowe our hie Priest hath obteined a more excellent office, in as much as he is the Mediatour of a better Testament, which is established upon better promises. . . . Not like the Testament [gloss 6: "or covenant"] that I made with their fathers (Heb. 8:6, 9).

> In that he saith a new Testament, he hath abrogate the olde: nowe that which is disanulled and waxed olde, is ready to vanish away (Heb. 8:13); [it consists of] . . . carnall rites, which were injoined, untill the time of reformation. (Heb. 9:10)

A new covenant or testament could be called a divine self-correction or palinode, an admission that the OT led its readers into an educative mistake. Such announcements of it may well have been the models for Spenser's closing palinodes privileging eternity over time (FQ VII.viii.1–2) and sacred love over sexual (*Fowre Hymnes*), especially since the palinodes echo the New Testament thematically as well. The problem of the degree of self-cancellation remains, but it remains both in the Bible and in Spenser, constituting still another filiation. Therefore this correction of law by gospel is likely to be a model formally and sometimes even thematically for all of Spenser's widely separated propositional corrections, and perhaps for those of other authors; it will provide the key to most of the rest of this chapter. First we will consider resolutions (corrections in general and supplementation in particular), then motives for irresolution (paradox and contrasting halves).

Despite its abrogation in some or all respects, the Old Covenant, and the Old Testament which contains it, is allowed to remain in the Christian Scriptures as if it retained some authority, or as if the exercise of putting it in its place were somehow beneficial to the reader, perhaps to make her appreciate grace by comparison. Retaining an initial error rather than just saying what one meant in the first place is the essence of the figure *correctio,* as we saw in Erasmus' explication of the *correctio* in 1 Corinthians 15:10. To this small extent, even abrogation is evolutionary as well as iconoclastic. Spenser's corrections bear the imprint not only of the palinodic tradition traced by Patricia Phillippy, not only of the rhetorical figure, but of the two-part Bible as well.[34]

I concede that the magisterial Reformers like Calvin and Luther mitigated by glosses the palinodic nature of passages such as Hebrews 8, 9, and 12 and the Antitheses. For example, the Calvinistic Geneva gloss 9 on Matthew 5:38–42, "Ye have heard that it hath bene said, 'An eye for an eye, and a tooth for a tooth,' But I say . . . ," reads, "He sheweth cleane contrary to *the doctrine of the Scribes,* that the summe *of the second table* must be understood . . ." (emphasis mine; see also gloss 5 on 5:21–24; gloss 8 on 5:33–37).[35] There is a semantic reason why exegetes in general do not come right out and say that gospel "corrects" law: the root *correct* both in Latin and in English (except for the rhetorical figure) almost always meant disciplining people, not rectifying propositions.

The mainstream nevertheless included two splitters—exegetes who perceive one or more genuine contradictions and/or dwell on apparent ones. The first was Andreas Althamer. His major work *Diallage* or *Conciliationes* was immensely popular in sixteenth-century Europe at large and at Cambridge University in particular.[36] At Cambridge, then, people would perceive at least apparent contradictions as being a feature of the Bible's method of presentation. Althamer insists that most contradictions are only apparent. In doing so, he distinguishes different kinds of law. The moral law is not abrogated and can be reconciled with the gospel by rightly discerning its abuses from its proper uses—such as to mortify the old man, to terrify the conscience, and to induce that despair which leads to dependence upon God (a concept presumably alluded to in the salutary despair that Red Cross feels in the House of Holiness); in other words, gospel just limits the applicability of the moral law (fols. 3v–4v). But unlike Beza and the Geneva glosses sampled above, he admits that Christ's "Antitheses" (Matt. 5:19–48) register genuine contradictions of some kind and that the gospel genuinely contradicts both the ceremonial and the judicial law.

Similarly, Matthias Flacius in Tractate 1 of his monumental and re-

---

34. Phillippy, *Love's Remedies.*

35. See also Calvin, *Institutes* II.xi, esp. sections 3 and 4.

36. Althamer (Latin, Althemerus; b. before 1500, d. 1539 or shortly thereafter), *Diallage* (var. *Diallages*), usually known by its (operative) subtitle *Conciliatio(nes) locorum scripturae, qui . . . inter se pugnare videntur.* It was first published in 1527; a second part appeared in the following year. I cite the augmented two-part edition known as *Conciliationes.* See Kolde, *Andreas Althamer;* Kolde's bibliography lists no less than twenty-four editions of the text, in one or both parts, up through the year 1597 (131–32). There were three editions of the German translation by Franck; see Kaczerowsky, *Sebastian Franck Bibliographie,* 23–26.

spected *Clavis Scripturae Sanctae* joins other splitters—such as Erasmus and Althamer—in describing Scripture in general as a labyrinth.[37] Like Althamer, Flacius declares that gospel both contradicts law and corrects it. Emboldened by Romans 10:5–9, he gradually gains the courage to say that law and gospel represent two kinds of teaching that are "seemingly contrary," "almost contrary," nay, "really through their very nature contrary": law says, "He who does these things shall live by them"; gospel says, as in John 3:16, "He who believes shall be saved." Moreover, "the first offers salvation only to the just and the worthy, the second, only to the most worthless of all." Gospel is better than law not only in its doctrine but also because it can really produce its intended effect of giving eternal life, whereas law cannot, because man is too depraved to be able to obey it. The covenants can be reconciled only if law becomes the servant of gospel, stepping down, as Althamer says about the moral law, to the ancillary function of revealing sin. This radical distinction and demeaning reconciliation, says Flacius, is "the surest key to all of Scripture." Limiting the primary statement to an ancillary function is a correction. Thus, these two splitters strongly imply that gospel corrects law.[38]

The Old Testament advocates violence; the New Testament, pacifism. Genuine and widely separated contradictions of this sort are noticed by Luther on vengeance, Martyr on animal sacrifices, and Herbert on calling down fire from heaven; the first two explain their contradictions by the abrogation of the Jewish civil and ceremonial law, the last by the diversity between the old moral law and the new. Gillian Evans reports that someone asked Luther in his Table Talk:

> The texts in Numbers 35.[6] and Deuteronomy 19.[3] seem to permit private revenge to a person who lays hold of the killer of a relative before he betakes himself to a city of refuge. These passages appear to be in conflict with the Scripture that forbids private revenge. He [Luther] replied, "That precept in Moses is judicial and is abrogated." (*Language . . . Reformation*, 113–114)

Thus Luther explains a contradiction in the Bible in terms of the abrogation of Moses' judicial law. Although this particular interpretation is fairly orthodox, it exemplifies the hermeneutic process employed frequently by radical splitters such as Bale.

A biblical contradiction might serve an educational purpose: according to Martyr, a contradiction between the law and the prophets regard-

---

37. *De ratione*, 40.
38. Ibid., Regula 14; see also "Causae Difficultatis" 20, Regulae 44–45.

ing animal sacrifices was intended to lead the Jews in the time of the Old Testament to see that a divine-human sacrifice was needed:

> They might consider, that God first said that he would be pleased with the bloud of sacrificed beasts [Margin: "Levit. 1,4 and in manie places more"]: and yet, that he afterward in the Psalmes, and in the Prophets [Margin: "Psalme 50, verse 8, etc. Esaie. 1.11, Jerem. 6,20 and 7,22. Amos 5,22"] testifieth that he is not delited with those sacrifices. These two places, seeming in outward shew to be repugnant, must so be reconciled, as the people, by meanes of the latter sentence, should be taught, that those sacrifices, of their owne strength and nature were not sufficient to please God, who onelie (for Christ his sake) sheweth himselfe to be gratious and mercifull: and in those sacrifices setteth foorth the Messias to be beholden.[39]

The prophet's correction shows the ceremonial law to be insufficient and merely typological. This historical relativism is an early specimen of what the seventeenth century was to label progressive revelation.[40] The hermeneutical steps that Martyr recommends model the experience of a reader of one of Spenser's contradictions: first, reading concordantially; second, perceiving a contradiction; third, reconciling by a distinction that reduces the primary statement to a heuristic and propaedeutic rather than an ultimate validity. William Streat always follows these steps, and in explaining Contradiction 261 appeals to the abrogation of the ceremonial law.

The poet George Herbert, too, advocates distinguishing law and gospel relativistically and temporally with regard to another kind of violence. After his instruction to read concordantially (quoted in Chapter 2)—an instruction that implies large-scale textual homogeneity—he notices a contradiction:

> To this may be added the consideration of any text with the coherence thereof, touching what goes before, and what follows after, as also the scope of the Holy Ghost. When the Apostles would have called down fire from Heaven, they were reproved, as ignorant of what spirit they were [Luke 9:51–56]. For the Law required one thing [1 Kings 10–14], and the Gospel another: yet as diverse, not as repugnant: therefore the spirit of both is to be considered, and weighed.[41]

In other words, calling down fire from heaven was virtuous then, but not now, especially not to punish enemies. This is the sort of historical rela-

39. CP 2.15,30:582a; see also CP 2.5:360a–361b; CP 3.6:184.
40. See, for example, Long, "More Shapes," 85–99.
41. "A Priest to the Temple," chap. 4, in *Works,* 229.

tivism recommended by T. Grashop in the 1594 edition of the Geneva Bible: "Marke and consider the . . . [c]ourse of times and ages, with such things as belong unto them." Thus Herbert too backs down as to both the Bible's unity and the perpetuity of the moral law of Moses, maintaining it is not repugnant to the gospel (though the difference is radical enough to be called so) but admitting it is "diverse" from it. This biblical model could be employed by students of Herbert to reconcile doctrinal contradictions in his poems. God's shifting evaluations of violence as registered by these three exegetes are relevant to Spenser's shifting evaluations of bloodshed.

A literary example in English of gospel correcting law which Spenser is likely have known is John Bale's polemical morality play *The Three Laws.* Not only does its plot consist of sweeping corrections in salvation history such as Spenser arguably imitated, but it embodies as well several motifs that later show up in FQ I and II. In this personification allegory of salvation history, the three successive laws—that of nature, Moses, and Christ (cf. the threefold mountain simile in I.x.53)—while basically in agreement, are said to be differentiated according to times and persons. The plot implies that by their distinctive features, Moses's law and Christ's each successively corrects the corruptions of its predecessor.[42] Moses' ceremonial law is explicitly abrogated (Sig. cv). In his moral aspects, Lex Moseh is not only freed from his corruptors (Ambition and Covetousness) but also corrected: he exults as Act Three ends: "Now will I to Christ, that he may me restore, / To more perfection, than ever I had afore." Most exegetes handle the abrogation of Mosaic law gingerly, as if it bred anxiety, but Bale treats it with heady postmodern exhilaration in a drama that thematizes progressive revelation. He takes us one step further down the road to the *mise en abîme,* mere pluralism, in which the second statement is just another perspective—the relationship we saw to obtain between the two cities. Bale foretells a fourth age, the age of the Holy Ghost, which is also the age of Henry VIII and Edward VI; thus he seems to see his own time of the Reformation as another correction, a still newer covenant. The age of the Holy Ghost, as its inventor Joachim of Fiore tells us, ushers in the end of the world—God's most sweeping *correctio* of all.[43]

---

42. Bale, *Three Laws,* Sig. A iii. For Spenser's use of the three laws, see Bergvall, "Eusebius," 22–23. Bale held an Anglican bishopric in Ireland and at midcentury performed a bibliographical census of British libraries, including Pembroke's.

43. Closing lines of Act Three. There is no lineation or foliation, and by this point in the volume, signatures appear erratically. On Bale's Joachism, see King, *English Reformation Literature,* 198–99; on his *Three Laws,* 276–77, 293, 351.

Supplementation

A more genial, both/and kind of correction than abrogation is supplementation, a kind applicable to something that merits preservation. According to most exegetes most of the time, this is what gospel does to the moral law. In Spenser, Despair finally persuades Red Cross to attempt suicide by invoking the "righteous sentence of th' Almighties law," and by conspicuously omitting God's grace and mercy (I.ix.46–50). When Una in I.ix.53 contradicts and corrects Despair's successful argument, she supplies these missing ingredients:

> In heavenly mercies hast thou not a part?
> Why shouldst thou then despeire, that chosen art?
> Where justice growes, there grows eke greater grace,
> The which . . . that accurst hand-writing doth deface.

Whereas she abrogates law (hand-writing), she merely supplements justice with grace, as gospel does (John 1:17). The grace Una is talking about is primarily forgiveness, which is external to the believer, a correction in God's mind, and to that extent not a supplement. But Una's "grace" could also include that grace that so transforms the believer's heart and will that he becomes able to obey the law if he so chooses. In II.i.33, Red Cross will state that grace supplemented his "goodwill." Statements that grace is a supplement, though without the precise word, are found in Flacius (*De ratione* 42) and Luther.[44] The personification Lex Moseh in Bale's drama *The Three Laws* expects not only "restauracion" but also "supportacion" when Christ shall come.[45]

Once the supplement arrives, the law returns in an ancillary role. Luther, echoed by Althamer, frequently argued that moral despair induced by law is a necessary stage in learning to depend entirely upon grace:

> The law wills that man despair of his own ability, . . . he who acts simply in accordance with his ability and believes that he is thereby doing something good does not seem worthless to himself, nor does he despair of his own strength.[46]

---

44. "Augustine says, 'The Law is given . . . in order that grace may be sought whereby the Law in turn may be fulfilled. That the Law is not fulfilled is not the fault of the Law. . . . This fault had to be shown by the Law but had to be cleansed by Grace.' Rom. 8:3–4: 'For God has done what the Law, weakened by the flesh, could not do.'" *Works,* vol. 25, *Comm. Rom.,* 243, on Rom. 3:21.

45. Near the end of Act Three. For a link between Una's refutation of Despair and the supplement in the Derridean sense, see Goeglein, "Utterances," 1–19.

46. *Works,* vol. 31, Heidelberg Disputation, 1518, Thesis 18, 51–52.

This despair is voiced by Spenser's poet-speaker when he says, "If any strength we have, it is to ill" (I.x.1.8). Even despair, despite Spenser's grisly first picture of it, is all right when properly supplemented—an adiaphoristic correction. That the realization to which Despair brought Red Cross was partly true and salutary is evidenced by his having to go through the whole experience again in the normative House of Holiness (I.x.21).

Spenser also uses these formal patterns for subjects that are not biblical. Just as he derived Una's corrective supplementation from this large-scale supplementation in the Bible, so too he seems to have derived the form of his far-flung three-stranded supplementation on food and sleep, the sexual organs, and art. The second and third statements each provide a missing ingredient that has been either denied or ignored in the predecessor. Emerging from his three-day sojourn in Mammon's Cave, Guyon faints "For want of food, and sleepe" (II.vii.65). To Guyon's watching and fasting in Mammon's Cave, the House of Alma supplies a correction; it holds up the value of food and sleep when Alma tells the reading Guyon that it is "so late" and that "supper did them long awaite" (II.x.77). But the episode of the House of Alma itself commits a conspicuous sin of omission by ignoring the sexual organs. This lack is then compensated by the celebration of the sexual organs in the Garden of Adonis (III.vi.43 et passim; see Hamilton's notes). While definitively correcting the House of Alma, the Garden of Adonis goes overboard in correcting the illusionistic Bower of Bliss by omitting art altogether, and this brings us to the four-stranded chain previously explored. When this conspicuous omission in turn is compensated by the celebration of a duly subordinated art in the Temple of Venus, we encounter the root of the word "supplementation": "and all that nature did omit, / Art playing second natures part supplied it" (IV.x.21). This correction occurs in the second instalment, which appeared six years after the first; as the Old Law reigned for centuries, so Spenser's black and white opposition between nature and art was allowed to stand for six years. These omissions and supplements reenact again and again the "progressive revelation" whereby gospel supplies an essential but hitherto missing ingredient to law. In heaping correction upon correction in his allegorical tableaux, Spenser follows Bale's exaggeration of the biblical structure, which portrays defective systems supplanted by more nuanced ones in the evolutionary and dialectical pattern that constitutes salvation history.

Paradox

Another trope often invoked by exegetes to at least acknowledge if not reconcile contradictions in the Bible is paradox. Christianity's troubled relation to its parent religion gave rise to paradoxes about the law, paradoxes ruminated on by Paul in Romans 7:

> What shall wee say then? Is the Lawe sinne? God forbid. . . . But sinne tooke an occasion by the commandement, and wrought in me all maner of concupiscence. (7, 8)

> Was that then which is good, made death unto me? God forbid: but sinne, that it might appeare sinne, wrought death in mee by that which is good. (7:13)

This passage contains two paradoxes: the law provokes sin, and (as Franck said in Paradox 56) the law brings death. Paul's first paradox about law gives birth to a third and even more fascinating paradox about the will: "For I alow not that which I do: for what I would, that do I not: but what I hate, that do I" (15), and so on, for eight miserable verses (7:15–23).

Although no critic has noticed it, this same Pauline paradox of a law working evil in Romans 7 is invoked in two lengthy passages in the *Vewe* as an analogy to the English Common Law being at once good yet inappropriate to the Irish. Eudoxus echoes Paul's rhetorical questions "Was that then which is good made death unto me?" (Rom. 7:13) and "Is the lawe sinne?" (7:7) when he objects,

> [W]hy Irenius. cane theare be anye evill in the lawes cane the thinges which are ordeyned for the good and safety of all, turne to the evill and hurte of them? (Var. 9:45)

Irenius answers precisely as Paul does:

> The Lawes Eudoxus. I doe not blame for themselves. . . . [T]he lawes weare at firste intended for the reformacion of Abuses and peaceable Continuance of the Subjecte, but are sithence either disanulled or quite prevaricated thoroughe Change and Allteracion of Tymes, yeat are they good still in themselves, But to that Comon wealthe which is ruled by them they worke not that good, which they shoulde and sometymes allsoe perhaps that evill which they woulde not. (Var. 9:46)

At the end of his answer, Irenius echoes Paul's corollary paradox as restated in Romans 7:19: "For I doe not the good thing, which I would, but the evil, which I would not, that do I." Irenius here ascribes to the law itself the failure Paul experiences in trying to obey the law. It was this failure that led to Spenser's abandoning the English Common Law, as allegorized by Artegall abandoning his shield.

In the second reference to Romans 7, Irenius puts the Irish in the position of Paul's persona. Irenius continues to resolve the paradox of the English Common Law by distinguishing: "[Y]eat is the lawe of it selfe/ (as I saide good) and the firste institucion theareof beinge given to all Inglishemen verye rightefull, but now that the Irishe . . ." (66). Both of Irenius' answers begin by echoing Romans 7:12–14: "[T]he Lawe is holy and that commandment is holy, and just, and good. But . . ." On the same page of the *Vewe,* Irenius has just given a concrete example of how the English Common Law fosters crimes: the Irish twist it by using their position on a jury to acquit any and every one of their countrymen no matter how guilty (66; quoted in Chapter 3). By tempting jurors to this abuse, the law causes them to sin, just as Saint Paul's "sinne might be out of measure sinfull by the commandement" (Rom. 7:13b); by occasioning the straining of their juridical oaths it could even be said, like Paul's law, to give damnation or spiritual "death." Spenser was interested in Romans 7 and particularly its paradoxes of law. He saw the same or similar paradoxes in the English Common Law.

This discovery lends force to my previously published interpretations of two objects that behave paradoxically—Red Cross's armor in the Dragon-Fight and the well in the episode of the Nymph's Well—as Mosaic law.[47] Spenser identifies Red Cross's armor in the Letter to Ralegh as the armor of a Christian man; in past action it has been miraculously beneficial (see I.ii.18), and on the next day of the battle it will perform adequately. But it is made by the dragon into an instrument of pain and imminent death:

> [The dragon] from his wide devouring oven sent
> A flake of fire, that flashing in his beard,
> Him all amazd, and almost made affeard:
> The scorching flame sore swinged all his face,
> And through his armour all his bodie seard,
> That he could not endure so cruell cace,
> But thought his armes to leave, and helmet to unlace.
> (I.xi.26)

Spenser comments on the paradox: "Whom firie steele now burnt, that earst him arm'd, / That erst him goodly arm'd, now most of all him harm'd" (I.xi.27). We have armor *in bono et in malo,* and *in malo* because it brings death. Despite its literal sameness, it cannot continue to symbolize the armor of a Christian man which it has symbolized up to now. (It

---

47. Kaske, "Dragon's Spark," 433–35, hereafter cited in text; "Augustinian Psychology," 95; "Amavia, Mortdant, Ruddymane," SE. Cf. Michael Leslie, *Spenser's "Fierce Warres,"* 104–15.

could still be of divine origin and good purpose, which would then be one pole of a paradox.) If the fire carries its traditional symbolism of sin ("Dragon's Spark," 426), then the armor's transmitting the heat resembles the law's second paradox as well. It does so especially in the martial terms in which Augustine summarized the two paradoxes in Romans 7:11: "Armis tuis te vincit: armis tuis te interemit" (With your own arms sin conquered you, with your own arms sin slew you). Both Augustine and Spenser build paradoxical figures out of words with the root *arm-*. Therefore Romans 7 and Augustine are Spenser's sources, and Romans 7 at least is also intended to be recognized as an allusion.

Once the general intertextuality is recognized, further correspondences can be seen. The personified sin in Romans 7, according to some commentators, is the devil; so too the dragon is the devil. The precise means by which the law caused or augmented sin—"Was then that which is good, made death unto me? God forbid" (7:13); "But sinne tooke an occasion by the commandement, and wrought in me all maner of concupiscence"(7:8)—is similar to the way the armor in Spenser causes sin (sin being the decision to doff one's armor). Law is classified by Peter Martyr (citing Rom. 7) as an occasion of sin along with the devil ("Dragon's Spark," n. 17). Similarly, the dragon and his spark take advantage of the armor; once a spark gains entry, the armor spreads "the scorching flame," symbolizing concupiscence, to "all his bodie." Commentators explain that law augments sin in that it spices the attraction of the object with the thrill of rebellion, what in modern terms would be called negative suggestibility; as Ovid paradoxically observed, "We strive towards the forbidden always, we covet what is denied" (*Amores* 3.4.11; see also *Metamorphoses* 15.138 and Montaigne, "That Our Desire Is Increased by Difficulty"). Thus the paradoxically destructive behavior of Red Cross's armor can be explained if not reconciled by reading it as law. We shall see the Nymph's Well behaving paradoxically in accordance with the same Scripture and interpretation.

Two Contrasting Halves

The Bible has as part of its overarching poetics a twofold structure—two mirroring halves with a medial shift between them. Even though the Old Testament (especially with the Apocrypha) bulks many times larger than the New, Christians persist in thinking of the two as symmetrical. As some of the splitters recognized, the "Antitheses," Hebrews, and the Pauline topos of the first and last or Old and New Adams imply that the testaments are reverse images of each other. To this twofold mirroring Bible one formal parallel is Milton's *L'Allegro* and *Il Penseroso*. The perfect Spenserian formal parallel is the *Fowre Hymnes,* of which one half, the latter, also draws most of its themes from the New Testament. In "November," too, the medial shift from "deade is Dido" to "Dido nis dead, but into heaven hent," parallels the Bible's medial shift from death as the end of life to death as the gateway to heaven.

The FQ contains a medial shift from private to public virtue,[48] and, as I will show, the public half both parallels and echoes the Old Testament. This distinction in kinds of virtue formed part of the Platonic tradition; the distinction between private and public roles was politically important at the time. Spenser in the Letter to Ralegh projected a poem—to say nothing of a queen—in two halves, the first exemplifying the private virtues, the second, the public. Certainly the titular virtue of Book V, Justice, is public. In Books IV and VI the demarcation, as Debora Shuger says in another context, is dotted; most critics see friendship becoming more and more public in the course of Book IV; and courtesy in Book VI, if occasionally private, is mostly social and hence to that extent public. Although Spenser in the Letter to Ralegh claims to have modeled his private-public diptych on that of the *Aeneid,* Spenser may have had more than one model; and another is needed because the *Aeneid* contains no such contradiction between its two halves regarding bloodshed such as we shall see in Spenser. Spenser, like the Bible, takes features of one half and reverses them in the other half: as Adam by his sin brought death, so Christ as the second Adam by his righteousness brought life (Rom. 5); so, in reverse of the biblical order, "grace" emanates mostly from God in Book I, mostly from man in Book VI.

This distinction between private and public virtue can serve to reconcile some of the Bible's contradictions, according to the splitters quoted above. It can reconcile some in Spenser, too, sometimes on the same topics. Spenser's shift from private to public, from spiritual to worldly, serves as the ultimate explanation for the contradiction about free will, to be considered below, between I.x.1.8–9 and the Hermit's remedy for slander, VI.vi.7: "in your selfe your onely helpe doth lie, / . . . and must proceed alone / From your owne will." We have seen that Luther, Martyr, and Herbert reconcile contradictions about violence by distinguishing the OT or Mosaic law from the NT or the gospel. As they imply, the OT advocates retributive justice; so does Artegall in FQ V.

---

48. Nohrnberg has explored the implications of the public and private halves and the mirroring of FQ I by VI and II by V (*Analogy,* x–xii, 60 et passim); but he has not aligned these pairs with the Bible.

One far-flung Spenserian contradiction is Una's punishment of Duessa versus Artegall's. We know that both are right in their place and time because their actions are endorsed by other authority figures on the scene. Una says, "To do her die . . . were despight, / And shame t'avenge so weake an enimy; / But spoile her of her scarlot robe, and let her fly" (I.viii.45); Artegall votes to execute her (V.ix.49). The first scene of judgment seems introduced in order to parallel and contrast with the second, and they must be considered together concordantially, yielding a rough distinction between mercy and justice, private and public, the first half from the second. Some readers feel that Una lets Duessa off too easily; most readers nowadays feel that Artegall's judgment on her is draconian. Startled by this difference in treatment, my ideal reader distinguishes the agents: Una represents truth, for whom exposure of Duessa's falsehood is enough, whereas Artegall represents retributive justice. Artegall's correction of Una is not sweeping; his perspective is not higher, just different. Both perspectives are necessary, and they must occur in this order, since execution by its very nature must come last. While Una's purely epistemological and relatively merciful verdict could be seen as fulfilling either a private or a public role here, Artegall's retributive justice is clearly a public virtue. Artegall certainly represents a public official, first as a knight on duty, second as the knight of Justice. As the reader strives to reconcile the verdicts, she finds that they are those of private and of public virtue.

Spenser could have gotten the idea for this distinction between public and private from the Bible as glossed by Beza in the "Protestant Vulgate." Una's relatively merciful verdict on Duessa somewhat resembles that of Christ on another unchaste woman—the woman taken in adultery in John 8. Just as Una considers intellectual exposure punishment enough for Duessa, Christ may have granted mercy to the defendant brought before him because he believed that exposure was punishment enough. (Una does not tell Duessa to "go, and sin no more," because Duessa is a personification.) As the Pharisees declare, according to Mosaic law, she should be executed. Thus the law's verdict on the woman taken in adultery is the same as Artegall's verdict on Duessa. Just as this pericope contains a contradiction between law and gospel, so Artegall's treatment is that of law, while there is a New Testament air about Una's mercy. Moreover, Beza sees this pericope as a contrast between public and private virtue, and this too can be related to Spenser. Christ's "Let him that is among you without sinne, cast the first stone" (John 8:7) means not that, in the absence of morally perfect judges, criminals should go scot free, but that Christ "would not take on himself the duty of the civil magistrate." Beza adduces Christ's abdication of responsibility when he refused to get involved in a property dispute: "who made me a judge, or a devider over you?" (Luke 12:14). Beza's comment implies that the verdicts of Moses (Old Law) and of Christ are both valid in their respective spheres, public and private. Whether one agrees with Beza's interpretation or not, it exemplifies a valid and hermeneutically useful *distinctio* between private and public roles, and it also identifies the public role with the Mosaic law. A more explicit connection between Artegall, the public sphere, and the Old Testament occurs in V.i.25–28 when he recapitulates normatively the judgment of Solomon. Therefore Spenser saw the distinction between private and public as deriving at least in part from the distinction between the two testaments.

It was not only Beza who equated public virtue with Mosaic law. The Old Testament, besides endorsing bloodshed, was often associated with public morality. Melanchthon frequently insists that the Old Testament, while not the way to salvation, lays out God's blueprint for law and order; for example, "In this fourth commandment [honoring parents] we should be able to see that God earnestly wants order and government instead of the kind of freedom in which everyone may exercise all his wantonness as a wolf in the forest."[49] Luther, too, for all his pacifism reluctantly allows some slight resistance to evil on behalf not of oneself but of one's neighbor, provided the bloodshed is delegated to the civil magistrate; he goes so far as to affirm the job of executioner to be appropriate to a Christian, even when enforcing the laws of a secular state; for this he appeals uneasily to the bloodthirsty feats of Old Testament heroes. Luther admits that all this seems to contradict the pacifism of the Sermon on the Mount but finds it necessary in our world where Christians are few and even they are not always good.[50] Andreas Althamer, after frankly admitting that "An eye for an eye and a tooth for a tooth" contradicts "Turn the other cheek," mitigates this Mosaic revenge by institutionalizing it, by making it public, cautioning that it was never (*contra* Luther) open to private individuals, but only to "*adiudices,* constituted by divine ordinance."[51] Historically speaking, the Ghibellinism of these three Germans, all Lutherans or quondam Lutherans (in contrast to the theocracy of Calvin), was motivated in part by revulsion at the antinomian excesses of radical Protestants such as the Anabaptists, who applied Paul's perceived scorn of Mosaic law also to civil law. In England, too, it was their

49. *Loci,* Article VII, 101.
50. "On Secular Authority," in *Selections,* 375–77.
51. Contradiction 34 on "An eye for an eye, a tooth for a tooth" (Exod. 21) versus "If anyone strike you on the right Jaw, offer him also the other" (Matt. 5), fol. 30r–v.

threat to public order that gave the Anabaptists a notoriety beyond what their pitiful numbers would warrant.

Besides these paired incidents, there is a propositional contradiction about bloodshed between Books I and VI. Its poles are far apart, but the wording is similar, and Nohrnberg has highlighted other symmetries between Books I and VI. Calidore protests, "Bloud is no blemish; for it is no blame / To punish those, that doe deserve the same" (VI.i.26). He echoes and corrects not only his interlocutor but also the pacifistic Hermit Contemplation five books earlier, who bids Red Cross after his earthly victories to

> Thenceforth the suit of earthly conquest shonne,
> And wash thy hands from guilt of bloudy field:
> For bloud can nought but sin, and wars but sorrowes yield.
> (I.x.60).

The Hermit's pacifism contradicts both his own endorsement of knightly "victorie" in Cleopolis (I.x.60) and farther back, in I Proem 1, Spenser's epic proposition which flaunts among its ingredients "fierce warres." If Spenser can contradict himself within a few cantos or even stanzas, then when he contradicts Book I in Book VI, it is not necessarily because he has forgotten what he previously said. In Book II, Guyon has tentatively agreed with the Hermit's pacifism, conjecturing that God made indelible the bloodstains on the baby Ruddymane "To shew how sore bloude-guiltinesse he hat'th" (II.ii.4). Shocked by this imagistic correction and propositional contradiction of both the Hermit and Guyon, the rereader notices that, like any knight on duty, Calidore as a minister of retributive justice is in a sense a civil magistrate, an agent of public virtue, whether or not one classifies Calidore's ruling virtue, Courtesy, as public. Moreover, he speaks here in the accents of Artegall, with whom he has just been talking. We can now see that Calidore here, like Artegall in V.ix.49, represents not only public virtue but a voice out of the Old Testament as well. Most of the violence praised in the second half of the FQ meets Luther's criteria, criteria he sometimes uneasily affirms to be met in the Old Testament: it is executed by the state, even, in V.x.4, by a monarch, Mercilla; and it is executed on behalf of others, not oneself.

Spenser's code of public virtue is no "higher" or more divinely sanctioned than is his private, though it is not ironized either; these are not corrections from a higher viewpoint. To shift from private to public virtue is to shift from gospel idealism not only to Mosaic retributive justice but also to pragmatism, as the *correctio* about abandoning one's shield.

This shift, too, is a *correctio,* but only in the weak sense of another perspective: it is not so biblical and authoritative as Una's initial *correctio* of Despair's law by gospel or the poet-speaker's world-denying correction of the Goddess Nature. Artegall's and Calidore's corrective reinstatements of bloodshed for the sake of public virtue are adiaphoristic.

Spenser's reversal of the biblical order reflects the hermeneutical distinction widespread in exegesis, that between importance and simple chronological priority: Hugh of St. Victor recommended that the NT be studied before the OT,[52] and Protestants too would have seen the NT as more important. Spenser also had a biographical reason for ending with an endorsement of law. The FQ first rejects law (Mosaic) in favor of grace (on the first day of the Dragon-Fight), as does the New Testament, but then reinstates law (civil with overtones of Mosaic in Books V–VI.i and the *Vewe*). Just as Luther and Melanchthon initially rejected Mosaic law in favor of grace, then reaffirmed law in general (Mosaic law as an example of civil law) because they witnessed the overthrow of public order by the Anabaptists, so I propose that Spenser early in the FQ rejected Mosaic law in favor of grace, then reaffirmed law in general because he witnessed the lack of public order in Ireland. (His culture's distinction between divine and positive law and his own distinction in the *Vewe* between English Common Law and draconian martial law are not important here.) Equating the lawless with wolves as did Melanchthon, Spenser's persona Colin in CCCHA states that England's public order sets it above Ireland in his eyes:

> For there [in England] all happie peace and plenteous store
> Conspire in one to make contented blisse:
> No wailing there nor wretchednesse is heard,
> No bloodie issues nor no leprosies,
> No griesly famine, nor no raging sweard,
> No nightly bodrags, nor no hue and cries;
> The shepheards there abroad may safely lie,
> On hills and downes, withouten dread or daunger:
> No ravenous wolves the good mans hope destroy,
> Nor outlawes fell affray the forest raunger.
> (310–19, YSP)

To achieve it, as the *Vewe* shows and Talus allegorizes, Spenser like Luther contradicts himself and reluctantly acknowledges the necessity for blood-

---

52. *Didascalicon* VI.6, 145.

shed. (I say "reluctantly" because we are not intended to forget that the Hermit Contemplation inscribes Spenser's pacifistic side.)

Akin to practical virtue is the virtue of being human as opposed to sub-human. When supposedly normative characters in the latter half of the FQ contradict Christian charity, the reader may reconcile the two by distinguishing the practical virtue of being human from theoretical virtue. Arthur rebukes the pusillanimous Turpine, saying that it would be better, given that he has taken up a wrongful quarrel, to prosecute it forcefully and openly (VI.vi.34–35); Calepine's diagnosis of him is that he "had no courage, or else had no gall" (VI.iii.35–36), no impulse to revenge. Although the violence recommended by these heroes meets no theoretical standard—for example, it is not on behalf of others, as Luther required—they still prefer it to his pusillanimous behavior, which falls below even the natural behavior of the human male. Again, the reason for Spenser's retention of the retracted hymns of earthly love may be that their sentiments are human and natural. That the Bible's all-controlling divine author has some respect for merely human behavior even though it is sinful is perceived by TJ when they condone vengeful and petulant sentiments in the Psalms as "spoken from a purely human point of view."[53]

Irreconcilable Contradictions:
Free Will and Justification

Contradictions about free will and justification are many and often obvious in Books I and II of the FQ. Do we obtain heaven by God's indefectible, irresistible grace, which springs ultimately from his predestination, or do we obtain it by our own good works? If we do so by works—winning merit, avoiding serious sin, and repenting when we fail to do so—are they performed through grace or through our own free will? Spenser presents all these positions. We have seen that I.ix.53 contradicts both I.x.41 (substantively) and II.i.32 (apparently) in its explanation of how we get to heaven; and insofar as it is by works, we shall see that I.x.1 contradicts both I.vii.41 and II.i.33 on what part free will plays in performing those works. Contradictions about free will occur in Book I; hence the contradictions cannot be explained away by any supposed shift in viewpoint between books. First there is the famous I.x.1, espe-

---

53. On Psalms 35:22–23; 56:9; 73:20; 109:14; 110:1.

cially "If any strength we have, it is to ill, / But all the good is Gods, both power and eke will" (8–9). In other words, whatever strength or power to do good a human action may exhibit—and it sometimes does if we have "gained" a "spirituall . . . victory" (3,7)—it has been bestowed by a special infusion of God's grace before any act of the will. Such grace is called "prevenient." These theological insights were invented by Paul, codified by the later Augustine, and rediscovered by Luther and Calvin. Prevenient grace is presented in FQ I.x.1 in such a way as to insist on its irresistibility, for the passage explicitly denies to man any moral center from which he could accept it or refuse it. Here Spenser says that prevenient grace is the foundation for everything in the moral life.

The principal contradicting text—unmentioned by Schiavoni yet stressed, indeed, overstressed, by Robin Wells—is I.vii.41. Here Arthur says to Una, "he, that never would, / Could never: will to might gives greatest aid." We know that this is a religious debate, not just a psychological one, because Arthur brings in "faith"; thus there are enough similarities to justify comparing this text with I.x.1. According to Arthur, "might" (God's or one's own) can help one only if one first wills it (in psychiatric discourse, one must want to change). Here, the foundation for everything in the moral life is free will. The only kind of power and might that one could receive from God is that which cooperates with a preexisting good will. This "cooperating grace" is the opposite of prevenient grace.

Intellectual background may be found to support both the rightness of each statement and yet its contradiction of the other. Arthur here echoes the ever-popular yet very un-Augustinian Greek father Chrysostom, who never tired of repeating, "God draws no one who does not will." Chrysostom's statement was often quoted with approval by Melanchthon. The disagreement between Chrysostom and Augustine about free will indicates the contradictory nature of the topic, says Bernardino Ochino. If mankind becomes virtuous and/or gets to heaven by God's inscrutable predestination, then Chrysostom and many other reputable Greek theologians must be heretics; if mankind obtains these things by his free choice, then Augustine and all his countless followers must be heretics.[54] As for cooperating grace, Luther always and Calvin usually denied its existence. Spenser undoubtedly read or heard of Chrysostom's and Augustine's positions at one time or another. Therefore, he must have realized

---

54. *Labyrinthi*, 254, translated into Latin from a rare Italian original, perhaps by Ochino's friend Sebastian Castellio; hereafter cited in text. Although another work of Ochino's was available at Cambridge, this one was not. Queen Elizabeth, however, obviously owned one.

that I.vii.41 and I.x.1 were both authoritative and at least partially contradictory, must, indeed, have deliberately so constructed them.

Arthur's statement occurs in the middle of a stichomythic debate, albeit on a different subject, namely, whether Una should tell Arthur what is troubling her. I propose that Spenser presents this stichomythia, this chain of corrections, as a model of that which the reader should assemble on free will (relying, in our day of weak memories, on a concordance or a word search of an electronic text) from the poem's own, more widely separated dialogue on this subject. The reader then sees that they are not echoes of one another, not a consistent development, but a debate formally resembling this stichomythia.

Some critics such as Daniel Doerksen take their stand on I.x.1 and try to adapt everything else to it.[55] Such critics would have to relativize I.vii.41, to limit its applicability. They might dismiss Arthur's affirmation of free will as springing from his heroic ethos. But two other speakers also affirm it, albeit less categorically; they are as authoritative as is the speaker of I.x.1: and they come only a few stanzas after I.x.1—Fidelia's syllabus (I.x.19) and Caelia's declaration that Red Cross and Una have chosen the right (I.x.10). Much later, in VI.vi.7, comes an intensification of Arthur's position, and an even sharper contradiction of I.x.1. Here, a hermit instructs people who have been bitten by the Blatant Beast, "For in your selfe your onely helpe doth lie / To heale your selves, and must proceed alone / From your owne will, to cure your maladie." To be sure, this contradiction is ultimately reconcilable by the *distributio* between public and private: the malady in question is a public one, slander; and in the public sphere, even Luther affirmed that man has free will. This reconciliation could only result from some later reading of VI.vi.7, however, and thus does nothing to alter the fact that its phraseology directly contradicts the phraseology of I.x.1, thus momentarily and formally destabilizing it.

Three critics have tried to mitigate I.x.1. Hume's relativization of I.x.1, on the grounds that it refers to the unregenerate, fails to take account of the fact that the people in question have won a "victory" over "spiritual foes."[56] Gless's mitigation—"all the good" in the moral life is *ultimately* from God—broadens the definition of divine grace so far that it includes, say, the precepts of the law, and thus is morally meaningless (149). Finally, according to Wells, I.x.1's apparent lapse into Augustinianism is purely rhetorical; it can be accounted for by analogy with one of Eras-

---

55. Doerksen, "'All the Good is Gods,'" 14–17.
56. Hume, *Edmund Spenser*, 68–69.

mus' habitual shifts from doctrinal to moral discourse (like the shift Erasmus projects onto 1 Cor. 15:10, cited earlier). Imposing his characteristic synergism upon predestinarian prooftexts, Erasmus says, "Our will is not inactive, even if man can reach the goal of his striving only with the final assistance of grace. But since it is a minimum which we contribute, the entire affair is attributed to God." Wells rightly comments, "Erasmus is not contradicting himself here and denying the goodness of human nature; he is merely arguing the need for a proper sense of humility." [57] But Spenser is arguing more than that in I.x.1. As Schiavoni objects, this analogue, while it might explain in what sense "All the good is Gods," fails to mitigate I.x.1.8; "If any strength we have, it is to ill," which does deny the goodness of human nature. [58] Perhaps for this reason, in 1982, in a book on another topic, Wells wearily decides "to accept [I.x.1] for the anomaly that it is," [59] dramatizing the growing consensus that the contradiction is both present and irreconcilable.

In his "Predestination and Free Will: The Crux of Canto Ten," Schiavoni not only admits but actually proclaims Spenser's presentation of free will to be contradictory. He proposes that Saint Augustine is the true source. At the same time, though, he claims that Augustine provides a way to reconcile free will and predestination. Schiavoni fails to deal with I.vii.41, a passage on which I focus, but he engages II.i.33, which, as we shall see, sends almost as voluntaristic a message. After incisively laying out those contradictions that fall within the tenth canto of Book I, he shows that all of Spenser's words on the will and on justification find an echo somewhere in the utterances of Augustine. He then tries to smooth down the contradictions in Augustine's thought to the level of paradoxes. He is able to do this, however, only by ignoring the fact that these positions were taken in different treatises at different points in Augustine's long career; that the later statements are not simultaneous paradoxes but revise and supersede earlier ones, sometimes explicitly. In the *Retractations,* Augustine enters into dialogue with his past selves, correcting them according to what he thinks now, or else reinterpreting their words so that they seem to have been saying that all along. [60] On the subject of free

57. Wells, "Christian Knight," 365, quoting *De libero arbitrio* from *Luther and Erasmus,* 85; see also 355, 358–59, 364.

58. Schiavoni, "Predestination," 181.

59. Wells, *Cult,* 45.

60. True, the word "retractation" in Augustine's title may not necessarily mean a revocation, for it can be taken in the weak sense of "revision" (see Lewis and Short s.v. "retractatio") and even of "a catalogue of one's works" (see Phillippy, *Love's Remedies,* 57–58); Peter Brown allows for both meanings in Augustine's *Retractations* (*Augustine,* 429–30).

will, he admits that he has at least been seen by others to contradict himself, to such an extent that his affirmations of free will in the early *De libero arbitrio* have been quoted against his own later anti-Pelagian tracts, such as the *Contra Julianum*.[61] Schiavoni is right that Augustine's final, anti-Pelagian position (for example, in the *Contra Julianum*) coincides exactly with I.x.1; his early position on the subject of free will in the Cassiciacum dialogues, however, resembles more the position of Arthur in I.vii.41 and of the perfected Red Cross in II.i.33. Whereas Augustine progresses linearly from reliance on free will to reliance on grace, as if he had changed his mind once and for all, Spenser vacillates. Consequently, this analogue, while helping to establish the reality of Spenser's self-contradictions, does not reconcile them so much as is claimed.

However self-contradictory Augustine may be, Schiavoni admits that even the saint did not assemble the paradoxes and set them in relief to the same degree as did Spenser, thus unwillingly confirming their irreconcilability. I agree with him that "[b]y asserting both human responsibility and divine sovereignty, Spenser insists on the mystery of the salvific process" (190). Schiavoni has taught us a great deal, but he backpedals and cobbles together a synthesis which I find unconvincing (191). More important, like Wells, he finally concedes that Spenser's treatment of free will and predestination is more contradictory than that of his source. These concessions are borne out by my own source-hunting: during various lengthy stints up to the present in the course of my thirty-odd years as a Spenser scholar, I have tried in vain to reconcile or trace to a single theologian all of Spenser's varied statements on free will and justification. More of them can be traced to Melanchthon than to Calvin or Luther, but not every single one. Although it is not an either/or question, it is more reasonable to suppose that the contradictory Bible is the single common source from which both Spenser—product of a culture whose motto is *sola scriptura*—and theologians such as Augustine derive their contradictions.

Analogues to all Spenser's contradictory statements about the will can be found in one place or another in the Bible. On one occasion, Philippians 2:12b–13, Paul even pulls the widely separated poles of this contradiction together in a paradox (Gless, 148): "Worcke out youre owne salvacyon with feare and tremblinge. (13) For it is God, whiche worketh in you, both the will and also the dede, even of good wyl." (I quote here from the Great Bible, essentially echoed by the Coverdale, the Vulgate, and the Rheims, because the Calvinistic Geneva translators mitigate the

---

61. *Retractations* I.8, cited by Brown, *Augustine,* 430.

human side of the paradox and shrink from the Pelagian agency in "work out," employing the less active verb "make an end of.") Spenser alludes to Philippians 2:12b–13 in I.x.1; but echoes explicitly only the Calvinistic verse 13.[62] By echoing only the God-centered part of the paradox, Spenser signals to the biblically trained reader that his apparently authoritative statement is too extreme. In other places (such as I.vii.41.6–9 and I.x.47.9), Spenser refers to salvation as the product of man's effort and thus in effect supplies the missing verse 12b. Thus he pries apart the paradox, giving it at least the appearance of a contradiction.

The Bible, too, generally presents the two poles of Philippians 2:12b–13 in separate passages that go all the way in one direction or the other. Romans 9 is the chief prooftext for predestination. There, God is responsible not only for "all the good" but also for damnation: "As it is written, I have loved Jacob, and have hated Esau. . . . So then it is not in him that willeth, nor in him that runneth, but in God that sheweth mercy. . . . Therefore hee hath mercy on whome he will, and whom he will, he hardeneth" (9:13, 16, and 18). It was Romans 9:13, Augustine admits in his *Retractations,* that compelled him to abandon his former defense of free will, thus belatedly correcting his early work.[63] Thus the Bible is the ultimate and extreme model of a single self-contestatory text for Spenser.

In Spenser's time, the Protestant Bible was more contestatory of Paul's predestinarianism and emphasis on grace because it still contained the deuterocanonical books, and so did the lectionary. For example, as previously noted, Ecclesiasticus is very works-righteous, placing the burden of salvation entirely upon man. Chapter 15 mounts the most categorical affirmation of free will and denial of predestination unto damnation to be found in all of Scripture:

11   Say not thou, It is through the Lord that I turne backe: for thou oughtest not to do the things that he hateth.
12   Say not thou, He hath caused me to erre: for he hath no neede of the sinnefull man. . . .
14   He made man from the beginning, and left him in the hande of his counsell, and gave him his commandements and precepts.
15   If thou wilt, thou shalt observe the comma[n]dements, and testify thy god [*sic*] will.

62. See Hamilton ad loc.; Schiavoni, "Predestination," 179–80 and 191; cf. Gless, *Interpretation,* 148–49.
63. *Retractations* II.27, quoted by Brown, *Augustine,* 154.

16   He hath set water and fire before thee: stretch out thine hand unto which thou wilt.

17   Before man is life and death, good and evil, what him liketh shall be given him. . . .

20   He hath commanded no man to doe ungodly, neither hath he given any man licence to sinne. . . .(15:11–20)

Erasmus seized upon this voluntaristic passage as a powerful defense of free will against Luther. The Geneva Bible passes over it without a gloss, while the "Protestant Vulgate" contains but one gloss, and it hastens to limit the applicability of the freedom in verse 15 (numbered 16 in this version) to Adam before the fall, glossing "Before man" ("coram homini-bus") as follows: "that is, before the human race in Adam."[64] Melanch-thon's interpretation is equally strained: either this freedom pertains only to man's external morality (a freedom agreed on by all parties) or, if it per-tains to salvation, the assistance of divine grace is tacitly presupposed.[65] The medieval and Romanist commentators gladly take the passage at face value, as applying to anyone, and even make it the touchstone of other scriptures; they adduce as a cross-reference to verse 15 Matthew 16:17, "If thou wilt enter into life, keep the commandments."

Unlike the tendentious Protestant synthesizers, at least three six-teenth-century exegetes stated or implied that on the subject of free will, the Bible contradicts itself. Erasmus in his *Diatribe on Free Will*, while grounding himself on Ecclesiasticus 15:11–20, does not sweep Romans 9 under the rug. I apply Erasmus to Spenser, not, as Wells does, in order to reconcile contradictions, but rather to confirm their existence and their biblical origin. At the very beginning of his *Diatribe*, Erasmus says, "Among the many difficulties encountered in Holy Scripture—and there are many of them—none presents a more perplexed labyrinth than the problem of the freedom of the will." And at the end he confesses his tendentiousness: "It is a fact that Holy Scripture is in most instances ei-ther obscure and figurative, or seems, at first sight, to contradict itself. Therefore, whether we like it or not, we sometimes had to recede from the literal meaning, and had to adjust its meaning to an interpretation." These introductory and final admissions amount to an admission that contradictions on the subject of free will are a feature of biblical herme-neutics and thus of biblical poetics. Indeed, Luther himself admitted to

64. So also Calvin, *Institutes*, II.v.18.
65. *Loci*, Article V, 65.

his inner circle (in his lectures on Deuteronomy at his house, 1523–24) that the Bible seems to contradict itself about free will versus grace:

> Moses recites variously in one place and in another, and so do almost all of the prophets . . . as, for example, about grace and free will: in Romans 2[10] "glory and peace to him who does good works" and 3[20] "for by the works of the law no person alive is justified." Likewise Zachariah 1 [3,4] "Turn ye unto me" and "Turn us, o God of our salvation" [Ps. 85:4] seem to conflict.[66]

As for resolutions, both Erasmus' rhetorical explanation quoted by Wells and Melanchthon's and Junius' mitigations of Ecclesiasticus 15:15 quoted above are fairly typical of their shared hermeneutical tradition: in a version of the hermeneutic circle, they first decide which pole represents the *scopus* or overall point of the Bible as a whole and then tendentiously adapt the other pole to it.[67] This hermeneutical maneuver is applied by some critics to Spenser's contradictions; but as we see in the case of Erasmus versus Junius and Melanchthon, though it may produce internal logical consistency, it is no guarantee of consensus, for Erasmus in the quotation by Wells explains away a grace-centered passage and Junius and Melanchthon as quoted above explain away a voluntaristic passage so that doctrinally they disagree with one another.

This debate between Erasmus and Luther over free will and predestination was known in England and fairly well represented at Cambridge,* where it must have functioned, up to my terminus ad quem of 1590, as the classic statement of the problem. Erasmus' works in general were immensely popular at Cambridge; Luther, while less popular, was in a good position here in that his hard predestinarian line concided with that of Calvin, whose thought dominated the English religious scene.[68] Although Englishmen had written on the subject (see the index to the Parker Society volumes), English intellectual leaders had not yet contributed their major debates—the Lambeth Articles, Hooker's *Laws,* and the controversies they generated. Hooker's "Sermon of Justification"

---

66. Erasmus, *Erasmus-Luther,* quotation 93–94; see also 3; 79. Luther, Weimar ed., 14, 550, *Comm. Deuteronomy* on 1:11.

67. Eden says that Melanchthon considered the predestinarian Epistle to the Romans to represent the *scopus* of the entire Bible; see *Hermeneutics,* n. 10, 85, and 81–86; this explains why he plays fast and loose with the voluntaristic Ecclesiasticus 15. For Erasmus' similar accommodation of everything to his own presumed and very different *voluntas scripti,* see *Hermeneutics,* 1–3, 8–13.

68. See Wallace, *Puritans,* 27–28.

preached at the Temple, along with his consequent exchange with Travers in 1585–86 attests to continued interest in the subject in the 1580s; but it had a small audience because it had not yet appeared in print.

Two theological precedents exist for Spenser's practice (according to Schiavoni, Wells, and me) of leaving contradictions about free will unreconciled within a single work: a letter by Melanchthon and Ochino's *Labyrinthi*. On certain occasions (not including Ecclesiasticus 15), Melanchthon was a splitter. He once gave a destabilizing account of free will and predestintion. He wrote to Calvin that a worthy man named Stadtianus said he could prove the existence of either free will or predestination and yet could not reconcile them. Melanchthon warns against disputes and affirms that some things are contingent, for example, that God helps those who are making an effort (a voluntarist doctrine echoed by Arthur in I.vii.41).[69] Melanchthon cannot resolve the contradictions presented by predestination but feels safe so long as he is quoting the Word of God. Melanchthon thus sacrifices consistency to the Bible's inconsistency. In his mature work, Melanchthon criticizes predestination, the corollary of I.x.1.8–9 voiced in I.ix.53; he also criticizes free will as affirmed in I.vii.41 and VI.vi.7. Because the Bible voices contrary opinions on this topic, Melanchthon put no article concerning predestination or God's foreknowledge into his creed, the Augsburg Confession of 1530.[70] Nor did the other original Protestant creeds contain such articles, presumably for the same reason, until the contentious 1560s.[71] Melanchthon thus functioned as a model for the self-contestatory way in which Spenser presents these topics.

External evidence, too, indicates that Melanchthon is a likely source and model. He was dear to two of Spenser's immediate audiences: Queen Elizabeth and, for varying reasons, the Cambridge students and faculty. Queen Elizabeth was—and still is—sometimes called a Lutheran; so were her mother, Anne Boleyn, Bishop Cheney, and a few others. Under her tutor Roger Ascham, "Queen Elizabeth I memorized large portions of the *Loci*," Clyde Manschreck notes in his preface to *Loci Communes,* and in 1559, she directed scholars to read Melanchthon "to induce them to all godliness." It was from Melanchthon, Carl S. Meyer tells us, that

69. Letter 2712 of May 11, 1543, in *Melanthonis* [sic] *opera,* CR 5, col. 109. Besides two *Opera,* one separately printed copy of Melanchthon's *Epistolae* was at Cambridge*.

70. "Catechesis Puerilis," 1532, in *Melanthonis opera,* CR 23, 179, translation mine, available at Cambridge*. See also CR 15, 678ff., in *Loci,* Preface, xii–xiv; and Intro. by Hans Engellond, xli.

71. Not even the Geneva Confession of Calvin himself, 1536; see Porter, *Reformation,* 338.

she imbibed adiaphorism.[72] Before Elizabeth's reign, as Manschreck writes, "Through Thomas Cranmer [and the Thirty-nine Articles, in which he had the controlling hand] Melanchthon's thought became current in England." At Cambridge, even though many there were strong Calvinists, *Loci Communes* was required reading. Six pages of BCI are devoted to all his works (not counting Carion's Chronicle), as compared to seven and one half of Calvin and three of Luther. Through his sacralization of the state as an avatar of Mosaic law, Manschreck continues, Melanchthon fathered the related notions of a state-supported church and of *cuius regio eius religio*. These notions in turn fed into Spenser's final rejection of pacifism (see above) in the FQ. The name of Melanchthon was unpopular, however, in England at large, for reasons good and bad, which included his reticence about predestination.[73] Thus, Spenser's similarities to Melanchthon represent a reaction against the Calvinist hegemony and an inscription of Spenser's personal convictions, those of his university community, and those of his patroness.

In the mid-sixteenth century came the most extreme splitter of all, a theologian who wrote a work that deliberately vacillated on free will in imitation of a Scripture which on this topic was contradictory. Bernardino Ochino (1487–1564), after strongly affirming double predestination in Geneva in some sermons which were published in England in 1550, changed his mind[74] and devoted a treatise, the *Labyrinthi,* to the irreconcilability of free will and predestination. From the point of view of reason, either leads to logical impasses. From the point of view of Scripture, either meets with contradictory prooftexts. From the point of view of moral results, either leads to a vice; for example, "He who believes that he is not free falls into the pit of moral sloth, but he who believes he is free falls into presumption." Although Ochino does not explicitly accuse Scripture of contradicting itself, choosing rather to stress its silences, after a long and frank discussion of Romans 9, he cries, "This labyrinth is inextricable."[75] The book proceeds by a recursive dialectic which Roland Bainton summarizes as follows: "Ochino set forth four dilemmas involved in predestination and four on free will, and then extricated him-

---

72. Meyer, *Elizabeth I,* 7; on her general Lutheranism, see 5–7, 11–12. For further information and some caveats, see Clebsch, "Elizabethans," 104–17.

73. Manschreck, Intro., *Loci,* xx and n. 99, citing T. W. Baldwin, *William Shakspere's Small Latine and Lesse Greeke* (Urbana, Ill., 1944), 1:259; and xxi and n. 106, citing Baldwin, 1:276.

74. See Wallace, *Puritans,* 16 and 203, n. 82, citing *Certayne Sermons of the ryghte famous and excellent Clerk Master Bernardine Ochine* (London, 1550), Sigs. F 7, F 8, G 6r, H 3v, K 6v–K 7r–v, L 6v, L 7, M 1r.

75. *Labyrinthi,* 97, hereafter cited in text.

self from the first four and then from the second four, and ended just where he began."[76] *Labyrinthi* is a self-consuming artifact, an exercise proving that it is impossible to form an opinion, and thus that neither view could possibly be essential to salvation.

Despite the difference in genre, Ochino's series of dialectical reversals is a more pointed version of that stichomythia which Spenser's reader would assemble if she collected his statements about free will and justification. Ochino's purpose was to unsettle the dogmatists and to recommend a complex moral and hermeneutical stance. He was obviously attacking the dogmatism of the Calvinist view of predestination, as Calvinists perceived;[77] at the same time, he was also attacking that Romanist dogmatism exemplified in Trent's anathema against anyone who denied free will (quoted in Schiavoni, 180).

To mitigate his complete theoretical impasse, Ochino adds a final chapter (XIX) of practical advice. He recommends a species of skeptical fideism:

> In order to avoid either of these evils [moral sloth fostered by predestination and presumption fostered by free will] the safe way is by wavering in opinion: that we on the one hand strive for the good with all our might just as if we knew ourselves to be free, lest we fall into inactivity, and on the other hand give God alone the honor and glory as if we knew that we aren't free. (253)

Of his various labels for this complex moral and hermeneutical stance, "wavering in opinion" (*dubitandum*) possibly alludes by anticipation to the pamphlet *De arte dubitandi,* to be composed in 1563 by Sebastian Castellio, his friend and the probable translator into Latin of the *Labyrinthi.* (Castellio's influence on Spenser will be assessed in a study that does not require its sources to be popular.) Ochino also calls it *docta ignorantia* (245), alluding to Nicolas of Cusa. By concluding with this, Ochino reveals his concern about the moral consequences of his positions.

Spenser's diametrically opposite stance(s) on predestination in I.ix.53 versus I.x.41 are as self-contestatory as Ochino's; so are the contradictions of the grace-centered I.x.1 by I.vii.41; by "choose" in I.x.10; by I.x.19; by the Hermit's voluntaristic counsel in VI.vi.7; and by II.i.33, to be examined below. While Spenser does not voice Ochino's *docta ignorantia* in

---

76. R. Bainton, *Travail,* 149–76, esp. 168; see also his book-length biography in Italian, *Bernardino Ochino,* 120–23, 165.

77. McNair, "Ochino's Apology," 362.

the FQ, in two places he dramatizes the moral results of his two positions. The hazard of believing that one is free, presumption on one's own moral strength, is a vice which the untested Red Cross exemplifies when he cries, "Vertue gives her selfe light, through darkenesse for to wade" (I.i.12), a vice of which Orgoglio is an allegory.[78] Then Una corrects Red Cross's voluntarism and urges him to the opposite extreme, the predestinarian pole of Ochino's double truth, in I.ix.53, "Why shouldst thou then despeire that chosen art?" and I.x.1 elaborates on it. The vice that (according to Ochino) results from positive predestinarianism, moral sloth, is allegorized in Book II by the Idle Lake and its inhabitant Phaedria (II.vi). That the sloth is not only physical but moral as well is shown by the lake's refusal to "quench" (as it had quenched the wrath of Cymochles, and as the Well of Life had quenched the "inward fire" of Red Cross, I.xi.28) the "inly flaming side"—in other words, the smoldering wrath—of Pyrochles (II.vi.44). To Pyrochles' complaint about his inability to control his wrath, Archimago responds in the spirit of the place by giving him a sword and leading him to a victim (II.vi.48–51; viii.10–12, 30). This cure is not physically slothful, but it gives wrath an outlet in accordance with moral sloth.

Spenser draws no explicit connection between this moral sloth and the predestinarianism of I.ix.53 or I.x.1; but he may have implied it, for a connection between moral sloth and dependence upon grace is contained in the Epistle to the Romans, near a passage to which Spenser alludes elsewhere: "where sinne abounded, there grace abounded much more: . . . What shall we say then? Shal wee continue stil in sinne, that grace may abound?" (Rom. 5:20–6:1). By portraying both presumption and moral sloth and tracing presumption to unmitigated voluntarism, Spenser seems to judge beliefs by their consequences and to transmit Ochino's warning against either/or thinking on these matters. This moral pragmatism reminds us of the political pragmatism which led Luther to reverse himself about law.

But was Labyrinthi well enough attested in England that Spenser could have known it, or at least known of it? In the first place, his patroness Queen Elizabeth could have substituted for Ochino. Elizabeth was a problematizer of predestination in her own right. Her speech of 1585 to Parliament reveals skepticism about predestination and enjoins that skepticism on others: "I see many ever bold with God Almighty, making too many subtle scannings of the blessed will as lawyers do with human tes-

78. See Torczon, "Spenser's Orgoglio," 123–28.

taments. The presumption is so great as I may not suffer it nor tolerate new-fangleness."[79]

Moreover, Elizabeth's skeptical pragmatism concerning predestination and free will could have been created and must in any case have been confirmed both by conversation with Ochino and by perusing his book's recursive dialectics. *Labyrinthi* is dedicated to her. Ochino was personally acquainted with her, and around 1551 she had frequently explored with him the problematics of free will and predestination.[80] This occurred in the period from 1547 to 1553, while Ochino was prebend of Canterbury; but in 1554 he was forced by the Marian persecutions to move to the Continent. It is perhaps a sign of Ochino's influence on her that, as Bainton recounts without documentation, Elizabeth opined sagely that grace can be resisted when it is not irresistible (*Travail*, 168). The concept of irresistible grace which she is satirizing here is an extreme version of the prevenient grace described by Spenser in I.x.1. Spenser would have known that Ochino was the queen's sometime religious mentor from the memories at court of an earlier event: in 1560 her advisers (Archbishop Parker among them) asked someone to enlist Ochino, who had remained on the Continent, to talk her out of a popish devotional practice.[81] Therefore Elizabeth was in a position to introduce Spenser to *Labyrinthi*, whether directly or indirectly.

As for Ochino's intrinsic appeal and reputation, his name, though not this work, was familiar because his other works continued to be published both in England and on the Continent, in Latin (one work in BCI), in Italian, and in English translation (this last consisting of sermon collections and a drama satirizing the pope). This evidence compensates for the paucity of evidence in Adams and James. It would seem that *Labyrinthi* educated or confirmed Spenser, either directly or through Elizabeth, in skeptical pragmatism about these issues and in dialogic presentation of them. Even Milton was to present at least one (to him) insoluble problem in this dialogic manner—the Ptolemaic versus the Copernican paradigm of the movement of the heavenly bodies.[82] Thus, Spenser's problematization of free will and predestination was probably influenced by his skeptical queen and by a theologian who was favored by her and her prelates.

79. D'Ewes, *Journal*, 328, quoted in Chamberlin, *Sayings of Queen Elizabeth*, 99.

80. Ochino, Preface to *Labyrinthi;* see also Bainton, *Travail*, 162.

81. Bainton, *Travail*, 162; on this and his general fame in England, see Bainton, *Bernardino Ochino*, 90–94.

82. See Mollenkott, "Milton's Technique," 101–11.

To this problem of "adjusting intrinsic to extrinsic causes . . . of salvation,"[83] no discursive resolution is given in Book I. The closest we get to
a resolution there is equivocations and the Melanchthonian compromise
that serious sinning can destroy one's divinely established communion
with God and hence preclude one's salvation. The antecedent of "his" in
I.xi.55, for example, remains mysterious. Therefore I agree with Schiavoni
and Gless, who say, when they are in their deconstructive modes, that in
Book I we should leave the contradiction unresolved. This might seem
an anachronistic imposition of twentieth-century indeterminacy on an
age of faith, were it not for the fact that contradictions, especially on this
topic, were sometimes perceived as a characteristic of the Bible, the book
of books, so that any biblical imitation would be likely to incorporate
some of them.

In all probability, Spenser had the same motive for problematizing free
will and predestination—and for treating justification by works in a similar way—as did Ochino. That is to say, amid the aporias inherent in these
topics and the complexities of experience, disagreement of authorities,
and tensions of ecclesiastical politics, he could not make up his mind. As
is not uncommon with people in this frame of mind, he wanted to unsettle those who had; and in order to do so, he adopted a stance like that
of philosophical skeptics who treated dialogue as an end in itself. More
remains to be said about this motive, but first I must note that Spenser
also had a more immediate and constructive purpose for adopting a self-
contestatory poetics in Book I.

In Book II, Spenser gives this contradiction an educative sequel when
he rounds it off with a compromise: "His be the praise that this atchiev'-
ment wrought, / Who made my hand the organ of his might; / More
then good will to me attribute nought" (II.i.33). Red Cross here affirms
that his will, his very own will, cooperated with grace. All critics agree
that this compromise is authoritative because it comes at or near the end
of a debate and because it is inclusive and judiciously qualified. Referring
only to the speaker, the perfected Red Cross, it does not totalize as does
Arthur in I.vii.41, and it does specify, as Arthur does not, that the "might"
comes from God. This gives it enough authority to count as a correction,
albeit not a palinodic one.

Red Cross's compromise position here is in modern theological terms
a kind of "synergism"—a doctrine which states that by exercising his
will in some way, man cooperates with God in his salvation. It also carries practical authority in fostering moral effort: continence is unthink-

83. Gless's phrase in *Interpretation*, n. 66, 250.

able without the will, and Book II celebrates not only temperance but also continence. Synergism was later embraced by Anglicans, but before Hooker, under the Calvinist hegemony, it was rejected and associated with the Pelagian heresy, with Romanism, with Greek Orthodoxy, or with the suspect Melanchthon.[84] Red Cross here supplies the discursive information necessary to sort out the ambiguous antecedent of the pronoun "his"; in a satisfying *distributio,* he retroactively itemizes what the ambiguity in I.xi.55 mystified.[85] Thus, not only is the indeterminate poetics of Book I Melanchthonian, but so are the compromises in both I and II as well: works prevent loss of salvation; works earn rewards in heaven; and they are performed by the will cooperating with grace.

The compromise is not an intellectual resolution—for to say that the will is all man's ("to me attribute") still contradicts I.x.1.8–9. This compromise is more voluntaristic and synergistic than Augustine's, echoed by Aquinas, that grace can cooperate with any will that has previously been moved by prevenient grace.[86] In Book I, Spenser unsettles the reader not just to prevent dogmatism on this topic but to engage her in the dialectical process of reaching the compromise, and to make her appreciate it when it comes. Spenser's delaying the compromise until Book II is a bit like postponing the answer to a study question to the back of a textbook.

Although Spenser's contradictions enable a hasty, superficial reader to find what she wishes in the text, and thus manifest complaisance, when they are understood by the cognoscenti, they manifest religio-political courage. In affirming the cooperation of free will with grace as he does in II.i.33, in saying with Melanchthon that God helps those who are making an effort, Spenser risked being stigmatized by his countrymen as a papist or a semi-Pelagian "Lutheran." In denying by his self-contradictions that any judgment on these topics can be definitive, Spenser (along with his patron the queen, and his probable sources Erasmus, Melanchthon, and Ochino) was resisting the hermeneutics of all the major confessions of Europe at the time. In the last third of the sixteenth century, each confession claimed to derive from Scripture its own consistent doctrine about these topics, demanded doctrinaire allegiance, and demonized the opposition. Western Christendom cast to the winds the caution of Erasmus and Melanchthon; none of the major confessions was able to see or willing to acknowledge that God has sent contradictory signals concerning so

84. Mackenzie, "Synergism."

85. Roche sorts out the ambiguous meanings of the phrase by ascribing God's might to the allegorical sense and man's might to the moral sense; see "Typology," 12.

86. Aquinas, ST I–IIae q. 111, Art. 2, citing Augustine, *De gratia et libero arbitrio* XVII (PL 44, 901).

important a matter. Spenser and Elizabeth were voting either with some of the earliest reformers such as Erasmus and Melanchthon, or with the skeptics such as Montaigne, or with radical reformers such as Sebastian Franck, or with all of the above. Spenser was also ahead of his time, for his biblically vacillating treatment is in harmony with what his classmate Lancelot Andrewes was to announce in the seventeenth century as Anglican policy: "nil temere definimus." Spenser's theological and hermeneutic avant-gardism is the reason why Spenserians have thought they could interpret him in the light of later thinkers, but in so doing they have ignored the Calvinist consensus reigning in his own time and obscured his loneliness, courage, and originality.

In this chapter the discussion has moved from less to more unsettling contradictions. I have argued that when Spenser contradicts himself on such topics as female independence, sexual love, death, change, the body, art, and violence, he is imitating the Bible thematically and/or formally—the Bible as seen by Protestant or proto-Protestant splitters. The presence of the adjacent contradictions witnesses that the far-flung too are intentional; if so, the far-flung are the most demonstrably biblical. The Bible's miscellaneous contradictions were reconciled by explaining one term either as an equivocation; or as a correction, be it palinodic, adiaphoristic, supplementary, or merely new, a turning point in history; or as a mere shift of perspective, perhaps to the merely human, perhaps to pragmatism. Resolutions offered by exegetes to biblical contradictions formed an arsenal of reconciliations from which Spenser prompts his reader to draw resolutions for his own contradictions, biblical and non-biblical—resolutions such as looking ahead to later supplementation and distinguishing between private and public, theoretical and practical virtue.

In regard to free will and justification, Spenser contradicts himself irreconcilably, and so does the Bible, as was recognized by Queen Elizabeth, Erasmus, Melanchthon, and Ochino. The Bible's indecision doubtless encouraged Spenser to express his own indecision. It may also form part of his announced educational project. Such indeterminacy impels the docile reader first to one attitude, then to its opposite; it fashions not a gentleman or noble person but an intellectual or indecisive person. Of what use is he? At least he does no harm. People were disowning, defrocking, excommunicating, and killing one another over free will and justification. Spenser may be making the same relativistic, irenic point about all these religious topics as did some of the exegetical splitters—that if they are so doubtfully revealed in what is for Protestants the sole guide to salvation, salvation cannot depend upon doctrinal precision about them, and therefore we must agree to disagree. If so, in this contradictory presentation, Spenser takes one step toward religious toleration. However that may be, in the course of tracing all these contradictions back to biblical models, I have discovered more complexity than has hitherto been perceived not just in the doctrinal climate but in the habits of reading in sixteenth-century England.

THE EPISODE OF THE NYMPH'S WELL:

CORRECTIVE IMAGES,

PARADOXES OF LAW, AND TAPINOSIS

In this final chapter, to obviate the distortion attendant upon quoting in isolation, let us focus on a single episode. Intersecting in the episode of the Nymph's Well are many strategies of biblical poetics: recurrences of images previously discussed (wells and other bodies of water, cups, armor, and washing blood off guilty hands); typology, both Edenic and Messianic; paradoxes of law; corrections and the resulting distinctions; and one uniquely biblical but not previously discussed, tapinosis. I will concentrate on the last three.

Guyon and the Palmer come upon the infant Ruddymane and his parents, the dying Amavia and the recently dead Mordant (in 1590, it was spelled Mortdant in II.i.49), beside a sylvan well or spring. Ruddymane sits in Amavia's lap, playing in the blood from her self-inflicted wound. She accuses fortune and the heavens of injustice, commends her child to fortune, and bids him live and testify by his bloody hands that she died guiltless of any crime. When she was pregnant with this child, she informs Guyon, her good and beloved husband left on a knightly quest, in the course of which he was drugged by Acrasia and seduced into an adulterous liaison. Taking the guise of a palmer, and undergoing en route a painful childbirth in a wood, Amavia tracked Mordant down. Finding that he had ceased to reason, she reformed him and implemented their departure. Just at this auspicious point, Acrasia "deceived" Mordant into one more sin—drinking, presumably for old time's sake, a stirrup cup of wine which she had secretly charmed with a delayed-action poison designed to activate "So soone as Bacchus with the Nymphe does lincke" (II.i.55). On their trip home, when Mordant happened on the Nymph's Well and drank its pure water, it catalyzed instead of tempering the wine within him and killed him. In despair, Amavia stabbed herself. Having told her story, Amavia expires. Guyon and the Palmer reflect sadly on this overthrow of reason by passion, bury the couple despite their crime or crimes, and vow vengeance upon Acrasia; here the first canto and the first half of the episode ends.

In Canto ii, Guyon tries unsuccessfully to wash Ruddymane's "guiltie" hands in the Nymph's Well. His explanations of why he cannot are "corrected" by the Palmer: the indelibility arises from no fault either in the well (whose feminine shape and soil- and wine-resistant property originated in its Nymph's resistance to the lustful Faunus) or, surprisingly, in the blood, valuable as a "sacred Symbole" (II.ii.10) of vengeance and of Amavia's innocence and chastity. Satisfied, Guyon gives Ruddymane to the Palmer and takes up Mordant's bloody armor and they depart. I will treat the following somewhat overlapping sections and aspects in the order in which they occur: Canto i, Mordant, Amavia, the cup, and the well; Canto ii, Guyon's indecisions and the Palmer's corrections of him both for these and for his legitimate distress about the bloodstain; and the biblical rationale behind the Palmer's somewhat arbitrary celebrations of both the bloodstain and the well.

More Paradoxes: Mordant, Amavia, the Cup, and the Well (II.i.35–61)

It is paradoxical that the wife, by reforming and reclaiming her husband, should allow and in a way cause his seemingly small but in fact fatal return to his mistress; and, furthermore, that a good well such as the Palmer later declares this one to be (II.ii.5–10) should kill someone for a trivial and indeliberate sin while he is reforming. In the second half of the episode come two final paradoxes: that this water will not wash blood off flesh, and that both this fact and the bloodstain can be interpreted positively. The tragedy of passion which is shaped by the first two paradoxes is open to a religious interpretation, because the blood on Ruddymane which is the focus of the second half is clearly theological and almost universally agreed to symbolize original sin or some aspect thereof.[1] This

---

1. Hamilton, "Theological Reading," 155–62; Fowler, "Image," 144. Lewis H. Miller ("Secular Reading," 300–302) once dissented, grounding himself on the Palmer's apparent dissent; but on this episode he seems not to have gained a following. Harold Weatherby's interpretation is theological but revisionary; he interprets Spenser in general, and this episode among others, as inscribing some Greek Orthodox convictions which free Spenser from Augustine's unpalatable doctrine of original sin: Ruddymane's stain represents not Augustinian

legacy from a man who ingested something proffered by a woman in a garden renders Mordant a type of Adam and Acrasia a type of the tempting Eve.[2]

The first two paradoxes are found also in Romans 7, and they are manifested in the behavior of law. In Amavia's flashback, four forces impinge upon Mordant: in chronological order, Acrasia, Amavia, the cup, and the well. There are also four forces or "laws" impinging on Paul in Romans 7. My first interpretive task here will be to prove that they are the same four. Fowler has made a beginning; but he skewed his interpretion of the well by mingling the theme of baptism into Romans 7, where the subject is Mosaic law and baptism is conspicuous by its absence.[3] Both the well and law behave paradoxically.

The fact that Mordant in the first phase of his adultery "knew not . . . his own ill" (II.i.54) parallels verbatim Augustine's paraphrase of the first condition of Paul in Romans 7:8, where "without the Law, sinne is dead": namely, he was *nescius malorum suorum*.[4] In this condition Amavia finds Mordant and "through wise handling and faire governance" recures him "to a better will, / Purged from drugs of foule intemperance" (II.i.54) and arranges for their escape. The first paradox—that just at this auspicious point Acrasia inveigles Mordant into one more sin, and does so precisely because he has reformed (II.i.55)—corresponds to Paul's first paradox, that the law increases sin: "For I once was alive, without the law: but when the commandement came, sinne revived, But I died. . . . For sinne tooke occasion by the commandement, and deceived me" (Rom. 7:9–11). (These are the verses, it will be recalled, which supplied the allegorical explanation for the armor's augmenting Red Cross's inward fire of concupiscence.) Mordant's peculiarly passive acceptance of it "With cup thus charmd, him parting she deceiv'd" (II.i.55), dramatizes the involuntary operation of concupiscence ("the evil, which I would not, that do I," 7:19), an operation perceptible only when one is trying to be good.

---

guilt but corruption and death—an interpretation inscribed in the "secret filth" and "great contagion" of II.ii.4.6–9. When the babe is called "innocent / Of that was doen" (II.ii.1), Weatherby reads it in the strong sense in which the non-Augustinian Fathers would have said it: innocent not only of actual but also of original sin (*Mirrors*, 174). In consequence, the second conjecture (II.ii.4.3–5) is simply wrong; the Greek Orthodox God does not do such things.

2. See Fowler, "Image," 144; Hamilton, *Structure of Allegory*, 108–9; Kaske, "Augustinian Psychology," 96; "Amavia, Mortdant, Ruddymane," SE, from which source also the plot summary above is copied and several of the points made below are elaborated.

3. Fowler, well as baptism, "Image," 139, 143, 145, 147; Romans 7, "Image," 141. See also Kermode, *Spenser*, 198.

4. FQ II.i.54.5; *Sermones in Scripturis* 153, PL 38, 828, on Rom. 7:7–8, faintly echoed in Hugh of St. Cher on Rom. 7:9, *Opera*, 7, fol. 42.4.

Spenser has allotted to Amavia the Pauline paradox that law revives sin. Since Amavia is a wife, not a law, this would seem to be an incongruous element, but it is only a slight adaptation. First, the foundation for this allotment is Amavia's symbolism of reason, noted by Hamilton and others: not only is her cure couched in language that elsewhere describes the Palmer (e.g., II.i.34), but also she has "wrapt [her] selfe in Palmers weed" (II.i.52) to find Mordant, indicating that she is a pale, fleeting double of the Palmer. Females could personify reason: in the *Roman de la Rose*, Reason is feminine; and in the *Orlando Furioso,* Logistilla both symbolizes reason and opposes Alcina, the main protoype of Acrasia (II.xii.76–87; *Orlando Furioso* 6.43–46). Finally, in Guyon's partial summary of the plot—"raging passion with fierce tyrannie / Robs reason of her due regalitie, / And makes it servant to her [passion's] basest part" (II.i.57)—since Acrasia obviously personifies "passion," it is likely that Acrasia's rival Amavia personifies "reason." And reason in mankind is traditionally identified as natural law, as subsequent citations will illustrate.

Spenser can transfer a paradoxical effect from law to Amavia because she allegorizes a law. As the other good law or force in her story, she corresponds in Romans 7 to the "Lawe of my minde" and the "inner man" which assents to Mosaic law's prohibitions but is balked by "the Law of sinne, which is in my members" (7:22–23); and this law-abiding force is glossed in Origenistic, medieval, and Romanist exegesis of Romans as reason and its equivalent, natural law.[5] If the reader will accept provisionally on the basis of previous evidence that the well represents Mosaic law, similarities of Amavia to natural law emerge. Amavia relates to the well the way the "inner man" or the "Lawe of my minde" relates to Mosaic law in Romans 7. As we saw in Chapter 2, in the mountain simile (I.x.53–54), natural law (the Muses as a kind of vision) is juxtaposed to Mosaic law. With or without conscious intent, Amavia leads her reformed husband to the well. In her personal ideals, Amavia assents to what the well stands for, which, as we shall see, is chastity—marital in her case, virginal in the Nymph's. In God's progressive revelation, as we have seen in Bale's account of salvation history, natural law represents a step toward Mosaic law; just so we have here natural law leading to Mo-

---

5. In Rom. 7:25, Paul seems to equate the "inner man" and "Lawe of my minde" with "mind" itself. The Origenistic and Romanist exposition of Rom. 7:22–23 interprets "the Lawe of my minde" and "the inner man" as reason and natural law; see, for example, Hanson, *Allegory and Event,* 299–300, and Aquinas, *Opera,* 5:467.1. Martyr, too, says natural law is equated by "some" with the "Lawe of my minde" which fights the law of sin in the members in Rom. 7:23ff. (CP 2: 223b). The law that revives sin in Rom. 7:9, which I have identified with Amavia, is identified with "the inner man" and "Lawe of my minde" in Rom. 7:21, 23ff., both by the *Glossa* (= PL 114, 491, 493, for readers without access to a better edition) and by Hugh, *Opera,* 7, fol. 42.4, in both his interlinear gloss and *Expositio Glossae.*

saic, making the Mordant-Amavia story an allegory of human history. The well is also allied with Amavia imagistically; to her alone is it cooperative, accepting the blood that falls directly into it like a tributary stream, blood that "the cleane waves with purple gore did ray" (II.i.40). This well's unmetamorphosed sisters gave Amavia some help in her maritally chaste childbirth in the forest: "The Nymphes . . . my midwives weare"(II.i.53). All these females symbolize either chastity or law or both. Spenser has merely reflected Paul's bifurcation between the good laws in Romans 7:22–25, introduced it earlier on in his story, and relegated one of the paradoxically bad effects of Mosaic law to natural law.

In *Vewe,* as we have seen, Irenius alludes in so many words to this paradox in Romans 7 (esp. 14, 15, and 19) when he says that the English Common Law may produce the very sin it prohibits in a sinful subject:

> Iren: . . . *So the lawes weare at firste intended for the reformacion* of Abuses . . . , yeat are they *good still in themselves,* But to that Comon wealthe which is ruled by them *they worke not that good, which they shoulde and somtimes allsoe perhaps that evill which they woulde not.* (*Var. Prose,* 46, emphasis mine)

In his oeuvre, Spenser replays three times with three kinds of law the paradox that the law revives or creates sin: first and purely biblically, in the heat-conducting effect of the armor as Mosaic law; second, in the sin-reviving effect of Amavia's tutelage as natural law; and then in the *Vewe* in the sin-reviving effect of English Common Law—a law that belongs to the coordinate category that jurists distinguish as positive law.

To Mordant, finding himself taking the cup not only despite but because of his reformation is paradoxical because it dramatizes, first, negative suggestibility—a temptation's being enhanced by a prohibition— just as Paul in Romans 7:7–8 (see also 9–11) finds that he "had not knowen lust, except the Law had said, Thou shalt not lust," because "sinne tooke an occasion by the commandement, and wrought in me all maner of concupiscence." This negative suggestibility in Mordant and Paul is the most striking manifestation of the underlying paradox of concupiscence as an involuntary sin (Rom. 7:19). The second paradox is that for having this concupiscence, law condemns one to death (Rom. 7:10– 11), meaning, according to exegesis, that it reveals that one is already spiritually dead. When the good well kills Mordant, it dramatizes the paradox that involuntary desires can be mortally sinful. When the Nymph's Well catalyzes the wine—which represents an indeliberate, trivial, and victimless sin committed while Mordant was trying to put his life back together—into a lethal poison, I propose, it both dooms him to hell and tells him that he is already spiritually dead. In Book I the law has produced death: Mosaic law is "The bitter doome of death and balefull mone" (I.x.53); the Bible-teaching Fidelia kills and resurrects; the "righteous sentence of th'Almighties law" (I.ix.50), upon admittedly greater actual sins (I.ix.49), dooms Red Cross to hell and thus makes him want to die; and, of course, the armor as law made the spark of concupiscence unbearable so that he wanted to die and divest himself of this armor. In Romans 7, Mosaic law is said to proclaim that concupiscence is enough to merit the penalty of spiritual death: Augustine says that it is the prohibition *non concupisces,* literally, "Thou shalt not have concupiscence"—the last and most inward of the Ten Commandments—which imposes spiritual death on Paul.[6] Spenser's friend Sir Walter Raleigh explains that "true divinity" regards having involuntary evil desires as a sin.[7] Gregory the Great, in his *Moralia in Job,* agrees:

> For what man's heart, whilst bound up with this corruptible flesh, does not slip in ill bent thought [like Mordant leaving the Bower], even if he be not plunged into the very pit of consenting? And yet to think these same wrong thoughts is to commit sin.[8]

Mordant progresses, as does Paul, from happily oblivious intemperance, to rational continence (having involuntary evil desires but not acting on them), to realization under the tutelage of the well or Mosaic law of the mortal sinfulness of this continuing concupiscence. Examination of the well's refusal to wash Ruddymane and of the Palmer's concurrence will clinch its symbolism as Mosaic law.

The paradoxes imply that all morality is self-defeating. What is the use of prohibitions if they just make the sin more attractive? What is the use of law if one cannot avoid what it condemns? Besides the social use mentioned in the preceding chapter, law has an educative use. Augustine explains that it prepares for the supplement:

> We must understand that the law was given not to introduce sin [though it did so] nor to extirpate it, but simply to make it known . . . in place of a secure sense of its innocence. . . . [T]he law was given to convert the soul by anxiety about its guilt, so that it might be ready to receive grace.[9]

Spenser frequently implies, however, such as, in the conspicuously pagan funeral given to the couple (see Kaske, "Hair," SE), that grace is unavail-

---

6. *De spiritu et littera* IV.6, cols. 203–4; and XIV.23, col. 215.

7. *History,* I.ii.4.13:286.

8. *Moralia* in Job 27:6, Book XVIII, 2:323–24.

9. *De diversis quaestionibus ad Simplicianum* (written ca. 397) I.i, on Rom. 7:7, in *Earlier Writings,* 377 (= PL 40, col. 103).

able to Mordant, Amavia, and Ruddymane. Just so Romans 7 contains no mention of grace (except in the very last verse), a silence that implies, as the early Augustine claimed, that Paul must be speaking in the persona of a well-intentioned unregenerate man under the dispensation of law.[10]

Indecisions and Corrections (II.ii.1–10)

The part of the episode which Spenser has reserved for Canto ii—the well's refusal to wash Ruddymane—contains two new paradoxes that bear some relation to law (that water will not wash blood and that a bloodstain can be good) and further evidence for the second paradox, that a well that kills can still be good. But first, let us pause to note the manner of presentation. Formally, the Palmer corrects Guyon, just as the Bible occasionally corrects itself at close quarters. Guyon's and the Palmer's speeches also illustrate both two kinds of contradictions—one unresolved and the other resolved as correction—and two stages in the hermeneutics of reading any contradiction, the indecisive stage and the decisive. The Palmer's survey of wells, by which he manages to defend the well despite its uncooperativeness, illustrates that *distinctio* which is a decisive, exhaustive scholastic *distributio,* the third stage to which every reader of contradictions aspires:

> . . . secret vertues are infusd
>   In every fountaine, and in every lake,
>   Which who hath skill them rightly to have chusd,
> To proofe of passing wonders hath full often usd.

> Of those some were so from their sourse indewd
>   By great Dame Nature . . .
>   But other some by gift of later grace,
>   Or by good prayers, or by other hap,
>   Had vertue pourd into their waters bace,
> And thenceforth were renowmd, and sought from place to place.

> Such is this well, wrought by occasion straunge,
>   Which to her Nymph befell. . . .

> From thence it comes, that this babes bloudy hand
>   May not be clensd with water of this well:
> (II.ii.5–7, 10)

---

10. See ibid. and editorial matter, 370, 374; and *Expositio . . . propositionum . . . Rom.,* 45–46, PL 35, col. 2071.

Thus the Palmer serves as a figure for the reader of an image that has shifted in value, a reader who constructs a *distributio* from a bird's-eye view. The first *distributio* is that wells may be endowed naturally or supernaturally; the ensuing story reveals this well to be supernatural. Although its actions seem destructive, it is really good if used properly. "This well" implies that some other well—such as the Well of Life (I.xi.29–30) and also, as I and a few other critics believe, Arthur's Standing Lake (II.xi.46)—would answer to Ruddymane's needs (and also those of Mordant). My first point is that this *distributio* shares a structural kinship with the *distinctiones.* The Palmer's second *distributio* is that wells may be used and abused. The Bible uses this trope of reconciliation about law. After Paul attacks law, he says of it in 1 Timothy 1:8, "And we know, that the Lawe is good, if a man use it lawfully." [11] So Irenius explains on the biblical model that English Common Law is good, but not for the Irish, who abuse it. These analogues also further my ongoing thematic argument: that the well symbolizes Mosaic law.

Let us finish that argument before proceeding to Guyon. The notion of the washing of a baby and the Palmer's praise of the well for something or other has seemed to some critics to necessitate the interpretation of the well as baptism; but, as the Palmer says, there are many wells, opening the possibility that this one could be a baptism manqué, and that he is just emphasizing its good side. Although the Palmer does not admit it, clearly some of Spenser's wells are *in malo* (e.g., the Well of the Lazy Nymph in I.vii.5). In the Bible, too, according to the *distinctiones,* washing an infant, while it may symbolize baptism, may also symbolize other and even unproductive things, and so may the images *fons, lacus,* or *lavacrum.* Of course, any inversion of baptismal symbolism is paradoxical and unsettling to the reader, but this inversion should be accepted and made a part of the interpretation.

The Palmer's etiological eulogy of the well clinches its symbolism as Mosaic law. Here we find images, not just a paradoxical plot, that suggest Mosaic law. The image of stone (associated with law in I.x.53) is repeated four times in six lines which Spenser has added to his sources. [12] "Lapis" is associated with law in exegesis; for example, in Lauretus, it symbolizes "the asperity and the heavy yoke of the law itself." Although the Palmer is ostensibly praising the well, the sinister aspects of Mosaic law are embodied concessively. A number of ancillary images reinforce this meaning. The imagery of "cold" (II.ii.9) is linked with the Nymph's thrice-

11. Or he was then thought to say it; Pauline authorship is now disputed. Martyr devotes an entire Common Place to the topic "Of the Use and Abrogating of the Law" (CP, 2.15:575b–582).

12. FQ II.ii.8.8–9.2; on the sources, see Fowler, "Image," 146.

mentioned fear (II.ii.8,9). A traditional distinction between law and gospel is that the former is obeyed out of "servile fear" and the latter out of love, the former out of psychological coldness and the latter out of psychological heat (see Lauretus, "Frigus").[13] The only thing that suggests baptism in the Palmer's celebration of the well is the analogy between a miraculous stone welling out water and that rock in the desert which, struck by Moses, gave out water for the thirsty Israelites to drink. Admittedly, the water from the rock is generally interpreted as symbolizing Christ or the sacraments.[14] But this well's recalcitrance shows that the symbolism of the Christian sacraments is being conspicuously inverted; this is water from the rock *in malo*.

The Palmer is not giving a balanced view but trying to tease out the good side of the paradox—law's educative function. Just as the well's Nymph, allegorizing man's original righteousness, rejects both Ruddymane and the lustful Faunus (who allegorizes both the Tempter and concupiscence; see II.ii.7–9),[15] so Mosaic law in its Tenth Commandment, "Thou shalt not covet" (Latin, *non concupisces,* literally, in the Protestant interpretation, "thou shalt not have concupiscence"), holds up original righteousness as an impossibly high standard and thereby serves only to condemn both adults and infants. Martyr—committed, like all extreme Protestants, to deconstructing law in order to exalt grace—says that even infants such as Ruddymane harbor concupiscence and are obliged by the Tenth Commandment to harbor instead that original righteousness which mankind has lost (CP 2: 223–224a). Preservation is also the goal of the Nymph's metamorphosis:

> And yet the stone her semblance seemes to show,
> Shapt like a maid, that such ye may her know;
> And yet her vertues in her water byde
>
> . . . .
> But ever like her selfe unstained hath beene tryde.
> (II.ii.9)

Like the Tenth Commandment, as the monument to man's created innocence, the Nymph is entitled to reject "any filth," whether acquired

---

13. See Hugh of St. Cher on Rom. 7:21–23: " . . . the servile fear by which the law of Moses is fulfilled" (*Opera,* 7, fol. 44.4).

14. E.g., Lauretus, "Aqua." This traditional meaning is firmly based on 1 Cor. 10:4. Fowler notes this tradition as evidence for his interpretation of the well as baptism ("Emblems," 145); but as we have seen, one image can have various meanings in Scripture.

15. Fowler, "Image," 146.

through a trivial and indeliberate act or through an inevitable and un-
conscious physical connection with a parent, just as Martyr says the Tenth
Commandment is entitled to reject what is "dishonest, although it seem
not so to us," and to require us to have that image of God which we have
lost.[16] Her proper use is for education; as Spenser's friend Raleigh says of
Mosaic law, quoting Augustine and Chrysostom, "not to helpe, but to
discover sicknesse."[17] The price of preservation has been petrifaction,
just as Mosaic law, to quote Raleigh again, is likened to "An Heart without affection, to an Eye without lust, to a Minde without passion."[18]
That the Palmer is something of a stuffed shirt, that his comfort, memo-
rialization, seems cold to a Christian audience and not worth the price of
a human life, could also be said of Paul in his portrayal, at once grim and
defensive, of Mosaic law. For all these reasons, the Nymph's Well represents Mosaic law or, at the broadest, law in general — not, as others have
previously suggested, baptism, natural purity, a too-sudden reformation,
the opposite extreme of insensibility to the erotic, or the female generative principle.

Since the Palmer speaks about both images, water and blood, from now
on let us organize by image, not by speaker. Regarding the blood, first,
Guyon constructs not an exhaustive scholastic *distributio* but "divers"
overlapping alternatives, the best *distinctio* he can achieve:

> He wist not whether blot of foule offence
>   Might not be purgd with water nor with bath;
>   Or that high God, in lieu of innocence,
>   Imprinted had that token of his wrath,

16. "Neither doth it . . . take away their sins [infants' infractions of the Ten Command-
ments] because they are not felt by them: for a thing is dishonest, although it seem not so to
us, yet in his own nature it is dishonest. That (saith he [Augustine]) which is dishonest, is
dishonest, whether it seem so, or no" (CP, 2:224b). Again, linking law to Original Righteousness: "And yet ought not God therefore to be accused of injustice [for prohibiting
concupiscence] . . . for it cometh not through his fault that his commandments can not be
observed. . . . The law was given, as a thing most agreeable unto our nature, as it was first in-
stituted. For the image of God could not otherwise more lively and plainly be expressed"
(*Commentaries on Romanes,* fol. 179r on Rom. 7). Again, Martyr's comment on 1 Tim. 1:8
sounds like the Palmer's defense of the well: "Wherefore, when as it seemeth that the lawe is
by Paule, either diminished, or reprooved; that is not in respect of it selfe, but for our fault
sake. For it meeteth with such, as be defiled" (CP, 2.16.8:585b).

17. *History,* I.ii.4.11:282–83. I agree with Fowler ("Image," 146) that the Nymph per se
symbolizes Original Righteousness. After her metamorphosis into well and stony source,
the Nymph symbolizes that law which requires Original Righteousness (cf. Frye, "Structure," 164).

18. *History,* I.ii.4.3:268.

> To shew how sore bloudguiltinesse he hat'th;
> Or that the charme and venim, which they druncke,
> Their bloud with secret filth infected hath,
> Being diffused through the senselesse truncke,
> That through the great contagion direfull deadly stunck.
> (II.ii.4)

Formally, this *distinctio* remains undecided and hermeneutically unsettling. Thematically, Guyon is trying out what amounts to different definitions of original sin; critics value this *distinctio* because it is the first overtly theological discourse in the episode and the basis for a religious interpretation of the whole. (I concede that Guyon's conjectures come nearer the truth than the Palmer's exhaustive, optimistic *distributio* of wells; but their rhetorical form is modest.)

The Palmer, however, in one gesture dismissively corrects all three conjectures, creating a contradiction:

> Whom thus at gaze, the Palmer gan to bord
> With goodly reason, and thus faire bespake;
> Ye bene right hard amated, gratious Lord,
> And of your ignorance great marvell make,
> Whiles cause not well conceived ye mistake.
> (II.ii.5)

Insofar as the Palmer contradicts Guyon, far from being exhaustive (as his survey of wells is), he compounds the confusion both of Guyon and of the reader; to this extent he brings us back to the second stage of understanding, the stage at which Stanley Fish stops.

Then Guyon and the Palmer perform an adjacent and internally debated shift in evaluation of one and the same image, the well, such as is typical of the second stage of reading a contradictory text. The Palmer's closing recurrence to the blood at the end of his speech does too. He announces that it does not need to be washed because it symbolizes something good—vengeance and, somewhat arbitrarily, innocence (II.ii.10). This revaluation is not equivocation, adiaphorism, or supplementation, but a radical contradiction: what according to Guyon was a "token" of "bloudguiltinesse" "in lieu of innocence" (II.ii.4) will now "tell" "his mothers innocence." (II.ii.10) One *distinctio* that can partially explain it is a shift to a higher viewpoint and to a typological level of allegory, making it a correction.

One source and explanation, both biblical and liturgical, for what Ruddymane undergoes here is a combination of the ceremonial law's lustrations such as the circumcision of the child (the forerunner of infant baptism) [19] and the Jewish and sometimes Christian rite of purification of the new mother. The foundational text for the latter rite declares the blood on the newborn to be the mother's menstrual blood, and hence polluting (Lev. 12:2, 5), as Ruddymane is said by his mother to be "defild" (II.i.50). Calvin affirms (in an opinion that was preceded by Aquinas and seconded by Archbishop Whitgift):

> This law (purification) is of itself abundantly sufficient to prove original sin. . . . For there could not be a clearer demonstration of the curse pronounced on mankind than when the Lord declared, that the child comes from its mother unclean and polluted, and that the mother herself is consequently defiled by childbearing. Certainly, if man were not born a sinner, if he were not by nature a *child of wrath* (Eph. ii.3), if some stains of sin did not dwell in him, he would have no need of purification. [20]

Just so the well serves not to remove original sin from the infant but, like purification, to dramatize its presence to the adults. Spenser wanted to define baptism by contrast, delineating what the purgative ceremonies of the Mosaic law did not accomplish. We have seen that, in its condemnation of Mordant's concupiscence, the well reflects the Tenth Commandment, a part of the moral law; in relation to an infant, who is outside the moral law, the well represents the ceremonial law.

One might put the synchronic question: Why does Spenser devote so much of the episodes of the Dragon-Fight and the Nymph's Well to casting aspersions on Mosaic law when, in the real world, Jews had been banished from England for centuries? Nowhere in his works does Spenser exhibit anti-Semitism. First, the use of Romans 7 in the *Vewe* shows that, for Spenser, as for Lutherans and Anabaptists alike, for better and for worse, Mosaic law could epitomize all law. Another motive is that the Epistles by and attributed to Saint Paul—Galatians, the Epistle to the Hebrews, and above all Romans—were the foundational scriptures of the Reformation, and they are concerned with Mosaic law. In Paul's qualified secession from Judaism, the faith of his fathers, the Reformers saw

19. See Heinrich Bullinger, *Decades,* Third Decade, Sermon viii, Parker Society 3:249; Thomas Rogers, *The Catholic Doctrine,* on Article 27, Parker Society 41:279; Martyr, CP 4:112b; 2:589a–b; Aquinas, ST I–IIae, qu. 102, art. 5, rep. obj. 3.

20. Quotation from Calvin, *Commentary on a Harmony* I:139–40 on Luke 2:22. Aquinas, ST I–IIae, qu. 102, art. 5, rep. obj. 4; Whitgift, "Defense of the Answer to the Admonition, Against the Reply of Thomas Cartwright," *Works,* IX.vii.1, Parker Society 2:558–59; 3:561.

their qualified secession from their parent religion, the Church of Rome. For Paul and the Reformers, Mosaic law represented in particular not only hypocrisy and legalism, as it does in the Gospels, but also justification by works; and works played for them a paradoxical role in relation to the passivity of justification by faith and the holistic ethics of grace, the indwelling Christ, and the Holy Spirit—a role they also play in FQ Book I.

Celebrations (II.ii.10 – 11)

The Palmer's revaluation of the repellent bloodstain is shockingly positive; at best, it can be smoothed down to a paradox. In context, as I said, it comes as a radical correction of Guyon. The shock prompts the reader to investigate its symbolic rationale. The Palmer's assertion derives its optimism, according to the greater number of those few critics who have interpreted it at all, from typology, from an attempt to turn Ruddymane into a type of Christ, but how he manages this is unclear. He has scattered precedents, doctrinal and imagistic. Another function of the ceremonial law according to Christians is to prophesy Christ.[21] The Crucifixion is suggested by blood that is "sacred," on Ruddymane's "hands," and "in" his flesh (II.ii.10). Zechariah prophesies Christ in terms of his crucified hands: "And one shall say unto him, What are these woundes in thine hands? Then he shal answere, Thus was I wounded in the house of my friends" (13:6). Portraying a Christ who is still an infant as undergoing some aspect of the Passion is traditional.

But if we examine the details of the contradiction in context, it remains as yet unresolved: how can the blood on Ruddymane, which is almost universally agreed (pace Weatherby) to represent original sin and which the Palmer himself has called "filth" in the previous stanza (II.ii.9.8), become a "sacred Symbole" not only to remind of "revengement" but also to tell Amavia's "innocence" and "be for all chast Dames an endlesse moniment" (II.ii.10)? Amavia too says at once that Ruddymane is "defild" with the blood and that the bloody hands are "pledges" "That cleare she dide from blemish criminall" (II.i.37). The Palmer called the blood "filth" because its overtones are obstetrical. Spenser mentioned

21. Calvin in the statement quoted above adds that the Mosaic rite of purification taught the Israelites that our pollutions are washed away by grace (*Commentary on a Harmony* I:139–40 on Luke 2:22). For a prefigurative purpose assigned to the ceremonial law as a whole, see Calvin, *Institutes*, II, vii, 1, 1:405–7; II, vii, 15, 1:421; Raleigh, *History*, I, ii, 4, 12:283; Aquinas, ST I–IIae, qu. 101, art. 2, 2:855.

an obstetrical image, midwives, in connection with Ruddymane's literal birth (II.i.53).

To understand the obstetrical overtones of Ruddymane's ineffectual bath, we must glance at the biblical source, Ezekiel 16—linked by many verbal and situational parallels, as I established in my 1976 article.[22] God finds blood on the infant Jerusalem "in thy nativity when thou wast borne," and does nothing about it: "thou wast not washed in water" (Ezek. 16:4). The commentators tell us the blood is the afterbirth (Latin, *secundina*), which includes, in the parlance of the day, not only the placenta but also the amniotic sac and other unpleasant material that comes out with the infant. The reader's gut reaction is anticipated by the "contempt" (Geneva) or "fastidio," "loathing," (TJ) of the babe which at first deterred God from rescuing it (Ezek. 16:5). This loathing is alluded to directly in the Palmer's "filth" and obliquely in Spenser's comment on Guyon's attempted washing: "So love does loath [not the victim but] disdainfull nicitee" (II.ii.3). Similarly, Amavia's description of Ruddymane as "with bloud defild" (II.i.50) echoes the biblical "polluted in thine owne blood" (Ezek. 16:6). These repellent echoes help to invest the blood on Ruddymane with overtones of the afterbirth. (The difference in sex of the infants does not appear to be significant.)

But before leaving Ezekiel 16, let us notice that it reinforces my previous point, that the well symbolizes not baptism but Mosaic law. Many commentators recognize the existence in Ezekiel 16 of a baptism manqué, a washing that was *in malo* because ineffectual, such as Ruddymane received: "thou wast not washed in water to soften thee" (verse 4; Vulg., "in salutem," "unto health" or "unto salvation"). Lauretus explains that this means not that no one had tried to wash her, but that someone had tried without effect—that is, without removing the blood. Lauretus attributes the ineffectual washing to someone who merely "goes through the motions"; among his sources for this gloss, Jerome and Rabanus Maurus adduce baptisms of pagans or heretics, or Christians who come unworthily.[23] Mosaic law, though never equated with the unsuccessful washing, is equated with the successful washing or with one of God's other favors to the babe (feeding, clothing, etc., 16:9–10).[24] From this it would seem that Spenser has, with typical Pauline animus, chosen as the vehicle

22. Kaske, "Exegetical Tradition," 149–79; see also my "Bacchus," 195–209; and Nohrnberg, *Analogy,* 288.

23. Lauretus, s.v. "Abluere"; the following are commenting on v. 4: Jerome, PL 25:127; Rabanus Maurus, PL 110:668; *Glossa,* citing Jerome, gloss c; Hugh of St. Cher, *Opera,* 5, fol. 56.3.

24. See, for example, *Glossa* quoting Jerome on 16:10, "ceremoniis legis."

for Mosaic law the unsuccessful washing implied in verse 4. He plays with a bifurcation of washings, as he did when he transferred to the "Lawe of my minde" another paradox of Mosaic law (Rom. 7:7–11, 23). Spenser does not incorporate the successful washing. Fradubio and Fraelissa in I.ii.28–45, the corresponding canto of Book I, are left similarly waiting in an unhappy plight "Till we be bathed in a living well" (I.ii.43).

The image of the afterbirth contains the rationale of the blood's positive as well as its negative valence. Another OT verse, Genesis 49:10, mentions an afterbirth, and two Protestant humanist commentaries see it as a symbol of Christ's birth and death. The verse reads: "The scepter shal not depart from Judah, nor a Lawgiver from betweene his feete, until Shiloh come." *Shiloh* means "filius eius," "his/her son," say TJ, and literally "secund[in]ae eius," "his/her afterbirth":

> his/her son] Hebrew, his/her afterbirth, that is Christ, as each of the Chaldee Paraphrases and almost all Hebrew translators agree: Metonymy, the container for the contained.[25]

Melanchthon's interpretation is more elaborate. Among other things, he says that "Messiah is named from that sheath on account of the human nature which he took on himself from the virgin." Just as the Palmer attributes to Ruddymane's repellent bloodstain the opposed meanings "innocence" and "revengement" (II.ii.10), so Genesis 49:10 calls Messiah *Shiloh* with reference to both his innocent birth and his vicariously sinful death. Most obviously and strikingly, the afterbirth symbolizes Christ at his death by its aesthetic overtones—its uncleanness, symbolizing his shed blood and his becoming for our sins the object of God's wrath. Melanchthon's notion, intrinsic to the latter meaning, that guilt can be shifted from one person to another, appeared also in Guyon's second conjecture about the bloodstain, that God "in lieu of innocence, / Imprinted had [on Ruddymane] that token of his wrath" (II.ii.4). Indeed, in retrospect, these lines also bestow on Ruddymane overtones of Christ, for just as Ruddymane was "innocent / Of that was doen" (II.ii.1), that is, of actual sin, so Christ was absolutely innocent, yet both have had imprinted on them a bloodstain as a "token" of God's "wrath."

According to the Palmer, the blood on Ruddymane incongrously symbolizes the "innocence" of his mother. But how can a token of original sin, whether innate or assumed, betoken a mother's innocence? Since it symbolizes the afterbirth, it can do so by physiological properties. To in-

---

25. Gloss d. The Chaldee Paraphrases are the Targums of Onkelos and of Jonathan.

tegrate TJ's gloss with Melanchthon's sermon, just as the amniotic sac contains the child, just as everyone's body contains his soul, so Christ's human nature, since it includes the body, can be pictured as containing his divine nature. A bloodstained sheath is donned by Guyon as the other avenger of Amavia's wrongs and thus to that extent another Christ figure when he takes up Mordant's "armes," which are, like Ruddymane, "with bloud defilde" (II.ii.11). Besides being a container, an afterbirth is maternal. Any afterbirth belongs to the mother though it is attached to the child, thus rendering visible her contribution to his makeup. Moreover, Christ's entire physical nature came from Mary; he had no more of his father in his entire physical inheritance than the afterbirth has. Thus the disgusting obstetrical blood on Ruddymane symbolizes not only original sin but also Christ's virgin-born human nature and the virgin Mary's genetic contribution thereto. It is defiling or innocent according to whether it is viewed as Mordant's or Amavia's. It can be considered Mordant's because, as Hamilton notes, Guyon's conjecture that "the charme and venim" which "*their* blood with secret filth infected hath" (II.ii.4, emphasis mine) implies that Amavia absorbed the venom, like a venereal disease, through intercourse; and intercourse was then thought to be a mixing of bloods (semen consisting of super-refined blood, the female contribution to generation consisting of the menses). The double symbolism is paradoxical, expressing the paradoxes of the Incarnation and of Christ's vicarious atonement—each both disgusting and sublime.

Furthermore, Melanchthon explains that "her afterbirth" is a synonym for "her seed" in God's prophecy addressed to the serpent after the Fall of Man: a virgin-born man will "bruise" the satanic serpent's head and be wounded by him in the heel (Gen. 3:15).[26] Melanchthon thus connects this obscure and repulsive prophecy of Christ as afterbirth and its Spenserian echo to a famous one of vengeance for the Fall. The famous one comes at the same point in its story as the Palmer's prophecy does in its—as a final prophecy of vengeance and thus a certain limited conso-

---

26. "Jacob [the speaker of the prophecy] looks back to the first promise [Gen. 3:15] and just as he is said there to be of the seed of the woman, so by *tapinosis* or an extreme *meiosis* he calls him Schiloh, which is *Khorion autés*, that is, 'her offspring.' *Khorion* signifies the sheath surrounding the offspring, but by synecdoche it is employed for the offspring itself. And Messiah is named from that sheath on account of the human nature which he took on himself from the Virgin. And then on account of infirmity: that sheath, which is called the *Khorion* and the afterbirth, is bloody and unclean, and the offspring, when first it is brought forth, is a tender and frail thing. Such is Christ sweating blood and hanging on the cross, where he felt the wrath of the Father poured out upon himself," a Christmas sermon on Gen. 49:10, CR 24:114. This point first appeared in Kaske, "Exegetical Tradition," chap. 4, 203–10; early versions of some of the previous points in this chapter also appeared in the same chapter.

lation for a tragedy. Christ's suffering—the "bruise" in "his heele"—accomplished vengeance on Satan and by analogy on Acrasia because it deprived these tempters of the souls they had seduced. Many Spenserians see in Mordant's and Amavia's story up to now other echoes of the Fall of Man in that a female in a garden tempts a man to ingest something which brings death to him and his child; this is the typological sense of the episode. Thus Genesis 3:15, while not explicitly mentioning blood, says that the woman's contribution to generation independent of the man's, that is, innocently, will produce an avenger. Although Amavia is certainly not innocent of male seed like the Virgin Mary, she has been until very near to her end morally innocent in that she bears no responsibility for the tragedy to which she has finally succumbed. This is enough to render her a pale copy of the Virgin Mary.

Spenser states elsewhere that Christ's innocence—his genetic freedom from original sin—was what qualified him vicariously to assume mankind's guilt. In order for his death to "clense the guilt of that infected crime, / Which was enrooted in all fleshly slime" (here another disgusting image is invoked, but only to be denied; *Hymne of Heavenly Love,* 167–68, YSP), he had to be genetically free of slime and crime himself:

> So taking flesh of sacred virgins wombe,
> For mans deare sake he did a man become.

> And that most blessed bodie, which was borne
> Without all blemish or reprochfull blame,
> He freely gave to be both rent and torne.
> (*Hymne of Heavenly Love,* 146–50, YSP)

Christ's being born "Without all blemish or reprochfull blame," that is, original sin, explicates Amavia's claim that the blood proves she died clear of "blemish criminall" (II.i.37), giving it an association with the intrinsically pure seed of the woman which flowed from Eve though Mary's ancestors to Mary to Christ.

The repellent symbol of the afterbirth exemplifies the final strategy of biblical poetics to be considered in this book—tapinosis, a breach of decorum between image and meaning. Melanchthon says that calling Christ an afterbirth is "tapinosis or an extreme meiosis," that is, an undignified or extremely diminishing epithet. These rhetorical terms also describe the Palmer's interpretation of the metaphorically obstetrical blood on Ruddymane as both Mary's chastity and Christ's assumption of human nature—and, vicariously, of its guilt.

Negative poetics in general are appropriate, according to patristic and medieval commentators, for three reasons. First, they are paradoxically appropriate for the Godhead in general because they foreground the ineptness of any language to describe him. While not employing the rhetorical terms later used by Melanchthon, Gregory the Great, in his *Moralia,* which is well represented at Cambridge in general and Pembroke in particular*, defends the practice of calling Christ by the names of undignified animals such as the ass:

> Nor let any consider it unbecoming that the Incarnate Lord can be typified by such an animal; whilst it is admitted by all that He is spoken of, in Holy Scripture, as, in a certain sense, . . . a worm. . . . As it is written; *But I am a worm, and no man.* . . . Since then He is typified by the mention of such vile and abject things, what is said offensively of Him, of Whom it is admitted that nothing is said appropriately? [27]

For the same reason, Pseudo-Dionysius the Areopagite, well represented at Cambridge*, devotes Chapter 2 of his *Celestial Hierarchies* to exemplifying and defending the "earthliest forms" (148), the "absurd, counterfeit, and emotional" (148), indeed, the "dissimilar and even entirely inadequate and ridiculous" (149) forms used by Scripture to describe the "Supramundane Natures" of God and the angels (152).[28] Even though "there is nothing which lacks its own share of beauty," the Areopagite concludes:

> Since the way of negation appears to be more suitable to the realm of the divine and since positive affirmations are always unfitting to the hiddenness of the inexpressible, a manifestation through dissimilar shapes is more correctly to be applied to the invisible. (150)[29]

Second, such imagery is genuinely appropriate to Christ as representing his condescension. John Scotus Eriugena's exposition on this chapter of the *Celestial Hierarchies* adds at the end: "nevertheless it [the worm] is made the image [*imaginatur* in Ambrose's Latin translation] for the very incarnation of God the Word, which transcends all perception and un-

---

27. *Moralia in Job,* chap. xxi on Job 39:5, Book 30, 3.2:409–10.

28. Pseudo-Dionysius, *Complete Works,* cited by page in text. Since the style of the Areopagite leaves much to the interpreter, see also both the Latin translation by John Scotus Eriugena, included as lemmata in his commentary, and *Dyonisii Celestis hierarchia, etc.,* translated by one Ambrose, an orator and monk of the Camaldolese Order (*Opera*), cap. 2, fols. 1.4–2.3.

29. In Ambrose's Latin, fol. 2.a.

derstanding"; and in the margins of two MSS is the comment, "Note on the moral level for promoting humility."[30]

Third, the shock from all negative poetics is intellectually stimulating. The Areopagite chronicles his readerly experience of such imagery:

> I myself might not have been stirred from this difficulty [Latin, *ambiguo*] to my current inquiry, to an uplifting through a precise explanation of these sacred truths, had I not been troubled by the deformed imagery used by scripture in regard to the angels. My mind was not permitted to dwell on imagery so inadequate, but was provoked to get behind the material show, to get accustomed to the idea of going beyond appearances to those upliftings which are not of this world.[31]

The shock promotes a further stage of reading, intellectualization; as with all negative poetics, each stage is predicated on an iconoclastic habit of mind; at neither stage is there any danger of verbal idolatry.

As exemplified in all three of these commentators, the locus classicus of the Bible's negative poetics is the Psalmist's cry, supposedly in the person of the crucified Christ, "I am a worme" (Ps. 22:6). Worms are used to symbolize Christ twice in the FQ. Fidelia's serpent discussed in Chapter 2 "That horrour made to all, that did behold" (FQ I.x.13; "worm" and "serpent" are interchangeable in earlier states of the language), alludes as we saw to Moses' brazen serpent in John 3:14, which is also said to be a degrading symbol for Christ.[32] Also "Infinite shapes of creatures," "Informed in the mud, on which the Sunne hath shynd" (III.vi.8) can be shown to symbolize Christ.[33] Spenser uses them explicitly to illustrate Belphoebe's and Amoret's virginal conception and birth, which is incongruous enough; he then implicitly alludes to the birth of Christ for the same purpose, as we shall see (III.vi.3 and 27), the connection being that both processes are asexual and hence without original sin, involving a divine or quasi-divine ray impregnating a passive female. The nymph Chrysogone "bore withouten paine, that she conceived / Withouten

---

30. *Expositiones*, 49, ll. 1068–73, esp. 1071(= PL 122, cols. 168–69), hereafter cited in text; the idea recurs passim to the end of the chapter. Rabanus Maurus: "No wonder if [Christ] is figured in vile significations [including "serpent" and "worm"], who, though he was the Son coeternal with the Father before the ages, not spurning the vileness of our nature, was born in time [as] the Son of Man" ("De laudibus Sanctae Crucis," PL 107, 154). On the degradation of Christ specifically in his being symbolized by the brazen serpent in John 3:14 (alluded to by the serpent in Fidelia's cup), see Luther, *Works*, 22: 340–41.

31. *Hierarchies*, 153; Ambrose's Latin, fol. 2.4.

32. Luther, *Works*, *Comm. John*, 22:340–41; Bruno of Asti, PL 165:470–71.

33. Hankins, *Source*, 242–46.

pleasure: ne her need implore/ Lucinaes aide" (III.vi.27) an offspring "Pure and unspotted from all loathly crime, / That is ingenerate in fleshly slime" (III.vi.3). Slime is mentioned and denied, but mud is not denied. The sunbeam is analogous to the Holy Ghost. Belphoebe's birth in particular, however, is described more directly in the sweet and exalted imagery that echoes Psalm 110:3, which is universally regarded as a prophecy of Christ's birth: her "berth was of the wombe of Morning dew" (vi.3). One might object that the two analogies are as unconnected as many of Shakespeare's are, but the biblical background forges a close link between them and thus a breach of decorum.

Augustine, while not mentioning the breach of decorum, sees the Psalmist's "worm" as foretelling the Virgin Birth: "a worm is born of the flesh without coition, as Christ was of the Virgin Mary."[34] John Scotus Eriugena's *Expositiones* on the *Celestial Hierarchies* concurs and confirms that worms are both among the creatures spontaneously generated from mud and, as images, indecorous:

> *I am a worm.* This is understood of Christ, who is not born of male seed but, like a worm from the simple nature of the earth, so he from the bowels of a perpetual virgin. . . . [N]othing in the nature of material things is more vile than a worm, who is conceived of the simple soil.[35]

The implications for women of the disgusting imagery for Christ's birth in II.ii.10 and III.vi.7–9 are twofold. Christ's parthenogenesis exalts woman. One might ask, did Spenser intend to humiliate Queen Elizabeth I by his disgusting comparison of the birth of Belphoebe to that of worms? That it was, as I have revealed, Christological removes some of the onus. Spenser's addition of Christological imagery that is exalted indicates that his primary concern was exaltation. In the portrayal of Belphoebe, Elizabeth is the central meaning of the images, and Christ serves an adjectival function, to glorify her. Also, in Canto vi in general, Spenser's concern is scientific—to explain generation, sexual or asexual, whether of Christ or of worms, whether disgusting or not. Here, too, Christ is adjectival; this scientific concern pertains chiefly to Belphoebe's lowly twin sister, Amoret, who is destined to play her part in generation.

The most unusual feature of the Christological tradition utilized by Spenser here to exalt Queen Elizabeth's birth is the description of Bel-

---

34. *On the Psalms,* 213 on Ps. 22:6; see also Rolle, "i am a worm, *that* is .i. am borne of the mayden, withouten mannys sede." *Psalter,* 77–78 on Ps. 22:5 [6].

35. 49 on Psalm 22.

phoebe's mother: "She bore withouten paine, that she conceived / Withouten pleasure: ne her need implore / Lucinaes aide" (III.vi.27). Lucina corresponds in function to midwives. The logic derives from the Romish legend, echoed for example in the midwives' speeches in the Nativity Play of the *Ludus Coventriae,* that the virginity of Mary was proved by her giving birth without afterbirth, blood, pain, or any need for midwives. Spenser thus gives Elizabeth a fictional parthenogenesis and implies that such superhuman ease and purity befits her. This parallels Spenser's gracing her with a fictional *genus* both by mythologizing her mother as the nymph Syrinx in "April" and keeping a fall and original sin out of her ancestry as he did in the "Antiquities of Faeryland" (II.x.70–76).

Thus, Spenser presents both Christ's birth and childbirth in general in both a good and a bad aesthetic light; to his disgusting portrayals, he presents at least an equal number of exalted (besides III.vi.3, 27, see also I.v.1; III.ii.11) or discreetly generalized ones (e.g., in this very canto, Genius releasing the babes into the world through the "fresh" gate, III.vi.31–2). Gaudentius (a minor Father of the church) observes that imagery for Christ in the Psalms is now dignified, now undignified.[36] The very frequency of images of childbirth testifies to Spenser's interest in this largely feminine activity.

We tend to forget this balance because of the power of the disgusting portrayals, among which the blood on Ruddymane ranks close to that of Error's brood. From such intensity, David Lee Miller argues that Spenser shared the misogyny of his culture. Clearly, one of the things Spenser is saying, in line with the second justification of undignified imagery for the divine, is: "Christ condescended to be born of (shudder) a woman!" Spenser contrasts Ruddymane's messy births—literal and metaphorical—with Belphoebe's birth and the Romish legend about Christ on which it is based: Ruddymane's mother complains of her pain and lack of midwives—"The Nymphes . . . my midwives weare, / Hard helpe at need. So deare thee babe I bought" (II.i.53)—and Guyon attempts to play midwife but cannot eradicate the bloodstain. Yet the defilement of these births, especially the second one, is equated with salvific things: Mary's virginal parturition and Christ's atoning death. The fact that a defiled birth can also symbolize that of Christ relativizes the Romish nativity legend and Elizabeth / Belphoebe's echo of it; the true Christian divinity typified in Ruddymane submitted to all human infirmities—if not at his birth then at his Passion. (Spenser is not necessarily questioning the truth of the legend, for Christ could be symbolized by an afterbirth even if he

36. A bishop of Brescia, fl. 420. See Sermon 19.9, PL 20:989.

did not actually have one himself.) Spenser is clearly more interested in the humble than the hieratic Christ.

Biblical commentators find in such ugly images for Christ a self-deprecating irony, an alienation effect, which is appropriate both generally to matters that transcend human language and specially to a divinity who humbles himself. Thus a long tradition underlies Fidelia's serpent, the "creatures" spawned by Nile mud, and the repellent blood symbolizing the afterbirth. This tradition, like the typology of which it is a part, originated solely in biblical exegesis; no one would call Zeus a worm. Its material cause was the sometimes quixotic project of the Christian community to appropriate the Hebrew Bible; its final cause was the inscription of negative theology, especially the paradox of the Incarnation. Tapinosis forms, along with paradox, part of that negative poetics which was later to bear bittersweet fruit in the witty religious grotesqueries of Andrewes and Crashaw and the absurd symbolism of Kafka and Beckett.[37]

37. See Andrewes's sermon, cited in Chapter 2, referring to the crucified Christ as "Zachary's Stone, graven and cut full of eyes, all over."

CONCLUSION

A Bible directly inspired by God throughout in form and content could be a model for merely human authors to emulate. Biblical hermeneutics was in the air at Cambridge; bibliographical statistics indicate that students and faculty viewed the Bible through the lenses of exegetes. Spenser felt that certain exegetes of the Middle Ages and the Reformation were literary critics: they revealed what the Bible is really like and indirectly showed how a serious literary work could be shaped by analogy and what an audience would expect of such a work.

Spenser imitates three biblical methods of presentation—varying repeated images *in bono et in malo,* propositional contradictions, and undignified symbols for the divine—singly or as a group in one or more of the following works: in the FQ, the *Fowre Hymnes,* the *Amoretti and Epithalamion,* "November," and the *Vewe.* Initially, the incongruity variously inherent in these three strategies produces a shock that is not just a problem for interpretation but part of the aesthetic experience. First, Spenser consciously chose to repeat images contrastively in the biblical manner. Aside from explicit *distributiones,* most of these contrasts entail contradiction, whether apparent or real, yielding an initial impression of self-contestation; when the reader distinguishes why one image is good and the other evil, she can usually achieve a *distributio* that is comfortingly exhaustive.

The second strategy is likewise one of internal contrast, but on the propositional level. Spenser's self-contradictions regarding death, bloodshed, free will, and justification by works imitate the irreconcilability of similar propositions in Scripture, contradictions highlighted by splitters such as Ochino. Spenser also presents in this manner topics having little or no biblical content such as change, art, sexuality, and female independence. In the FQ, while explicit pairings of bad and good figures may be iconoclastic, most of Spenser's unsettling self-corrections are adiaphoristic: they modify the primary statement to accommodate different circumstances, thus expressing situational ethics. The existence of deliberate contradictions in Spenser, noted as early as 1973, can no longer be doubted. Such contradictions appear even more obvious and deliberate when assigned a purpose or function. On those about free will and justification, Spenser could have taken biblical vacillation as a precedent for expressing his own or his sovereign's skepticism. Those between the ecclesiastical images are designed to encourage religious toleration; those regarding law, to promote at one and the same time personal reliance on divine grace and public law and order. Although some of his purposes remain debatable, it is nevertheless true that all Spenser's contradictions consciously imitate, to a greater or lesser extent, biblical form and content as these were perceived by medieval and Renaissance exegetes.

At the same time, Spenser constructed many propositional contradictions that invite resolution through viewing them as tropes—such as equivocation, paradox, and self-correction—the way some splitters reconciled contradictions in the Bible. Some of these tropes are advocated for various reasons in secular rhetorical manuals, but only on a small scale. Only in the Bible do we find widely spaced examples, such as the contrasts between the OT and the NT. Thus Spenser interlaced his vast major work and his volume of love poetry with various forms of cross-reference, forms that exegetes found in the Bible.

The third strategy—the choice of undignified symbols (tapinosis) for divine subjects—is employed at three important moments in the FQ and originates in the typological interpretation of the OT. The incongruity between image and meaning can first be enjoyed as exemplifying the paradoxes of the incarnation and of human language, then resolved by transcending their affect and excogitating the analogy that connects them—a thought process that is itself, according to Platonic Christians, both redemptive and verbally iconoclastic. By assigning to different, successive, and equally necessary stages of reading—the self-contestatory and the exhaustive—the approaches of reader-response critics such as Fish, Gilman, and Gless on the one hand and of synthesizers such as the New Critics, Fowler, and King on the other, I have offered a way of accommodating both.

Within Spenser's work, I have explicated passages by parallel or contrast with other passages linked to them by hook-word, topic, or rhetorical figure (for which see Appendix Two and Index). Blood winds like a red thread though the FQ; bloodshed, a bloodstain, bloodguiltiness, and propositions about them serve to exemplify, as it turns out, all three of the major biblical strategies under consideration here: both the bloodstain on Ruddymane and bloodshed in general switch valence from bad to good; the blood on Ruddymane is rechristened as good, that is, symbolizes Christ, by tapinosis; and the shedding of blood can be reconceived as good because the FQ, like the Bible, is divided into two halves which contradict each other. These strategies could be investigated in the works of other early modern authors: in Lancelot Andrewes in particular, but also in Sidney, Donne, Herbert, Crashaw, and Milton.

STATISTICS ON AVAILABILITY
OF SOURCES AT CAMBRIDGE

For purpose and sources of this appendix, see Introduction. In these tools, belletristic authors are scantily represented and Spenser not at all. Leedham-Green followed Adams's rationale; both took care to avoid duplicate entries. Therefore, when these tools list as a separate entry a fragment, part of a multiauthored book, or part of a multivolume set, I follow suit. For consistency and brevity—though at the risk of inflating statistics on MSS—I similarly count as wholes both incomplete MSS and MSS of parts. Books are listed here only if they bear a pre-1590 imprint. When my reader will need help in identifying a text, I supply Adams's reference numbers (and, once, those of the STC, with #. In the columns, numbers stand for copies. The "Pem" column denotes pre-1500 works (printed and MS) certainly or probably in Pembroke's library in Spenser's time as listed in James's *Catalogue*. Of printed books from 1500 to 1590, Pembroke's holdings, if any, are specified in the Adams column. Works are printed books unless otherwise specified. MS = manuscript, E = English, L = Latin. Authors with a * beside their names receive explanatory notes at the end. In my text, "available" means 1–5 copies in all; "well attested" or "widely available" means more than 5.

The numbers of copies of Calvin's *Institutes*—Adams 27 + BCI 31 = 58—provide a standard of popularity against which other numbers can be measured.

Work	Pem	Adams	BCI
Works Written before 1500:			
Alexander Anglicus/Carpentarius	2	0	0
Bersuire, *Repert.*	0	5	1
" " *Reduc.MSBib.*	2 (1 MS)	7	1
" " *Metamorph.*	0	3 ("Walleys")	0

Boraston	1 MS	0	0
Bromyard	1	4	0
Byard	1 MS	0	0
Cassiodorus (*Op.&Pss.*) #870–74	0	7	5
Ps.-Dionysius *Opera* & *C. Hier.*	0	24 (1 Pem)	11
Divina Commedia	0	66	0
*Glossa	?	12	25
Gregory, *Moralia*	2 (1 MS)	0	2
Opera	n/a	22	14
Hugh of St. Cher #1020	5	5	10
*Nicolas (in Adams, always accompanied by *Glossa,* i.e., #982,993, 1010,1035,1094, in BCI once without it)	3 MSS + 2 = 5	12	26

Works the MSS of Which Are Nonexistent or Insignificant (Pem N/A):			
*Althamer (Althemerus) *Diallages* L	7	13*	
Bibles, JTB			
1 Entire	0	2	
2 Tremellius OT #1249	4	9	
3 *Beza NT, comprising #1711–12, 1754 and, in BCI, STC #2802–09	5	3	
4 Junius Apocrypha	1	0	
Bible Concordances	39 (2 at Pem)	50	
Brocard, James, on Rev.	1L	2E	
Erasmus			
Diatribe #591–98	12	5	
Ratio . . . v.t. #817–25, 407	11	18	
Fisher, John, *Sermons,* E	n/a	1	
Flacius, *Clavis*	4	10	
Franck, *Paradoxa*	1	0	
Lauretus, *Sylva*	3	0	
Luther, *De Servo Arbitrio* #1898–1902	5	3	
*Martyr, Peter (Vermigli) CP E = STC #24667–9; Adams L = #791–92	4	3 E + 2L = 5	
Melanchthon			
Catachesis puerilis #1098	2	1	
Epistolae #1210–12, 1214	5	1	

In this epilogue I give discursive notes on figures marked with a * whose importance the statistics fail to represent adequately.

*Althemerus (Althamer), Andreas. My thirteenth copy is listed in BCI under "Anonymous" because Leedham-Green did not recognize it, listed as it was under a fragment of its subtitle *Loci repungantes* [*sic*], but another exemplar so titled is so attributed in the *British Museum Catalogue*. I count either or both parts as one.

*Beza. These statistics are probably too low. Adams by definition does not list those Beza L NTs printed in England (= STC #2802–9); and I did not count books that BCI designates merely as "NT cum annotationibus/scholiis," though some of these could well be Beza's.

*Glossa. Plentiful but difficult to tabulate. All but one ed. of Nicolas apparently contains it—that being the one BCI specifically mentions as "sine glossa" (hence we have 26 Nicolases but only 25 Glossas). These tools do not mention that every copy of Hugh automatically contains the interlinear gloss and snippets of the rest, hence we should really count the Hughs again (Pem 5 + Adams 5 + BCI 10) along with the Glossas for a total of 5 (?) + 17 + 35 = 57 Glossas. Among James's MSS, an individual book or part of the Bible will frequently be labeled "gl[ossata]" without specifying whose; because of the slight uncertainty as to whether these represent *the* Glossa and because a MS of an individual book is in any case not strictly comparable to a printed Bible or even testament, I have left a ? here.

*Nicolas. BCI occasionally mentions "biblia cum glossa" without specifying Nicolas, but Leedham-Green thinks Nicolas is included in these too, so I count such Glossas again in the total number of Nicolases.

*Vermigli, Peter Martyr, known as Peter Martyr (but not to be confused with Peter Martyr Anghierra), *Common Places . . . Vermigli . . . ,* trans. Anthony Marten (t.p. 1574, translator's preface 1583!). These statistics are probably too low because Adams by definition does not list this English translation, the version from which I quote. The Latin original which he does list, the *Loci Communes,* was compiled from Martyr's works (which were also in Latin) by Robert Masson, pastor of the French congregation in London. According to John Patrick Donnelly, the first edition of the Latin was London, 1576, of which 13 more editions followed in the next 50 years; see his *Calvinism and Scholasticism,* 172.

IMAGES REPEATED *in bono et in malo*

AND TREATED IN THIS BOOK

To find discussions of these images, look up the Spenserian references in "Index of Spenser References."

ALTAR. I.viii.36, Orgoglio's, *in malo;* III.xi.47, of Cupid at Busirane's, *in malo;* IV.x.39–43, in Temple of Venus, *in bono;* V.x.28, xi.21, Geryoneo's, *in malo;* VI.xii.25, in monastery, *in bono.* Am. 22 ambivalent; Epithalamion 215–30, *in bono.*

ARMS, ARMOR, ESP. HARMFUL, DEFILED, +/OR ABANDONING. I.xi.26–28, Red Cross's, ambivalent; II.ii.11, Mordant's, *in malo.* See SHIELD.

BEADS = rosary. I.iii.13, Corceca's, *in malo;* I.x.8, Coelia's, *in bono.*

BIRDS, various. I.xi.34, Eagle simile for Red Cross; in Spenser's works in general, see Cheney, *Spenser's Famous Flight.*

BLOOD, BLOODSHED, BLOODGUILTINESS. I.x.60, Hermit on bloodshed, *in malo;* VI.i.26, Calidore on bloodshed, *in bono;* II.i.50–II.ii.4 passim, blood on Ruddymane, *in malo;* II.ii.10, blood on Ruddymane, *in bono.*

BIBLE, NEW TESTAMENT. I.ix.19, Red Cross gives Arthur NT, *in bono;* I.x.19, Fidelia's book, ambivalent.

CITY. All *in bono* unless otherwise noted. I.vii.46; I.x.59; II.x.72; III.ix.51, Cleopolis. I.x.57–59, New Jerusalem. II.x.46, III.ix.38, 51; IV.xi.28, Troynovant. III.ix.51, IV.xi.39, Lincoln. I.v.47, Babylon, *in malo.*

CUPS. I.viii.14, 25, Duessa's, *in malo;* I.x.13, Fidelia's, *in bono;* II.i.55, Acrasia's, *in malo;* II.xii.36, Excess's, *in malo,* perhaps same as preceding;

II.xii.49, Genius's "mighty Mazer bowle," *in malo;* III.i.51, Malecasta's, *in malo;* III.ix.30–31, Hellenore's and Paridell's "sacrament prophane in mystery of wine," *in malo;* IV.iii.42ff., Cambina's cup of Nepenthe, *in bono;* V.i.15, the Squire's metaphor, *in malo.*

FASTING. I.ii.14, Corceca's, *in malo;* I.x.48, 52, Hermit Contemplation's precept and practice, *in bono.*

GARDENS. I.xi.1–II.i.1, Eden, *in bono* (mostly); II.xii, Bower of Bliss, *in malo;* II.vii.53ff., Garden of Proserpina, *in malo;* III.vi, Garden of Adonis, *in bono;* IV.x, garden around Temple of Venus, *in bono* (see TEMPLES).

GARLANDS. I.i.48, *in malo;* ii.30, 37, *in malo;* vi.13, *in bono;* vii.4, *in malo;* x.54, *in bono;* xii.8, *in bono.*

GENIUS. II.xii.47, in Bower of Bliss, *in malo;* III.vi.31, in Garden of Adonis, *in bono.*

GLORY-PRAISE-HONOR. All *in bono* unless otherwise noted. I.x.59; Gloriana gives earthly-heavenly (equivocal) g. to those who have earned it; I.x.62, God inexplicably ordains heavenly g.; II.i.32, Palmer says Red Cross has earned heavenly g.; II.iii.4–40, comments on Braggadocchio's "pleasing vaine of glory," *in malo;* II.vii.1, Guyon comforts himself with thought of his own virtues and deeds; II.vii.46–48, Philotime, *in malo.*

HANDS, WASHING. Always *in bono* unless it fails, as in last two cases. I.x.60; I.xi.36, "baptized hands"; II.ii.3–4; II.vii.61–62.

HERMITS. I.i, Archimago, *in malo;* I.x, Contemplation, *in bono;* VI.v–vi, Hermit who is a veteran, *in bono.*

HONOR, see GLORY.

LAUREL LEAF. Am. 28, emblem of his profession, *in bono;* Am. 29, of her dominance, *in malo.*

LOCUS AMOENUS. VI.x.5–31, Mount Acidale, *in bono;* see GARDEN.

MAGIC. *In malo:* Archimago, I.i.36ff.; II.vi–viii; Duessa's, I.viii.14–15; *in bono:* the Palmer's, II.xii.26; Merlin's, III.iii.11; Cambina's, IV.iii.40.

MOUNTAINS, always *in bono* unless otherwise noted. I.x.53–54, Mount of Contemplation compared to Sinai (*in malo* or ambivalent), Olivet, Parnassus; III.vi.43–48, Mount of Venus; VI.x, Mount Acidale; VII.vii.3ff., Arlo Hill.

NIGHT. I.x.8, time for Caelia's devotions, *in bono;* I.xi.32–50 passim, during Dragon-Fight, *in bono;* III.iv.35ff., *in malo,* if speaker is correct;

I.i.33–ii.6, Archimago's magic works at night, *in malo;* I.v.20–45, personified, *in malo.*

SELF-ASSURANCE, THE LADY'S. Am. 58, *in malo;* Am. 59, *in bono.*

SERPENTS, DRAGONS, and other reptilians. I.i, Error, *in malo;* I.vii.31, on Arthur's helmet, *in bono;* I.viii, Duessa's Beast, *in malo;* I.x.13, serpent in Fidelia's cup, *in bono;* I.xi, "that old Dragon," *in malo;* IV.x.40, Ouroboros, *in bono.*

SHIELDS, RELINQUISHING IN BATTLE. I.vii.8, Red Cross failed to get it on in time, *in malo;* I.xi.27ff., intended to relinquish, *in malo;* I.xi.43, refuses to let go, *in malo;* V.xi.54, Arthur refuses to let go, *in malo;* Artegall relinquishes and wins thereby, V.xii.22, *in bono.*

TEMPLES. III.xi–xii, Busirane's House, really Temple of Cupid, *in malo;* IV.x, Temple of Venus, *in bono.*

TOWERS. All *in bono* unless otherwise noted. I.x.56 and 58, of New Jerusalem; I.x.58–59, of Panthea in Cleopolis, except fragile; Let. to Ral. I.xi–xii, brazen tower (or castle vii.44) in which Una's parents are imprisoned, ambivalent; II.ix, Alma's tower, except fragile and compared to Babel; III.ii, built by Ptolemy for Phao, except fragile and eventually shattered.

TREE. I.ii, two trees into which Fradubio and Fraelissa have been transformed, *in malo;* I.xi.47, Tree of Life with Tree of Knowledge beside it, *in bono et in malo;* II.vii.53ff., trees in Garden of Proserpina, *in malo.*

WELLS and other bodies of water (does not include rivers or the sea, or those which are just part of the landscape). I.ii.43, well for which Fradubio hopes, *in bono;* I.vii.5, of lazy nymph, *in malo;* I.xi.29 et passim, Well of Life, *in bono;* II.i.56–ii.10, pure Nymph's Well, *in malo* or ambivalent; II.v.30, Acrasia's stream of forgetfulness, presumably the same as that at II.xii.71, since they both bear a part in music, *in malo;* II.vi.2 (where called a river) et passim, Idle Lake, *in malo;* II.vii.56–63, the River Cocytus in Mammon's cave, *in malo;* II.xi.46, Arthur's standing lake, *in bono;* II.xii.60, fountain of bathing beauties in Bower of Bliss, *in malo;* VI.x.7, "gentle flud" at foot of Mount Acidale, *in bono.*

WORKS CITED

Primary Sources

Alciati, Andrea. *Andreae Alciati . . . Emblemata*. With Mignault's commentary. Leiden, 1591.

Alexander Anglicus (Carpentarius). *Destructorium Vitiorum*. Nuremberg, 1496.

Althamer, Andreas. *Conciliationes locorum scripturae qui specie tenus inter se pugnare videntur, Centuriae duae . . . interspersas hincinde additiones . . . huic editioni triginta locorum bini seu paria*. Nuremberg, 1534.

Andrewes, Lancelot. *The Works: Ninety-six Sermons*. Oxford, 1842–43.

Aquinas. See Thomas.

Augustine, Aurelius, St. *Earlier Writings*. Translated by J. H. S. Burleigh. Philadelphia, 1953.

——. *On Christian Doctrine*. Translated by D. W. Robertson. New York, 1958.

——. *On the Psalms*. Translated by Dame Scholastica Hebgin and Dame Felicitas Corrigan. New York, 1960.

Bale, John. *A Comedy Concerning Three Laws of Nature, Moses and Christ* (1st ed., 1538). London, 1908.

Bersuire (Berchorius, Berthorius, Bercharius), Pierre. *Dictionarium vulgo Repertorium morale*. 4 vols. in 2; vols. 3–6 of *Opera omnia*. Cologne, 1730–31.

——. *Metamorphosis Ovidiana moraliter a Magistro Thoma Walleys Anglico . . . explanata*. Falsely attributed to Walleys. Vol. 1 in transcription of Paris, 1509, ed., titled *De formis figurisque deorum (Reductorium morale, XV.1)*. Edited by J. Engels et al. Utrecht, 1960–62. Cited by entry, not page.

[Bible]. *The Bible, that is, the Holy Scriptures conteined in the Olde and Newe Testament*. London, 1594. (Geneva version; contains T. Grashop and Lectionary.)

——. *Biblia cum glosis ordinariis et interlinearibus, cum expositione Nicolai de lyra . . .* I consult two eds., both in 6 vols: Venice, 1495, and Venice, *Biblia sacra. . . .* Venice, 1588. The reader is free to use other eds. because I cite chapter and verse. The ed. in PL 113–14 omits the interlinear gloss and avowedly abridges long quotations; moreover, it omits Nicolas of Lyra.

——. *Domini nostri Jesu Christi Testamentum Novum, sive fedus novum . . . Theodoro Bezae interprete . . . Franciscus Junius recensuit, auxit, illustravitque.* Geneva, 1590.

——. *Libri Apochryphi* [*sic*]. Translated and edited by Franciscus Junius. London, 1585.

——. *Psalmorum Davidis et aliorum prophetarum libri quinque: argumentis et Latina paraphrasi illustrati. . . .* Edited and translated by Theodorus Beza. London, 1580.

——. *Testamenti veteris Biblia Sacra . . . Latini . . . ex Hebraeo facti.* Translated and edited by Emmanuel Tremellius and Franciscus Junius. London, 1585.

The Book of Concord: The Confessions of the Evangelical Lutheran Church. Edited and translated by Theodore Tappert et al. Philadelphia, 1959.

Brocard, James. *The Revelation of S. John reveled.* Translated by James Sanford. London, 1582.

Calvin, John. *Commentaries.* 22 vols. Calvin Translation Society, various translators. Edinburgh, 1844–56. Unless otherwise specified, all references to Calvin's exegesis are from here, by book, chapter, and verse.

——. *Institutes of the Christian Religion.* 3 vols. Translated by Henry Beveridge. Calvin Translation Society. Edinburgh, 1845.

Cassiodorus. *Explanation of the Psalms.* Translated by P. G. Walsh. New York, 1990.

——. *Expositio Psalmorum.* Edited by M. Adraien. Turnholt, 1958.

——. *An Introduction to Divine and Human Readings.* Translated by Leslie Webber Jones. New York, 1966.

Donne, John. *Sermons.* Vol. 1 of 10. Edited by Evelyn Simpson and George Potter. Berkeley, 1962.

Erasmus, Desiderius. (See also Luther.) *Erasmus-Luther Discourse on Free Will.* Edited and translated by Ernst F. Winter. New York, 1961.

——. *Opera omnia.* 10 vols. Edited by Jean LeClerc. Leiden, 1703–6.

Eriugena, John Scotus. *Expositiones in Ierarchiam coelestem.* Edited by J. Barbet. Corpus Christianorum Latinorum. Turnholt, 1975.

Fisher, John. *The English Works of John Fisher.* Part I (no more published). Edited by John Mayor. Early English Text Society, Extra Series 27. London, 1879.

Flacius, Matthias. *Clavis Scripturae Sanctae, seu de Sermone sacrarum literarum. . . .* 2 vols. Basel, 1680–1.

——. *De ratione cognoscendi sacras literas.* Latin-German ed. of first four sections of the first tractate of *Clavis* reproduced from Frankfurt edition (1719). Edited and translated by Lutz Geldsetzer. Düsseldorf, 1968.

Franck, Sebastian. *280 Paradoxes and Wondrous Sayings.* Edited and translated by E. J. Furcha. Lewiston, N.Y., 1986.

Gregory the Great. *Moralia in Job.* Anonymous translator. Oxford, 1847.

Herbert, George. *The Works of George Herbert.* Edited by F. E. Hutchinson. Oxford, 1941.

Hugh of St. Cher. *Opera.* 8 vols. Lyons, 1645.

Hugh of St. Victor. *The Didascalicon.* Translated by Jerome Taylor. New York, 1961.

Lauretus, Hieronymus. *Sylva Allegoriarum Totius Sacrae Scripturae.* Lyons, 1622.

Luther, Martin. *Luther and Erasmus: Free Will and Salvation.* Translated by P. S. Watson. London, 1969.

——. *Luther's Works.* 55 vols. Edited by Jaroslav Pelikan et al. Various translators. St. Louis, 1955–76.

——. *Selections.* Edited by J. Dillenberger. Garden City, N.Y., 1961.

——. *Werke.* Kritische Gesamtausgabe. Vol. 14. Weimar, 1895.

Lutheran Church. *The Book of Concord: The Confessions of the Evangelical Lutheran Church.* Edited and translated by Theodore G. Tappert. Philadelphia, 1959.

Martyr, Peter. See Vermigli.

Melanchthon, Philipp. *Philippi Melanthonis opera quae supersunt omnia.* 28 vols. Edited by K. G. Bretschneider. Halle, 1834–60. Part of CR.

———. *Melanchthon on Christian Doctrine: Loci Communes, 1555.* Edited by Hans Engellond with Clyde Manschreck. Oxford, 1965.

Migne, J.-P., ed. *Patrologiae cursus completus . . . series graeca.* 161 vols. Paris, 1857–66. Individual vols. not listed here.

———. *Patrologiae . . . series latina.* 221 vols. Paris, 1844–65. Individual vols. not listed here.

Montaigne, Michel, Sieur de. *Complete Essays.* Translated by Donald Frame. Stanford, 1965.

Nicolas of Lyra. See *Biblia.*

Noot, Jan Van der. *A Theatre for Voluptuous Worldlings* (London, 1569). Edited by William A. Jackson and Louis S. Friedland. New York, 1939.

Ochino, Bernardino. *Labyrinthi, hoc est, De libero aut servo arbitrio, de divina praenotione, destinatione, et libertate disputatio. Et quonam pacto sit ex iis labyrinthis exeundum . . . nunc primum ex italico in latinum translati* [by Sebastian Castellio?]. Basel, 1561. Microfilm courtesy of Folger Library.

Pareus, David. *A Commentary upon the divine revelation of . . . John Translated out of the Latine into English.* Translated by Elias Arnold. Amsterdam, 1644.

Pseudo-Dionysius the Areopagite. *Complete Works.* Translated by Colm Luibheid and Paul Rorem. New York, 1987.

———. *Opera.* Translated into Latin by "Ambrose, an orator and monk of the Camaldolese Order." Strassburg, 1503. Reprinted in Frankfurt, 1970.

Raleigh, Sir Walter. *History of the World.* London, 1614.

Rolle, Richard. *The Psalter, or the Psalms of David and Certain Canticles.* Edited by H. R. Bramley. Oxford, 1884.

Sidney, Sir Philip. *Miscellaneous Prose.* Edited by Katherine Duncan-Jones and Jan van Dorsten. Oxford, 1973.

Spenser, Edmund. *The Faerie Queene.* Edited by A. C. Hamilton. London, 1977.

———. *Spenser: Selections from the Minor Poems and "The Faerie Queene."* Edited by Frank Kermode. Oxford, 1965.

———. *Works: A Variorum Edition.* 10 vols. in 11. *Prose,* though unnumbered, is really vol. 9; vol. 8 is Judson's *Life.* Edited by Edwin Greenlaw et al. Baltimore, 1932–58.

———. *The Yale Edition of the Shorter Poems of Edmund Spenser.* Edited by William A. Oram et al. New Haven, 1989.

Streat, William. *The Dividing of the Hoof: Or, Seeming-Contradictions Throughout Sacred Scriptures, Distinguish'd, Resolv'd, and Apply'd. . . .* London, 1654.

Thomas Aquinas. *Opera* (Indicis Thomistici Supplementum). 7 vols. Edited by Robert Busa. Stuttgart–Bad Canstatt, 1980.

———. *Summa Theologiae.* References can be accessed using any edition because they are by part, article, quaestio, etc., not by page.

Vermigli, Peter Martyr, *The Common Places of . . . Vermigli. . . .* Translated by Anthony Marten. London, 1583 (t.p. 1574!).

———. *Most Learned . . . Commentaries on Romanes.* Translated by H. B[illingsly]. London, 1568.

Visitation Articles and Injunctions. 3 vols. Edited by W. H. Frere and W. M. Kennedy. London, 1910.

Secondary Sources

Adams, H. M. *Catalogue of Books Printed on the Continent of Europe, 1501–1600, in Cambridge Libraries.* Cambridge, 1967.

Alford, John. "Biblical *Imitatio* in the Writings of Richard Rolle." *ELH* 40 (1973): 1–23.

——. "The Role of the Quotations in *Piers Plowman.*" *Speculum* 52.1 (January 1977): 80–99.

Allen, Don Cameron. *Mysteriously Meant: The Rediscovery of Pagan Symbolism and Allegorical Interpretation in the Renaissance.* Baltimore, 1970.

——. "On the Closing Lines of the *Faerie Queene.*" *Modern Language Notes* 64 (1949): 93–94.

Allen, Judson Boyce. *The Ethical Poetic of the Later Middle Ages: A Decorum of Convenient Distinction.* Toronto, 1982.

——. "Malory's Diptych *Distinctio.*" In *Studies in Malory.* Edited by James W. Spisak, 237–55. Kalamazoo, Mich., 1985.

Alter, Robert. *The Art of Biblical Poetry.* New York, 1985.

Altman, Joel. *The Tudor Play of Mind.* Berkeley, 1978.

Anderson, Judith H. *The Growth of a Personal Voice: Piers Plowman and The Faerie Queene.* New Haven, 1976.

Anonymous. "MS Notes to Spenser's Faerie Queene." *N&Q* 202 (1957): 509–15.

Asals, Heather A. R. *Equivocal Predication: George Herbert's Way to God.* Toronto, 1981.

Aston, Margaret. *England's Iconoclasts.* Oxford, 1988.

Auerbach, Erich. *Scenes from the Drama of European Literature.* New York, 1959.

Bainton, Roland. *Bernardino Ochino, esule e riformatore senese del Cinquecento, 1487–1563.* Florence, 1941.

——. *The Travail of Religious Liberty: Nine Biographical Studies.* Philadelphia, 1951.

Barney, Stephen. *Allegories of History, Allegories of Love.* Hamden, Conn., 1979.

——. "Visible Allegory: The *Distinctiones Abel* of Peter the Chanter." In *Allegory, Myth, and Symbol.* Edited by Morton W. Bloomfield. Cambridge, Mass., 1981.

Berger, Harry. *The Allegorical Temper: Vision and Reality in Book II of Spenser's "Faerie Queene."* New Haven, 1957.

Bergvall, Åke. "Between Eusebius and Augustine: Una and the Cult of Elizabeth." *ELR* 27.1 (Winter 1997): 3–30.

Blench, J. W. *Preaching in England in the Late Fifteenth and Sixteenth Centuries: A Study of English Sermons, 1450–c. 1600.* New York, 1964.

Borris, Kenneth. *Spenser's Poetics of Prophecy in "The Faerie Queene" V.* Toronto, 1991.

Brady, Ciaran. *The Chief Governors: The Rise and Fall of Reform Government in Tudor Ireland, 1536–1588.* Cambridge, 1994.

——. "The Road to the View: On the Decline of Reform Thought in Tudor Ireland." In *Spenser and Ireland.* Edited by Patricia Coughlan, 25–45. Cork, 1989.

Brown, Peter. *Augustine of Hippo.* Berkeley, 1967.

Bullinger, E. W. *Figures of Speech Used in the Bible.* London, 1898.

Burrow, J. A. *Langland's Fictions.* New York, 1993.

Bush, Douglas. *English Literature in the Earlier Seventeenth Century.* Oxford, 1945.

Chamberlin, Frederick. *The Sayings of Queen Elizabeth.* New York, 1923.

Charity, A. C. *Events and Their Afterlife.* Cambridge, 1966.

Cheney, Patrick. *Spenser's Famous Flight.* Toronto, 1993.

Clebsch, William. "The Elizabethans on Luther." In *Interpreters of Luther.* Edited by Jaroslav Pelikan, 104–17. Philadelphia, 1968.

Collinson, Patrick. *The Elizabethan Puritan Movement.* Oxford, 1967.

——. *The Religion of Protestants: The Church in English Society, 1559–1625.* Oxford, 1982.

Cullen, Patrick. *The Infernal Triad: The Flesh, the World, and the Devil in Spenser and Milton.* Princeton, 1974.

Davies, Horton. *Worship and Theology in England: From Cranmer to Hooker.* Princeton, 1970.

Demaray, John G. *The Invention of Dante's Commedia.* New Haven, 1974.

Dix, Dom Gregory. *The Shape of the Liturgy.* London, 1945.

Doerksen, Daniel. "'All the Good is Gods': Predestination in Spenser's *Faerie Queene,* Book I." *Christianity and Literature* 32 (1983): 11–18.

Donnelly, John P. *Calvinism and Scholasticism in Vermigli's Doctrine of Man and Grace.* Leiden, 1976.

Dorsten, Jan A., van. "Sidney and Franciscus Junius the Elder." *HLQ* 42.1 (1978): 1–13.

Duffy, Eamon. *The Stripping of the Altars: Traditional Religion in England c. 1400–c. 1580.* New Haven, 1992.

Dunseath, T. K. *Spenser's Allegory of Justice in Book Five of "The Faerie Queene."* Princeton, 1968.

Dupriez, Bernard. *A Dictionary of Literary Devices: Gradus, A–Z.* Translated and adapted by Albert W. Halsall. Toronto, 1991.

Eden, Kathy. *Hermeneutics and the Rhetorical Tradition: Chapters in the Ancient Legacy and Its Humanist Reception.* New Haven, 1997.

Edwards, David. "Beyond Reform: Martial Law and Tudor Ireland." *History Ireland* 5 (1997): 16–21.

Empson, William. *Seven Types of Ambiguity.* 3d ed. New York, 1955.

Evans, G. R. *The Language and Logic of the Bible: The Earlier Middle Ages.* Cambridge, 1984.

——. *The Language and Logic of the Bible: The Road to Reformation.* Cambridge, 1985.

Fish, Stanley. *Self-Consuming Artifacts: The Experience of Seventeenth-Century Literature.* Berkeley, 1972.

Fletcher, Angus. *The Prophetic Moment: An Essay on Spenser.* Chicago, 1971.

Fowler, Alastair. "Emanations of Glory: Neoplatonic Order in Spenser's *Faerie Queen* [*sic*]." In *A Theatre for Spenserians.* Edited by Judith Kennedy and James Reither, 53–82. Toronto, 1973.

——. "Emblems of Temperance in *The Faerie Queene,* Book II." *RES,* n.s. 11 (1960): 143–49.

——. "The Image of Mortality: *The Faerie Queene,* II.i–ii." In Hamilton, *Essential Articles,* 139–52.

——. *Time's Purpled Masquers: Stars and the Afterlife in Renaissance English Literature.* Oxford, 1996.

Freccero, John. "The Sign of Satan." In *Dante: The Poetics of Conversion.* Edited by Rachel Jacoff. Cambridge, Mass., 1986.

Frye, Northrop. "The Structure of Imagery in *The Faerie Queene*." In Hamilton, *Essential Articles,* 153–70.

Gallacher, Lowell. *Medusa's Gaze: Casuistry and Conscience in the Renaissance.* Stanford, 1991.

Gellrich, Jesse. *The Idea of the Book in the Middle Ages: Language Theory, Mythology, and Fiction.* Ithaca, 1985.

Gilman, Ernest. *Iconoclasm and Poetry in the English Reformation: Down Went Dagon.* Chicago, 1986.

Gless, Darryl J. *Interpretation and Theology in Spenser.* Cambridge, 1994.

Goeglein, Tamara. "Utterances of the Protestant Soul in the *Faerie Queene:* The Allegory of Holiness and the Humanist Discourse of Reason." *Criticism* 36.1 (1994): 1–19.

Green, Thomas Andrew. *Verdict According to Conscience: Perspectives on the English Criminal Trial Jury, 1200–1800.* Chicago, 1985.

Greenblatt, Stephen. *Renaissance Self-Fashioning: From More to Shakespeare.* Chicago, 1980.

Greene, Thomas. *The Descent from Heaven: A Study in Epic Continuity.* New Haven, 1963.

Hamilton, A. C., ed. *Essential Articles for the Study of Edmund Spenser,* Hamden, Conn., 1972. Individual articles are listed.

——. *Structure of Allegory in "The Faerie Queene."* Oxford, 1961.

——. "A Theological Reading of FQ Book II." *ELH* 25 (1958): 155–62.

——. "The Vision of *Piers Plowman* and the *FQ*." In *Form and Convention in the Poetry of Edmund Spenser.* Edited by William Nelson, 1–34. New York, 1961.

——, ed., et al. *The Spenser Encyclopedia.* Toronto, 1990.

Hankins, John E. *Source and Meaning in Spenser's Allegory: A Study of "The Faerie Queene."* Oxford, 1971.

Hanson, R[ichard] P. C. *Allegory and Event: A Study of the Sources and Significance of Origen's Interpretation of Scripture.* Richmond, Va., 1959.

Hieatt, A. Kent. *Chaucer, Spenser, Milton: Mythopoeic Continuities.* Montreal, 1975.

——. "Scudamour's Practice of *Maistrye* upon Amoret." In Hamilton, *Essential Articles,* 199–201.

Higham, Florence. *Lancelot Andrewes.* London, 1952.

Hollander, John. *The Figure of Echo: A Mode of Allusion in Milton and After.* Berkeley, 1981.

Hollander, Robert. *Allegory in Dante's Commedia.* Princeton, 1969.

Hughes, Phillip Edgcumbe. *The Theology of the English Reformers.* London, 1965.

Hume, Anthea. *Edmund Spenser: Protestant Poet.* Cambridge, 1984.

Imbrie, Ann. "Playing Legerdemaine with Scripture: Parodic Sermons in *The Faerie Queene*." *ELR* 17 (1987): 142–55.

James, M. R. *Descriptive Catalogue of MSS in the Library of Pembroke College, Cambridge, with a Handlist of Printed Books to 1500.* Cambridge, 1905.

Jauss, H. R. *Toward an Esthetic of Literary Reception.* Translated by Timothy Bahti. Minneapolis, 1982.

Jayne, Sears. *Library Catalogues of the English Renaissance.* Foxbury Meadow, Godalming, Surrey, 1983.

Judson, A. C. *The Life of Edmund Spenser.* Baltimore, 1945.

Kaczerowsky, Klaus. *Sebastian Franck Bibliographie.* Wiesbaden, 1976.

Kahn, Victoria. "Revising the History of Machiavellism: English Machiavellism and the Doctrine of Things Indifferent." *RenQ* 46.3 (1993): 526–61.

———. *Rhetoric, Prudence, and Skepticism in the Renaissance.* Ithaca, 1985.

Kaske, Carol. "Another Echo of the Tremellius-Junius Bible in Sidney's Biblical Poetics." *ANQ* 5.2–3, n.s. (1992): 83–86.

———. "The Audiences of *The Faerie Queene:* Iconoclasm and Related Issues in Books I, V, and VI." *Literature and History* 3.3/2 (1994): 20–21.

———. "Augustinian Psychology in *Faerie Queene* Book II." *University of Hartford Studies in Literature* 15.3 (1983), 16.1 (1984): 93–98.

———. "The Bacchus Who Wouldn't Wash: FQ II.i–ii." *Renaissance Quarterly* 29.2 (1976): 195–209.

———. "The Dragon's Spark and Sting and the Structure of Red Cross's Dragon-Fight: *The Faerie Queene,* I.xi–xii." In Hamilton, *Essential Articles,* 425–46.

———. "Mount Sinai and Dante's Mount Purgatory." *Dante Studies* 79 (1971): 1–18.

———. "'Religious Reuerence Doth Buriall Teene': Christian and Pagan in *The Faerie Queene,* II.i–ii." *RES,* n.s. 30.118 (1979): 129–33.

———. "Spenser and the Exegetical Tradition: The Episode of the Nymph's Well, FQ II.i–ii." Ph.d. diss. Johns Hopkins University, Baltimore, 1964.

———. "Spenser's Pluralistic Universe: The View from the Mount of Contemplation (*F.Q.* I.x)." In *Contemporary Thought on Edmund Spenser.* Edited by Richard C. Frushell and Bernard J. Vondersmith, 121–49, 230–33. Carbondale, Ill., 1975.

———. "Surprised by Puritanism." In session 515, "Protestant Poetics," Modern Language Association, Houston, 1980.

Kaske, R. E. (in collaboration with Arthur Groos and Michael W. Twomey). *Medieval Christian Literary Imagery: A Guide to Interpretation.* Toronto, 1988.

Kermode, Frank. *Spenser: Selections.* Oxford, 1965.

King, John N. *English Reformation Literature: The Tudor Origins of the Protestant Tradition.* Princeton, 1982.

———. *Spenser's Poetry and the Reformation Tradition.* Princeton, 1990.

———. *Tudor Royal Iconography: Literature and Art in an Age of Religious Crisis.* Princeton, 1989.

Kolde, Theodor. *Andreas Althamer der Humanist und Reformator in Brandenburg-Ansbach.* Erlangen, 1895.

Lake, Peter. *Anglicans and Puritans? Presbyterianism and English Conformist Thought from Whitgift to Hooker.* London, 1988.

———. *Moderate Puritans and the Elizabethan Church.* Cambridge, 1982.

Landrum, Grace Warren. "Spenser's Use of the Bible and His Alleged Puritanism." *PMLA* 41 (1926): 517–44.

Lanham, Richard A. *A Handlist of Rhetorical Terms.* Berkeley, 1991.

Leclercq, Jean. *The Love of Learning and the Desire for God: A Study of Monastic Culture.* Translated by Catharine Misrahi. New York, 1974.

Leedham-Green, Elizabeth. *Books in Cambridge Inventories: Book-lists from Vice-Chancellor's Court Probate Inventories in the Tudor and Stuart Periods.* 2 vols. Cambridge, 1986.

Leslie, Michael. *Spenser's "Fierce Warres and Faithfull Loues": Martial and Chivalric Symbolism in "The Faerie Queene."* New York, 1983.

Lewalski, Barbara K. *Protestant Poetics and the Seventeenth-Century Religious Lyric.* Princeton, 1979.

Lewis, C. S. *The Allegory of Love.* Oxford, 1936.

Long, Anne B. "'She May Have More Shapes Than One': Milton and the Modern Idea that Truth Changes." *Milton Studies* 6 (1975): 85–99.

Lubac, Henri de. *Les quatre sens de l'Écriture.* 4 vols. Paris, 1959–64.

Mackenzie, D. "Synergism." In *Hastings Encyclopedia of Religion and Ethics.* Vol. 12. New York, 1960.

MacLachlan, Hugh. "The Death of Guyon and the *Elizabethan Book of Homilies.*" *Sp. Studies* 4 (1983): 93–114.

Mann, Jill. "Eating and Drinking in *Piers Plowman.*" *Essays and Studies* 32 (1979): 26–43.

Mann, Thomas. "The Leitmotiv or Thematic Phrase." Reprinted from his *Rede und Antwort* in *Ten Modern Masters: An Anthology of the Short Story.* Edited by Robert Gorham Davis. New York, 1972.

McNair, Philip. "Ochino's Apology: Three Gods or Three Wives?" *History* 60.200 (1975): 353–73.

McNamee, Maurice B. *Honor and the Epic Hero: A Study in the Shifting Concept of Magnanimity in Philosophy and Epic Poetry.* New York, 1960.

Meyer, Carl S. *Elizabeth I and the Religious Settlement of 1559.* St. Louis, 1960.

Miller, David Lee. *The Poem's Two Bodies.* Princeton, 1988.

Miller, Lewis H. "A Secular Reading of *The Faerie Queene,* Book II." In Hamilton, *Essential Articles,* 299–312.

Mollenkott, Virginia R. "Milton's Technique of Multiple Choice." *Milton Studies* 6 (1975): 101–11.

Nelan, Thomas. *Catholic Doctrines in Spenser's Poetry.* Abridgment. Ph.d. diss. New York University, 1946.

Nesselhof, John Morrison. "Spenser's Book of Friendship: An Aspect of Charity." Ph.d. diss. Princeton, 1955.

Nohrnberg, James. *The Analogy of "The Faerie Queene."* Princeton, 1976.

——. *Like unto Moses: The Constituting of an Interruption.* Bloomington, Ind., 1995.

Norton, David. *A History of Bible as Literature.* Vol. 1. *From Antiquity to 1700.* Cambridge, 1993.

Oram, William. "The Invocation of Sabrina." *SEL* 24 (1984): 121–39.

Panofsky, Erwin. *Gothic Architecture and Scholasticism: An Inquiry into the Analogy of the Arts, Philosophy, and Religion in the Middle Ages.* New York, 1957.

Parker, Patricia. "Dilation and Delay: Renaissance Matrices." *Poetics Today* 5.3 (1984): 519–35.

Parker Society. Editors vary. Cambridge, 1840?–55. 55 vols. including index. Individual authors (Bullinger, Rogers, Whitgift) and titles (Index, *Liturgical Services . . . Elizabeth*) will not be listed here.

Pfander, H. G. "The Medieval Friars and Some Alphabetical Reference-Books for Sermons." *Medium Aevum* 3.1 (1934): 19–29.

Phillippy, Patricia B. *Love's Remedies: Recantation and Renaissance Lyric Poetry.* Lewisburg, 1995.

Phillips, James B. "Spenser's Syncretistic Religious Imagery." *ELH* 36 (1969): 110–30.

Pollard, A. W., G. R. Redgrave, et al. *A Short-Title Catalogue of Books Printed in England,*

Scotland, and Ireland, and of English Books Printed Abroad, 1475–1640. 2 vols. 2d ed. London, 1976–86.

Porter, H. C. *Reformation and Reaction in Tudor Cambridge.* Cambridge, 1958.

Prescott, Anne L. "King David as a 'Right Poet': Sidney and the Psalmist." *ELR* 19 (1989): 131–51.

Quilligan, Maureen. *The Language of Allegory: Defining the Genre.* Ithaca, 1979.

——. *Milton's Spenser.* Ithaca, 1983.

Rathborne, Isabel Elizabeth. *The Meaning of Spenser's Faeryland.* New York, 1965.

Rendall, Steven. *Distinguo: Reading Montaigne Differently.* Oxford, 1992.

Ricks, Beatrice. "Catholic Sacramentals and Symbolism in Spenser's *Faerie Queene.*" *JEGP* 52 (1953): 322–31.

Rix, Herbert D. "Rhetoric in Spenser's Poetry." *Pennsylvania State College Bulletin* 34. State College, 1940.

Robertson, D. W., Jr., and Bernard F. Huppé. *"Piers Plowman" and Scriptural Tradition.* Princeton, 1951.

Roche, Thomas P., Jr. *The Kindly Flame: A Study of the Third and Fourth Books of Spenser's "Faerie Queene."* Princeton, 1964.

——. "Typology, Allegory, and Protestant Poetics." *George Herbert Journal* 13.1–2 (Fall 1989/Spring 1990): 1–17.

Røstvig, Maren-Sophie. *Configurations: A Topomorphical Approach to Renaissance Poetry.* Oslo, 1995.

Rouse, R. H., and M. A. Rouse. "Biblical *Distinctiones* in the Thirteenth Century." *Archives d'histoire doctrinale et littéraire du moyen âge* 41 (1974): 28–36.

——. *Preachers, Florilegia, and Sermons: Studies on the Manipulus florum of Thomas of Ireland.* Toronto, 1979.

Sandler, Florence. "*The Faerie Queene:* An Elizabethan Apocalypse." In *The Apocalypse in English Renaissance Thought and Literature.* Edited by C. A. Patrides and Joseph Wittreich, 148–74. Ithaca, 1984.

Schiavoni, James. "Predestination and Free Will: The Crux of Canto Ten." *Spenser Studies* 10 (1992): 175–95.

Schuldiner, Michael. *Gifts and Works.* Macon, Ga., 1991.

Shaheen, Naseeb. *Biblical References in "The Faerie Queene."* Memphis, 1976.

Shuger, Debora K. *Habits of Thought in the English Renaissance: Religion, Politics, and the Dominant Culture.* Berkeley, 1990.

——. *The Renaissance Bible: Scholarship, Sacrifice, and Subjectivity.* Berkeley, 1994.

——. *Sacred Rhetoric: The Christian Grand Style in the English Renaissance.* Princeton, 1988.

Smalley, Beryl. *The Study of the Bible in the Middle Ages.* Oxford, 1952.

Spearing, A. C. "The Development of a Theme in *Piers Plowman.*" *RES,* n.s. 41.3 (1960): 241–53.

Stambler, Bernard. *Dante's Other World.* New York, 1957.

Stern, Virginia F. *Gabriel Harvey: His Life, Marginalia, and Library.* Oxford, 1979.

Thompson, Bard. *Liturgies of the Western Church.* Philadelphia, 1980.

Tonkin, Humphrey. *Spenser's Courteous Pastoral: Book Six of the "Faerie Queene."* Oxford, 1972.

Torczon, Vern. "Spenser's Orgoglio and Despair." *TSLL* 3 (1961): 123–28.

Tyacke, Nicholas. *Anti-Calvinists: The Rise of English Arminianism, c. 1590–1640.* Oxford, 1987.

Verkamp, Bernard J. *The Indifferent Mean: Adiaphorism in the English Reformation to 1554.* Athens, Ohio, 1977.

Von Nolcken, Christina. "Some Alphabetical Compendia and How Preachers Used Them in Fourteenth-Century England." *Viator* 12 (1981): 271–88.

Wallace, Dewey D. *Puritans and Predestination: Grace in English Protestant Theology, 1525–1695.* Chapel Hill, N.C. 1982.

Waters, D. Douglas. *Duessa as Theological Satire.* Columbia, Mo., 1970.

Weatherby, Harold L. *Mirrors of Celestial Grace: Patristic Theology in Spenser's Allegory.* Toronto, 1994.

Wells, Robin H. *The Faerie Queene and the Cult of Elizabeth.* Totowa, N.J., 1982.

———. "Spenser's Christian Knight: Erasmian Theology in the *Faerie Queene,* Book I." *Anglia* 97 (1979): 360–66.

Wenzel, Siegfried. *Preachers, Poets, and the Middle English Lyric.* Princeton, 1986.

Whitaker, Virgil K. *The Religious Basis of Spenser's Thought.* Stanford, 1950.

Wilmart, Dom André, O.S.B. "Un répertoire d'exégèse composé en Angleterre vers le début du xiiie siècle." In *Mémorial Lagrange.* Cinquantenaire de l'École biblique et archéologique française de Jérusalem. Paris, 1940.

Wittreich, Joseph. *Visionary Poetics: Milton's Tradition and Its Legacy.* San Marino, Calif., 1979.

Woodhouse, A. S. P. "Nature and Grace in the *Faerie Queene.*" In Hamilton, *Essential Articles,* 58–83.

Woods, Suzanne. "Spenser and the Problem of Women's Rule." *HLQ* 48.2 (1985): 141–58.

Yates, Frances. *The Art of Memory.* Chicago, 1966.

INDEX OF SCRIPTURE REFERENCES

GENERAL INDEX

For specific Spenserian images, see Appendix Two.